More Praise for *Think Like a*

"As an EdTech consultant advising c[...] say this book is a game-changer for L&D leaders. It brilliantly bridges the gap between traditional L&D and modern marketing, offering invaluable insights for creating compelling digital learning experiences."
—**Lori Niles-Hofmann,** EdTech Strategist and Global Adviser, NilesNolen

"This is the L&D and marketing crossover you are looking for. Discover how to transform dull learning content into engagement gold with skimmable writing, snappy headlines, and calls to action that demand action."
—**Cara North,** Founder and Chief Learning Consultant, The Learning Camel

"*Think Like a Marketer, Train Like an L&D Pro* presents a compelling argument for combining marketing ideas and strategies with current L&D techniques to create a powerful combination with the potential to take the L&D function to the next level. Bianca Baumann and Mike Taylor have created a work that will help you envision and achieve a future in which employees eagerly take charge of their learning journeys, acquire new skills, and apply them in real time through this unique intertwining of disciplines. The writing team provides actionable strategies, ideas, and concepts that empower L&D professionals to create training that captivates, motivates, and delivers lasting impact. This book will change the way you think about developing instruction forever."
—**Karl M. Kapp, EdD,** Professor of Instructional Design and Technology, Commonwealth University

"So much value on every page! Bianca and Mike have struck the right balance of instilling high-impact strategies and tactical design advice. *Think Like a Marketer, Train Like an L&D Pro* is essential reading for any learning and talent leader who is looking to elevate their practice and bring fresh perspectives to their teams. Keep this one beside your desk at all times."
—**Josh Cardoz,** Chief Creative and Learning Officer, Sponge Learning Group

"'Get attention, influence behavior'—the book recognizes that these are the central concerns of both learning designers *and* marketers, and that learning designers have a lot to learn from marketers on these topics. Packed full of useful tools and frameworks, this book has so much material to help create more engaging and impactful learning."
—**Julie Dirksen,** Author, *Design for How People Learn*

"Dang! I love this book. Bianca and Mike have written the go-to resource for what-to and how-to for instructional designers and the leaders who guide them. Insightful, readable, actionable, and chock full of activities, this is a must-read for you and your team."
—**Megan Torrance,** CEO, TorranceLearning; Author, *Agile for Instructional Designers* and *Data and Analytics for Instructional Designers*

Think Like a Marketer, Train Like an L&D Pro

Strategies to Ignite Learning

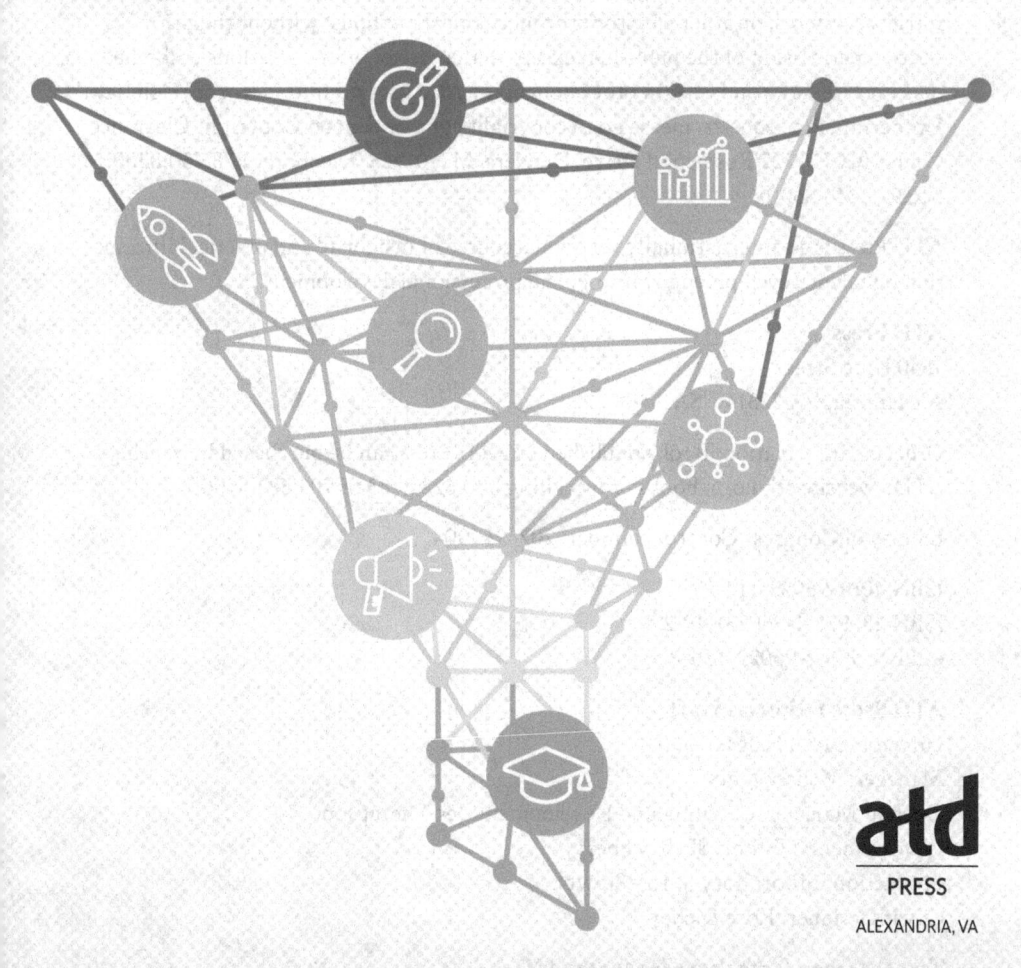

atd
PRESS
ALEXANDRIA, VA

BIANCA BAUMANN AND MIKE TAYLOR

© 2025 ASTD DBA the Association for Talent Development (ATD)
All rights reserved. Printed in the United States of America.

28 27 26 25   1 2 3 4 5

No part of this publication may be reproduced, distributed, or transmitted in any form or by any means, including photocopying, recording, information storage and retrieval systems, or other electronic or mechanical methods, without the prior written permission of the publisher, except in the case of brief quotations embodied in critical reviews and certain other noncommercial uses permitted by copyright law. For permission requests, please go to copyright.com, or contact Copyright Clearance Center (CCC), 222 Rosewood Drive, Danvers, MA 01923 (telephone: 978.750.8400; fax: 978.646.8600).

ATD Press is an internationally renowned source of insightful and practical information on talent development, training, and professional development.

ATD Press
1640 King Street
Alexandria, VA 22314 USA

Ordering information: Books published by ATD Press can be purchased by visiting ATD's website at td.org/books or by calling 800.628.2783 or 703.683.8100.

Library of Congress Control Number: 2024950004

ISBN-10: 1-96023-119-7
ISBN-13: 978-1-960231-19-2
e-ISBN: 978-1-96023-120-8

ATD Press Editorial Staff
Director: Sarah Halgas
Manager: Melissa Jones
Content Manager, Learning and Development: Jes Thompson
Developmental Editor: Shelley Sperry
Production Editor: Katy Wiley Stewts
Cover Designer: Rose Richey

Text Designer: PerfecType, Nashville, TN
Printed by BR Printers, San Jose, CA

Contents

Preface vii

**Introduction: The Power of Marketing for Learning
and Development** 1

Chapter 1. Design Learning for the Way People Think 5

Chapter 2. Create Learner Personas That Inspire 27

Chapter 3. Map Learner Journeys From Awareness to Action 63

Chapter 4. Maximize Learning With an Effective Content Strategy 95

Chapter 5. Captivate Learners With Writing That Clicks! 127

Chapter 6. Leverage Visuals for Maximum Impact 153

Chapter 7. Execute a Successful Learning Campaign 185

Chapter 8. Level Up Learning With Marketing Technology 209

Chapter 9. Measure the Impact of Your Efforts 239

Conclusion: Small Steps, Big Impact 269

Recommended Resources for Deeper Learning 271

References 281

Index 291

About the Authors 297

About ATD 299

Preface

Hey there, friends! We're Mike and Bianca, and we're thrilled to be your guides on a journey to revolutionize the way you approach learning and development (L&D). Before we discuss the strategies and insights that we hope will transform your practice, we want to share a bit about the paths that led us to write this book.

In 2017, we met at an online Learning Guild conference. We were both speakers at the event, sharing our passion for a topic we thought had never been fully explored: the intersection of marketing and L&D. Despite being relative strangers, we felt an immediate connection as we listened to each other's presentations and engaged in a lively panel discussion. We were both giving voice to ideas that had been percolating for a while but hadn't yet found an outlet—and it was an exciting moment.

The session crackled with high-voltage energy. By the end, it was clear that we had tapped into something powerful: a hunger for fresh perspectives and new approaches. We knew we couldn't let that momentum fade, so we committed to continuing our conversation, diving deep into the challenges facing modern L&D professionals and envisioning what a new frame of reference for workplace learning could look like. Our conversation is still going on more than eight years later and has resulted in this book and a consulting partnership that has enriched our work.

Our varied professional experiences inform the questions we ask and the conclusions we've arrived at during the process of writing. We've had the privilege of working with all types of learning organizations, from small startups to Fortune 500 giants, and with marketing firms. Bianca worked at Eloqua, a marketing automation company now owned by Oracle. Mike spent time at Mindset Digital, a digital marketing agency. In these roles, we first discovered the powerful connection between marketing and L&D.

For Mike, the "aha" moment came while leading a workshop for a room full of skeptical marketers, introducing them to adult learning principles and instructional design techniques. As he watched the lightbulbs switching on for each of the participants, Mike suddenly realized that L&D could also learn a ton from marketing.

Meanwhile, Bianca was geeking out over the way her marketing colleagues used data and analytics to optimize their campaigns in real time. She couldn't help wondering how those same tools could be used to personalize learning and measure its impact.

These experiences, coupled with our recognition of the challenges facing L&D, sparked a fundamental shift in our thinking and a deep conviction that the future of learning lies at the intersection of these two disciplines. We knew we had to spread the word, so a few years ago, we designed a workshop together. We poured our combined energy into crafting an experience that would engage learners, demonstrate the power of a marketing mindset, and provide practical takeaways that attendees could implement immediately.

On the opening day of the workshop, we met in person for the first time and clicked immediately. The energy and feedback we experienced over those few days were incredible. Participants told us this was an entirely new perspective, and they were eager to apply our marketing strategies and techniques in their own L&D projects. For us, that workshop solidified the importance of integrating these two powerful disciplines.

Fast forward to today, and here we are, putting the finishing touches on the book you now hold in your hands or see on your screen. The journey has included long days, countless revisions, moments of doubt, and flashes of inspiration. But through it all, we've been driven by a deep belief in the potential of our approach.

In the pages that follow, we'll break down the key principles of a marketing-driven approach to L&D. We'll share stories from our own experiences and provide you with practical, actionable steps you can take to start infusing a marketing mindset into your work right away.

We want this book to be the start of a conversation that challenges assumptions, embraces new possibilities, and unlocks the potential of L&D innovators. We invite you to join us in a larger discussion about the future of L&D. Visit us at TrainLikeAMarketer.com to join the conversation and access bonus resources and case studies, or find us on social media using the #TrainLikeAMarketer. You can also join a community of like-minded professionals who are ready to reimagine L&D in our Train Like a Marketer LinkedIn group at linkedin.com/groups/14552471. We can't wait to hear about your "aha" moments, answer your questions, and celebrate your successes.

Your partners in learning,
Mike Taylor
mike@trainlikeamarketer.com

Bianca Baumann
bianca@trainlikeamarketer.com

Introduction
The Power of Marketing for Learning and Development

> Creativity is just connecting things.
> —Steve Jobs

Organizations spend more than $350 billion globally on training each year, but only a fraction of that investment results in improved performance. That's a problem that needs a solution, and we believe the best solution is for L&D professionals to adopt the strategies, techniques, and mindset of modern marketers.

In an uncertain and evolving business landscape, organizations of all kinds are facing the challenge of helping their employees keep up with rapid changes in the knowledge, skills, and abilities they need for success. As workplace learning strategists, we often see traditional L&D approaches fail to deliver what organizations and employees need, leaving everyone grappling with a widening skills gap. We think it's time for a bold new approach to training that builds on the science and art of marketing to transform the way employees learn and grow.

Get Attention, Influence Behavior

At first glance, marketing and L&D may seem like an unlikely combination. But upon closer inspection, these fields share two core goals: getting people's attention and influencing their behavior.

Marketing is about captivating and persuading, which is the bread and butter of learning designers. It's about finding and engaging the hidden levers of human motivation and decision making. When done well, marketing speaks to our brain's automatic processing system on an intuitive, emotional level. The same is true of a great training experience: It captures participants' attention and engages them emotionally as well as intellectually. The experience then helps change participants' behavior through information, stories, and shared activities. As Nobel laureate and psychologist Daniel Kahneman (2011) eloquently explained in his groundbreaking book *Thinking, Fast and Slow*, our actions are often swayed more by compelling narratives and emotional connections than by mere facts and figures.

Marketing and L&D are both about *creating value*. Marketing is never just about selling products; it's also about the valuable experiences, emotions, and practical solutions attached to those products. Marketers try to understand what people want and need, sometimes even before they realize it themselves, and create products or services that meet those needs. As L&D professionals, we design our products to provide the ultimate value—new knowledge and skills for learners that will help them become more effective and improve the bottom line for their organizations.

Marketing and L&D share other characteristics too: Both require research, strategy, creativity, and a good grasp of human psychology. Both must effectively communicate ideas by crafting compelling narratives that resonate with the target audience, using a variety of content types and channels, including print, video, social media, and email. All these connections between marketers and L&D pros are compelling, aren't they?

When we imagine the future of marketing-inspired L&D, we see a workplace where employees are fully engaged in their learning journeys, eagerly acquiring new knowledge, skills, and abilities and applying them to their work in real time. Data-driven insights guide and optimize learning programs to align with the organization's changing needs. We see companies in which L&D initiatives are seamlessly integrated into the flow of work, delivering the right content at the right moment, all in fresh, engaging formats.

What to Expect in This Book

In the chapters that follow, we will explore the potential of marketing-inspired L&D, diving into essential principles and practical strategies that can help you transform your learning experiences. Here is a brief look.

In chapter 1, we consider how our brain's automatic processing system determines what we pay attention to and what drives our behavior. And in chapter 2, we explore how to create detailed learner personas that capture your audience's unique needs, preferences, and motivations.

Every great marketing campaign starts with a clear understanding of the customer journey. In chapter 3, we'll apply that idea to L&D, showing you how to create learner journeys that take participants from awareness to mastery.

Chapters 4, 5, 6, and 7 guide you through the process of creating content that ignites the learner's interest and inspires them to act. We'll explore proven marketing techniques to craft a comprehensive strategy and develop captivating copy and visuals. We'll bring it all together as we consider how to produce a learning campaign that resonates with your audience. In chapter 8, we'll see how we can bring all the elements to life by harnessing the power of marketing technology. Finally, in chapter 9, we'll dive into the world of learning analytics, showing you how to measure the true impact of your programs and continuously optimize for better results.

Our Call to Action

We see this book as both a how-to manual and a call to action. We hope to convince other L&D pros to embrace a new way of thinking and working that can transform our organizations and change our working lives for the better. When L&D has a more tangible, positive impact on business performance, we can also elevate its strategic role to secure a seat at the table as a trusted partner.

In the end, we're guided by one fundamental principle: The learner should be at the heart of everything we do. By applying marketing strategies to L&D, we can create learning experiences that resonate on a deep, emotional level, driving real behavior change and inspiring employees to achieve their full potential. It all starts with a simple shift in perspective and, as Steve Jobs might say, a willingness to connect things.

We're excited for you to join us on this journey to explore the untapped potential of marketing-inspired L&D. The future of learning awaits. Let's get started!

Chapter 1
Design Learning for the Way People Think

> We are very influenced by completely automatic things that we have no control over, and we don't know we're doing it.
> —Daniel Kahneman, psychologist, economist, and author of *Thinking, Fast and Slow*

Imagine two trainers, Jen and Juan, each leading a remote training course on effective sales techniques for LuxeKitchens, a high-end kitchen design company. Jen, who has a background in marketing, designs her program to engage the learners' fast, intuitive, and automatic thinking processes at every turn. She begins with the gripping story of a struggling salesperson's journey to success. She creates an emotional hook that illustrates the real-world impact of the strategies she'll share during the training. Her slides feature striking before-and-after visuals of contrast and progress that elicit a visceral, immediate response in the audience.

Throughout the session, Jen puts herself in her audience's shoes, constantly linking abstract concepts to their everyday challenges and goals. Participants actively practice techniques in interactive, realistic simulations, and afterward, Jen provides targeted feedback and encouragement. She uses other techniques, including visually impressive slides that trigger recognition of key concepts and brief quizzes that reinforce automatic recall of essential tasks.

Juan takes a more traditional approach to crafting his version of the training experience. He only uses text-heavy slides to methodically work through definitions and models, with few examples or stories to provide context and illustrate abstract concepts around customer centricity and data analysis. Juan's exercises lack opportunities to actively build practical skills. His delivery relies heavily on logical analysis and deliberate reasoning, and he rarely tries to connect with learners' emotions or motivations.

As you might expect, these two approaches yield dramatically different results. Jen's participants rate their training experience highly, with most saying they feel confident applying the techniques they've learned on the job. Their sales metrics support these instinctive assessments, showing sustained increases in their sales. Juan's learners don't rate their experience highly, report lackluster engagement, struggle to remember key points, and see little, if any, improvement in sales after the training program.

In designing her course, Jen drew on her education and experience in marketing, especially the application of insights from cognitive psychology about the way people process information. Juan relied on an approach dominated by a lecture-style presentation that didn't engage learners' attention, emotions, or imagination. Using what she knew about the human need for novelty, narratives, and deeper social and emotional connections, Jen succeeded in capturing her learners' attention, engaging all dimensions of their thinking, and driving their actions going forward. In this chapter, we'll explore how understanding a little more about how our audience thinks can help us design more effective learning experiences.

Intuitive Plus Deliberative Thinking

Research in cognitive psychology and behavioral economics, led by luminaries like Nobel laureate Daniel Kahneman, revolutionized our understanding of how people think—how they process information and make decisions. The dual process theory of the mind, developed gradually from the 1960s to the 1990s, was a central tenet of this research (Kahneman 2011). Kahneman and others popularized the theory in the 2000s, suggesting that we all have two distinct modes of thinking:

- A fast, automatic, and intuitive mode, or System 1 thinking
- A slower, more deliberate mode, or System 2 thinking

Many researchers emphasize the interconnectedness and interaction of intuitive and deliberative thinking rather than viewing them as rigidly separate processes. They argue that thinking is highly complex, with multiple cognitive processes occurring simultaneously and influencing one another. However, we believe that more effective learning and behavior change involves the activation of both "fast" (intuitive) and "slow" (deliberative) thinking.

Taking the evolving research into account, we still find it helpful to discuss two approaches to processing information and making decisions. Although some aspects of Kahneman's cited studies have sparked academic discussions, his work remains highly influential in marketing and behavioral economics because it has proven so useful. For example, Udo Kannengiesser and John Gero (2019) applied the "two systems" approach in their studies of information systems and design science (Table 1-1).

In this book, we'll refer to *intuitive thinking* and *deliberative thinking* with the understanding that both operate simultaneously and can lead to rational or irrational conclusions.

Table 1-1. Characteristics of Intuitive and Deliberative Thinking

Characteristic	System 1. Intuitive Thinking	System 2. Deliberative Thinking
Speed	Fast	Slow
Effort	Effortless	Effortful
Automaticity	Automatic	Controlled
Intuition	Intuitive	Analytical
Heuristics	Relies on heuristics and mental shortcuts	Uses deliberate reasoning
Emotion	Influenced by emotions and gut feelings	Less influenced by emotions, more rational
Capacity	High capacity for parallel processing	Limited capacity, focused processing
Conscious awareness	Often operates outside conscious awareness	Requires conscious awareness

Source: Adapted from Kannengiesser and Gero 2019.

Kahneman describes intuitive (System 1) thinking, which marketers often aim to exploit, as an always-on kind of mental radar that rapidly processes environmental cues. He suggests that it evolved to keep our ancestors alive in dangerous environments by enabling lightning-fast decisions. These rapid judgments rely on emotion, instinct, and mental shortcuts called *heuristics*, bypassing the slower process of deliberative reasoning. The intuitive system operates in parallel with our more analytical thought processes (Gilovich et al. 2002).

While we no longer encounter saber-toothed tigers or other lethal predators regularly, our intuitive thinking—the rapid, automatic cognitive process—remains perpetually active in our daily lives. We still continually scan for signs of social threats and opportunities, primed to make snap judgments and react instantaneously. This explains the outsized impact of first impressions: Our rapid, intuitive thinking swiftly forms lasting assessments. System 1 prioritizes emotionally charged and seemingly urgent information, which is why we tend to respond more strongly to vivid, emotive experiences than dry, statistical data.

Deliberative (System 2) thinking is a slower program that can weigh trade-offs and consider decisions from multiple angles. This is vital for complex problem-solving and planning but is always in communication with other programs running at the same time, including the intuitive rapid-response thinking marketers and educators are trying to engage (Stanovich and West 2000).

Think of your brain as an incredibly advanced computer system that is always running multiple programs simultaneously. Deliberative and intuitive thinking are partners in a never-ending dance—although our intuitive thinking often leads because it reacts in less time than it takes to blink. Deliberative thinking jumps in to collaborate with intuitive thinking when more deeply thoughtful reasoning is needed.

Effective learning design orchestrates a delicate balance between intuitive and deliberative thinking. It captures immediate attention through emotional resonance and relevance while simultaneously satisfying the need for structured, substantive content. The goal is to avoid both overly sensational approaches that feel manipulative and dry academic presentations that fail to engage. The ideal learning experience harmonizes these elements and ensures that information is both intuitively appealing and intellectually satisfying, leading to potentially more effective and lasting learning outcomes.

Six Ways to Engage Intuitive Thinking for Learning

Marketing researchers have identified a small set of meta-biases that may underlie many of our cognitive biases, the systematic mental shortcuts we take in decision making. In *The Persuasion Code*, neuromarketing experts Christophe Morin and Patrick Renvoise (2018) distill these meta-biases into six stimuli, or ways to engage intuitive thinking. When information aligns with these stimuli, learners are likelier to engage with and remember it. For example, learning content that evokes strong emotions or provides immediate solutions to urgent problems tends to be more effective because it resonates strongly with our instincts.

Let's now consider six ways to engage a learner's intuitive thinking like a marketer might and some specific tactics for applying them in learning design.

1. Make It Personal

We all crave personal relevance, tuning out generic information and perking up when content feels directly applicable to *me*, *here*, and *now*. As instructional designers, our job is to create experiences that feel tailor-made for each learner's needs, goals, and context.

Consider our two trainers again, Jen and Juan. Jen frames her content around how it will benefit learners directly. She uses relatable examples and case studies to show how the skills she's teaching will help them build stronger work relationships, advance their careers, and reduce daily stress. Juan, meanwhile, delivers content only in broad, theoretical terms without connecting it to his learners' personal situations. Guess whose training is more engaging and effective?

Research backs up the power of personalization. Studies have shown that personalized content can result in longer attention spans, improved memory retention, and greater willingness to engage with information (Tam and Ho 2006; Kalyanaraman and Sundar 2006; Walkington and Bernacki 2020).

We must put ourselves firmly in our learners' shoes to reap these benefits. What are their pain points and aspirations? How can our content help them achieve their goals? One powerful tool that we'll explore in the next chapter is the *learner persona*, which helps us understand our learners' needs and guide the creation of content that connects with them more deeply.

You can also try a quick litmus test: Scan your materials and tally how often you use the word *we* versus *you*. If the word *we* dominates your content, your learners may check out because it's not about *them*. Reframing the way you present the information to center on the learners can make it feel more immediate and relevant.

The bottom line is that if we want our training to stick, we must make it personal. By appealing to learners' core needs and goals and making that personal relevance crystal clear, we engage intuitive thinking and pave the way for real behavior change. In the battle for attention and retention, personalization is our not-so-secret weapon.

2. Make It Contrastable

Our brains are wired to notice differences and to quickly spot something that stands out from the surrounding environment. Learning content packed with vivid contrasts jolts learners to attention because they associate contrast with importance. If something stands out, it must be worthy of attention (Heath and Heath 2007). This has significant implications for learning design. By incorporating contrasts into our content and delivery, we can keep learners alert and focused.

Try some of these techniques:

- Introduce surprising twists or juxtapose different outcomes in your storytelling. For example, start with a story about a dramatic failure caused by poor communication, then contrast it with an example of how effective communication saved the day in a similar situation.
- Highlight key differences between concepts, historical periods, or case studies. Comparing and contrasting helps learners understand similarities and differences, aiding critical thinking and retention.
- Create visual contrast in your slides and materials, using bold colors, striking images, and varied layouts to draw the eye and maintain interest.

- Alternate between different types of content, including stories, facts, discussions, and practical exercises. Variety keeps learners engaged.
- Design "before and after" scenarios that demonstrate the influence of learning. Show the painful consequences of not having a skill, then contrast that example with the positive outcomes of mastering the skill.

Returning to our two trainers: Jen's program is full of contrasts. She starts with a dramatic story of an initial communication failure and a later success, uses visually striking slides, and skillfully mixes different teaching methods. Her approach combines short, focused talks with team activities where learners solve real-world problems together. Her learners are alert and engaged throughout.

Juan's workshop, on the other hand, lacks contrast. He presents a long series of similar text-heavy slides, rarely varies his tone or delivery, and provides few opportunities for interaction. His learners quickly tune out.

As L&D professionals, we must embrace contrast to capture and keep learners' attention. By creating learning experiences full of variety, surprise, and visual interest, we can drive deeper engagement and retention.

3. Make It Tangible

In addition to responding to contrasts, we tend to prefer the concrete—anything we can see, touch, smell, hear, or feel. Consider two different active-listening training sessions:

1. "Imagine communication as a game of tennis," Jen says in her workshop. "Before you can hit the ball back, you first have to let it land fully in your court. That's active listening at work, fully receiving your partner's message before formulating your response." By using this visual analogy, Jen gives learners a *tangible framework* for understanding an abstract skill.
2. Juan packs his presentation with dense jargon about "multimodal discourse competencies." Because he lists concepts without grounding them in real-world examples, the audience is unable to find a way to connect.

The difference between the two learning experiences is that one focuses on grounding abstract concepts in concrete examples, analogies, and sensory language. Concrete examples tend to reduce extraneous mental "noise" during learning, freeing up energy for deeper engagement (Sweller 1994). When we can see, hear, and feel an idea, it is more likely to stick.

One way to make learning more tangible is by simplifying your content. Break down complex topics into their core elements and strip away academic and other specialized jargon. Relate abstract ideas to familiar objects and situations, like Jen's tennis analogy. Analogies facilitate learning by mapping relationships between familiar and novel concepts (Gentner et al. 2003). Use sensory language to paint vivid mental pictures, describing concepts in terms of sights, sounds, and textures. Sensory language can evoke mental simulations that aid comprehension (Zwaan 2016).

By giving learners some sort of handle with which to grasp our learning content, we prime them to engage and retain the ideas and information. For learning designers, this can transform experiences from mind-numbing to memorable, which brings us to our next way to engage intuitive thinking.

4. Make It Memorable

Memorable learning experiences depend on the information we're sharing and the way we deliver it. Learning must be novel, emotionally evocative, and vividly imagined if we're going to create a lasting impact.

As we've already noted, we are more likely to encode and retain information that stands out from the ordinary and sparks an emotional response (Heath and Heath 2007). This is because our brains constantly filter the barrage of stimuli they receive, prioritizing the things that seem most important for survival or success. What key factors influence how memorable your learning experiences will be?

- **Repetition.** Just as it takes multiple exposures to learn a new language or master woodworking, it takes repeated encounters with information for it to stick in our long-term memory. The more frequently learners engage with a concept, especially over spaced intervals, the more deeply embedded it becomes.

- **Emotion.** Experiences that evoke strong feelings, whether positive or negative, leave a more vivid imprint on the mind. When we're emotionally invested, we pay closer attention and process information more deeply. That's why storytelling, humor, and suspense are such powerful tools for memorable learning.
- **Primacy and recency.** We tend to remember best what comes first and last in a sequence, with the middle being more of a blur. This means the opening and closing moments of a learning experience have outsized importance for retention.

Let's examine an example to see these principles in action. Jen designs her learning experiences around hands-on activities that allow learners to experience concepts viscerally. She uses a card-sorting game that simulates information overload and a tense role-play negotiation. These emotionally charged exercises burn lessons into participants' memories. Jen also bookends each session with a powerful story and a clear recap of core takeaways, leveraging the primacy and recency effects.

By designing her content to make ideas memorable, Jen not only engages her learners in the moment but also ensures they will recall and apply the lessons long after the workshop ends.

5. Make It Visual

Imagine you're a veteran sales associate at LuxeKitchens, the company mentioned at the opening of this chapter. You and your colleagues are called into a workshop on new sales strategies. You're not sure why your team was required to attend. Sales seem a little sluggish but nothing to worry about. The facilitator moves to a new slide. Before you can process the words at the bottom of the screen, you see the logo of your primary competitor and a graph with a large red upward arrow, tracking their stunning growth in sales revenue over the past six months. You get a sick feeling in the pit of your stomach and direct your full attention to the facilitator. That's the power of great visuals. They grab our attention in a way that text simply cannot.

The human brain is remarkably adept at processing visual information. A significant portion of the brain is dedicated to visual processing, enabling the rapid and efficient interpretation of images. In other words, we're wired to prioritize visual input.

This has huge implications for learning design. Too often, we rely on text-heavy slides and wordy lectures to convey vital information. However, as John Medina (2014) notes in his book *Brain Rules*—and a wide array of evidence demonstrates—people usually remember just a fraction of information delivered orally, but understanding and retention skyrocket if relevant images are added.

Why such a dramatic difference? It again comes down to how we process information. Reading text engages both the auditory cortex (the part of the brain that processes sound) and the visual cortex (the part that processes images) because our inner voice silently pronounces the words we are reading. But images (without text) hit the visual cortex first, allowing for fast and efficient processing. We can extract meaning from a picture in as little as 14 milliseconds, compared with 140 milliseconds for a single word (Ware 2010). Materials that blend traditional text and striking visuals enhance learning by engaging both verbal and visual processing.

Consider this example: If someone asked you to count the number of windows in your kitchen, you'd probably visualize the room and "see" the answer quickly. That's your rapid visual processing in action. Now think about a compelling advertisement you saw recently. Do you remember the words on the screen or the narrator's voice? Or are you seeing and imagining the feel of leather seats in a sleek black car, the pop of bright red lipstick, or the taste of a cheesy slice of pizza? The most effective ads rely heavily on striking visuals as well as words to convey their messages and evoke emotional and sensory responses. It's a cliché because it's true: A picture is worth a thousand words.

As learning designers, how can we harness the power of visuals? Jen is leading your workshop on effective sales strategies—the one that started with the scary graph of competitors' upward-trending sales. To drive home the importance of preparation, she displays a ticking 24-hour countdown clock on the screen. "What would you do if you only had 24 hours to prepare for a make-or-break sales pitch?" she asks. As participants brainstorm, Jen captures their ideas in a colorful, striking mind map next to the clock. The map helps focus everyone's attention and cement the essential steps to formulate a pitch.

Jen taps into our minds' natural processing preferences by putting visuals, in the form of a colorful, evolving mind map, at the center of her learning design. The images grab attention and help participants grasp and retain the core concepts more effectively.

6. Make It Emotional

"We are not thinking machines that feel. We are feeling machines that think." In this quote, widely attributed to Antonio Damasio, an eminent neuroscientist at the University of Southern California, we find a fundamental truth: Our emotions are not peripheral to cognition; they are central to that process.

Emotions play a crucial role in memory formation, motivation, and decision making (Phelps 2006). They are the intuitive thinking signal that something matters, driving attention and action. Yet, too often in designing learning experiences, we focus solely on conveying information and neglect the emotional dimension of learning. We assume learners will engage with and apply the knowledge we present if the facts are organized clearly and logically. This approach ignores the constant interplay between intuitive and deliberative thinking.

As Damasio suggests, deliberative thinking isn't alone in swaying our decisions. Emotions are the fuel that powers behavior. They shape what we pay attention to, what we remember, and what we do. This has profound implications for learning designers. We must engage learners emotionally to create experiences that truly resonate and inspire change. Let's revisit Jen one more time.

Jen is now leading a new workshop on conflict resolution. Rather than diving straight into a list of techniques, she structures the session as an emotional arc. She begins by evoking the tension and frustration of an unresolved conflict, the despair of stalled projects and frayed relationships. As she introduces new tools and techniques for resolving conflicts, she builds a sense of hope and possibility for the learners. They practice their new skills in role plays, experiencing the triumph of successful resolution. Throughout the workshop, Jen shares vivid stories and interactive exercises to make the emotional stakes feel real and relevant.

By designing for emotional resonance, Jen *motivates* learners while also informing them. She creates an experience that speaks to their core challenges and aspirations, priming them to internalize and apply the information.

A Toolkit for Engaging Learners

Let's now put our understanding of intuitive and deliberative thinking into practice. Try one, several, or all of the tools and techniques discussed here, which combine elements of intuitive and deliberative thinking in a way both Jen and Juan would appreciate.

Story-Based Learning

From case studies to simulations to role plays, stories are a powerful way to make learning personal, emotional, and memorable. They activate natural empathy and pattern-seeking circuits in our minds, allowing us to step into someone else's shoes and vicariously experience the consequences of different choices (Andrews et al. 2009). They can introduce concepts, illustrate their application, or reinforce key takeaways. Stories can be told through various media, including text, audio, video, and interactive scenarios. The key is to make the stories relatable, emotionally compelling, and connected to learning objectives (Reamy 2002).

Scenario-Based Learning

Realistic scenarios, whether presented as branching e-learning modules or live group challenges, immerse learners in authentic contexts and force them to grapple with the messy complexities of real-world decision making (Clark 2013). By providing a safe space to experiment, fail, and reflect, they build the kind of flexible expertise that transfers to actual performance.

Microlearning and Performance Support

Short, focused bursts of content, delivered at the point of need, cater to our preference for the immediate and applicable but can demand both intuitive and more deliberative ways of thinking (Kapp and Defelice 2019). Microlearning modules or performance-support tools that provide just-in-time guidance and feedback can help learners apply new skills when it matters most—in the heat of the moment, when the stakes are high and they're overwhelmed.

Visual Design
From graphic organizers to data visualizations to animated explainers, visuals can make complex information more accessible, engaging, and memorable (Malamed 2015). When designed with intention and restraint, they not only capture attention but also clarify key concepts and connections. The best visual aids don't decorate your content; they integrate with and elevate it.

Emotional Design
Small touches like warm color palettes, reader-friendly fonts, and encouraging language can make a big difference in how learners feel about a learning experience (Um et al. 2012). More elaborate techniques like gamification, humor, and surprise can inject moments of delight and discovery that keep learners motivated and engaged. The goal is not to manipulate emotions, but to create an authentic sense of connection and care.

Analogies and Metaphors
Analogies and metaphors help learners grasp unfamiliar ideas by relating them to familiar experiences. By linking abstract concepts to concrete images and sensations, we offer learners a new handle to grab onto. Effective analogies are vivid, memorable, and emotionally resonant (Bulgren et al. 2007).

Social Learning
Humans are intensely social creatures, wired to learn by watching and mimicking others. Social learning leverages this natural inclination by providing opportunities for people to observe, collaborate with, and learn from peers and experts (Bandura 1977). From discussion forums to group projects to mentoring relationships, social learning taps into our need for belonging and validation and can also allow for slower, more deliberative thinking during conversations.

Experiential Learning
Learning by doing is perhaps the most powerful way to engage intuitive thinking. Experiential learning activities, such as simulations, role plays, and real-world projects, allow learners to apply new skills in authentic contexts and learn from direct experience (Kolb 1984). By engaging both mind and body,

they create the kind of rich, multisensory memories that are easy to retrieve and apply.

Intuitive Thinking and Instructional Design

At this point, some learning designers might be skeptical of our emphasis on instinct, emotion, and experience. What about the tried-and-true principles of instructional design (ID)? What about the need for clear objectives, structured content, and rigorous evaluation?

We believe that an approach to learning design that pays attention to intuitive thinking doesn't replace traditional design foundations; it builds on them. We are not abandoning instructional design best practices; we are simply infusing them with a deeper understanding of how people learn and become inspired to act on their newfound knowledge.

Consider your go-to instructional design model. Whether you swear by the time-tested ADDIE framework, prefer the agility of the Successive Approximation Model (SAM), or use another approach, the intuitive thinking techniques we've explored can elevate every phase of your design process.

This doesn't replace your existing model; it enhances it. By infusing intuitive thinking principles into each stage, from initial analysis to final evaluation, we can create learning experiences that are not just effective but truly engaging. It's about marrying the structured approach of traditional models with the power of intuition, resulting in a flexible methodology that adapts to diverse learning contexts and design philosophies.

Imagine ADDIE, but with an emotional intelligence upgrade, or SAM, but with an intuitive edge that makes each iteration more effective. That's the transformative potential we're tapping into. Keep these core principles in mind:

- **Emotional connection.** Engage learners' emotions and personal experiences.
- **Intuitive processing.** Leverage rapid, instinctive cognitive processes.
- **Deliberative thinking.** Balance intuitive elements with opportunities for deep, analytical thinking.

- **Flexibility.** Adapt to different learning contexts and design models.
- **Iterative refinement.** Continuously improve based on feedback and outcomes.

Elevate Your Current ID Model

When we advocate for using insights from marketing, behavioral economics, and cognitive psychology in instructional design, it's not about reinventing the wheel—it's about adding a new set of gears. The strategies outlined in this section are designed to seamlessly integrate with your existing ID model. These tactics will help you transform your current model into a more holistic, learner-centered approach that not only imparts knowledge but also inspires action and fosters lasting change. Let's explore some strategies to elevate your practice, one phase at a time.

Needs assessment and analysis:
- Investigate learners' attitudes, motivations, and emotional connections to the topic.
- Identify potential cognitive biases or preconceptions.
- Balance intuitive insights with data-driven analysis.
- Explore the learner's hopes and fears, as well as and how the content connects to their identities and aspirations.

Design and development:
- Craft learning objectives that address both cognitive and affective domains.
- Use storytelling, analogies, and vivid examples to make content relatable and memorable.
- Incorporate visual design elements that guide intuitive understanding.
- Create opportunities for both quick, instinctive responses and in-depth analysis.
- Make each point personal, contrastable, tangible, memorable, visual, and emotional.
- Design activities that help learners discover and apply concepts intuitively.

Implementation:
- Set an emotional tone that promotes psychological safety and openness to learning.
- Use a mix of rapid, engaging activities and deeper, reflective exercises.
- Model vulnerability and growth mindset to encourage learner engagement.
- Create a sense of safety, belonging, and purpose in the learning environment.
- Provide feedback that feels supportive and constructive.

Evaluation:
- Assess both immediate, intuitive reactions and long-term, deliberative learning outcomes.
- Gather qualitative feedback on emotional engagement and personal relevance.
- Measure changes in attitudes and behaviors, not just knowledge acquisition.
- Collect stories from learners about their experiences and how they're applying what they've learned.

Dual Process Instructional Design: Intuitive and Deliberative Questions

Intuitive questions:
- What immediate reactions or emotions might learners have to the subject matter?
- What preconceptions or biases might learners bring to the topic?
- How can we use visual cues or intuitive layouts to guide learners?
- What metaphors or analogies can quickly convey complex ideas?
- What elements can we include to capture immediate attention (e.g., striking visuals or compelling stories)?
- How can we chunk information for easy processing?
- How can we create a positive first impression to engage our learners' emotions?
- What quick, interactive elements can maintain engagement?
- How can we gather immediate, intuitive feedback from learners?

Deliberative questions:
- What in-depth knowledge or skills do learners need to acquire?
- How can we encourage learners to critically examine their existing beliefs about the topic?
- What problem-solving activities will require deep, analytical thinking?
- How can we scaffold learning to gradually increase mental complexity?
- What opportunities can we provide for learners to practice deliberate, step-by-step reasoning?
- How can we incorporate reflective exercises to encourage deeper processing?
- How can we allocate time for learners to engage in deep discussion or complex problem solving?
- What strategies can we use to help learners overcome cognitive biases?
- How can we evaluate learners' ability to apply concepts in novel, complex situations?

By applying these strategies, considerations, and questions, you can enhance any instructional design model with principles of intuitive thinking, creating learning experiences that are both emotionally engaging and intellectually rigorous. Remember that emotion and cognition are inextricably intertwined in the learning process. By addressing both, we create more effective and memorable learning experiences.

Integrating these principles into each phase of your instructional design model helps to create learning content that is affective and effective, touching hearts as well as minds. The rigid separation of emotion and cognition is a false dichotomy. Intuitive and deliberative thinking are inextricably intertwined (Immordino-Yang and Damasio 2007). We cannot learn without feeling, and we cannot feel without learning. Emotion is not the enemy of reason but its essential partner.

Moreover, intuitive thinking is not a primitive, irrational impulse to be suppressed—it's an important part of how our brains work. The brain has different areas that do different jobs, like thinking logically, feeling emotions, and making choices. Intuition works with these other parts to help us understand complex situations and the world around us. When these brain areas work together, they shape who we are. Our brain's interconnection and teamwork influences our beliefs, motivates us, and helps us be creative. It's a big part of what makes us human.

Tap Learners' Emotions and Drive Action

To design learning that ignores intuitive thinking is to design for machines, not people. It is to assume that learners are empty vessels to be filled with facts and concepts rather than active, meaning-making agents with their own goals, desires, and perspectives.

Design attuned to our intuitive thinking recognizes and respects learners' humanity. It meets them where they are, not just intellectually but emotionally and experientially. It treats them as partners in the learning process, not just passive recipients. This is not to say that the techniques we've discussed should be used manipulatively or excessively. Like any powerful tools, they must be wielded with care and integrity. The goal is not to titillate or distract but to engage and empower. Whether you're designing technical training, a leadership development program, or an onboarding curriculum, considering how to make it personal, contrastable, tangible, memorable, visual, and emotional will only improve its effectiveness.

Marketers have long understood the power of engaging intuitive thinking. From Nike's energizing "Just Do It" ads to Subaru's emotionally resonant "Love" campaign, the world's top brands know that to drive action, you must first tap emotion.

Many L&D professionals have been stuck in an information-driven paradigm for too long. This is no longer viable in a world of increasing distraction. To cut through the noise and have a real influence, we must take some insights from marketers to recognize and respect the full complexity of the human mind and craft learning experiences that inform, inspire, and transform.

A Final Thought

As L&D professionals, we can amplify our results by embracing marketing principles that engage both intuitive and deliberative thinking. Let's harness the power of emotion, weave compelling narratives, and craft multisensory experiences that capture attention and drive lasting change. By making our content personal, contrastable, tangible, memorable, visual, and emotional, we'll see immense rewards. Our learners will be more engaged, our organizations will see improved outcomes, and we'll grow as professionals. So, let's take a page from the marketer's playbook and design learning programs that don't just inform, but truly transform.

Activity 1-1. Emotion-Infused Onboarding Makeover

Objective
Reimagine a portion of your current onboarding program by incorporating elements that engage intuitive thinking and emotions. (Note: If you would rather work on another initiative that's currently top of mind for you, feel free to use that idea instead.)

Steps
1. **Think about your current onboarding program.** Choose a specific module or section that is particularly information heavy or uses a traditional approach.
2. **Understand the emotional connection.** Consider the emotional journey of a new employee experiencing this part of onboarding. What might they be feeling? Excited? Overwhelmed? Curious? Anxious? Write down two to three key emotions.
3. **Apply the six principles.** Using the six principles discussed in this chapter, brainstorm ways to transform your chosen onboarding section. For each principle, write down at least one idea:
    » *Personal.* How could you connect the content to the new employee's role or goals?
    » *Contrastable.* What before-and-after scenarios or striking comparisons could you introduce?
    » *Tangible.* How could you make abstract concepts more concrete or hands-on?
    » *Memorable.* What story, analogy, or unexpected element could you incorporate?
    » *Visual.* How could you represent key information visually instead of just relying on text?
    » *Emotional.* How could you tap into or address the emotions you identified earlier?

4. **Review your ideas.** Choose the one you think would have the best ability to engage new employees and make the information stick. Write a brief paragraph describing how you would implement this change and what influence you think it would have.

Follow-Up

As you continue your learning journey, consider gradually applying these principles to other aspects of the onboarding program. Remember, the goal is not to completely overhaul everything at once but to incrementally enhance engagement and effectiveness by tapping into intuitive thinking and emotions.

Chapter 2
Create Learner Personas That Inspire

> When dealing with people, remember you are not dealing with creatures of logic, but with creatures of emotion.
> —Dale Carnegie, author and self-improvement lecturer

Years ago, Bianca ran design thinking workshops in which the goal was to identify the right learning strategy to solve a problem. (Design thinking is a problem-solving process popularized by designer Tim Brown, who leads the design firm IDEO.) In one of Bianca's workshops, participants rapidly created learner personas during the *empathize phase*. Personas 1 and 2 elicited lots of engagement, but the third was a different story. Once the group had identified the job role for Persona 3, the session came to a standstill, with the participants saying almost nothing. Bianca was baffled.

After a short break, Bianca asked a co-worker to function as a facilitator. When that didn't work, she decided to put a pin in the Persona 3 discussion, hoping to revisit the session the next day. That evening she felt frustrated and had a tough time coming up with solutions because she couldn't identify what had shut down the group discussion so suddenly and completely.

The next morning, Nabeeha, the training lead who had been in the workshop the previous day, took Bianca aside for a presession chat. "I'm so sorry about what happened yesterday," she said. "I think I can shed some light on the situation. You were trying to create a persona for an aspiring new partner in the firm, and there were two senior partners in the room. One of them is publicly on record as being in favor of promoting more people to partnership, and the other is strongly against it." The difficulty of the situation started to become clear.

"To make matters worse," she continued, "An aspiring partner—a real-life version of Persona 3—was sitting *in between the two partners* during the exercise." Talk about an awkward moment! Bianca thanked Nabeeha and quickly came up with an alternate exercise to use in the session. The lesson learned that day is something Bianca still tries to impress upon anyone interested in developing and using learner personas: It's all about knowing your audience, whether they're far away or in the room with you.

As L&D professionals, we all tend to focus most on the content we want participants to learn. We rarely take enough time to think deeply about the target audience who will be consuming the content, and that's a mistake. We need to explore the audience in terms of both basic population demographics (age, gender, location, language, and so on) and their personal qualities, including likes, dislikes, thoughts, and emotions. The key to creating learning solutions that are relevant and effective for our audience isn't about more interactivity or louder bells and whistles; it's about understanding their motivations and what drives them to do what they do. If we can unlock our participants' motivational DNA, our training programs can be much more effective.

Marketers are keenly aware of the importance of tailoring their campaigns to their target audience. They also employ a tactic called *segmentation*, which further customizes the message to specific interests or buying intentions. Without this tactic, most recipients would receive irrelevant content. Segmentation makes organizations 60 percent more likely to understand customers' challenges and an amazing 130 percent more likely to know their intentions. When segmentation is based on personas, companies have 90 percent better knowledge about their audience (Baker 2024).

As L&D professionals, we have to ask: Knowing how valuable they are, why *wouldn't* we adopt segmentation and personas to create more targeted and relevant learning content?

> **Terms You Should Know**
>
> **Segmentation**
> *Segmentation* is the process of dividing a large group into smaller, more targeted subgroups based on shared characteristics or behaviors. In the context of marketing, segmentation can help organizations better understand their customers' challenges and intentions and increase their overall knowledge about their audience. The same holds true for L&D pros who want to understand their learners better.

Over the past few years, the L&D community has had useful conversations about learner personas, and they are now more widely used. But even as learner personas have increased in popularity, some designers consider them just another item to check off during a project's analysis phase before moving on to focus on the content design phase. We believe personas are integral to the design phase of any project. In this chapter, we will discuss what a learner persona is, why the concept is so important in learning experience design, and how to create and use them in your projects.

What Are Learner Personas?

Learner personas are fictional characters who represent typical learners. By using personas, we can gain valuable insights into our audience and effectively tailor our approach to meet our learners' preferences and needs. Typically, one part of the learner persona consists of demographic information—such as job role, department, level of education, location, and tenure at the organization—to create a story about the learner.

We believe it's best to name and produce a profile image of a persona while developing this story to bring it to life. We also like to add information about the persona's interests and connections outside work and some personal goals to the story we generate. Some of this information is what a typical target audience analysis would uncover, but personas go beyond basic analysis to capture more about the learner, including whatever they might see, hear, think, do, and feel every day.

Origins

In marketing, personas originated as a way for organizations to better understand and target specific customer segments. For example, a *buyer persona* would be a fictional representation of an organization's ideal customer, based on data and research about that person's characteristics, goals, challenges, and behaviors. When you create an extremely detailed picture of the customer, marketing efforts can be tailored more precisely to meet their needs and preferences.

Personas have been used in advertising since the 1950s and became common in marketing in the 1990s, but were only recently applied to the field of L&D. As organizations began to recognize the importance of creating more engaging and effective learning experiences, they adopted the persona approach to better understand and cater to the needs of all learners. Learner personas are similar to buyer personas in that they are based on extensive research about learners' characteristics, goals, challenges, and behaviors. They can be used to create tailored experiences that are much more engaging, effective, and relevant to the people we want to reach.

Human-Centered Learning

We see learner personas as part of our larger effort to create more human-centered learning experiences for employees. Solid research supports the notion that human-centered learning experiences motivate modern learners (Deloitte 2019). These experiences happen at the intersection of *employee-led experiences* (which consider the employee's pre-existing tendencies to optimize working conditions) and *personal experiences* (which focus more on employees' psychological and emotional needs).

When we create learner personas, we take the first important step toward designing human-centered learning and examining how work helps employees achieve their goals and aspirations. We also pay closer attention to work environments—including co-workers, managers, tools, and equipment—in the workplace. We shift our initial focus as learning designers away from content and toward the people who are interacting with an organization's customers and clients. In establishing this human-centered focus, we try to help employees answer the question: *Am I making a difference?*

On a practical level, when we move from an abstract concept of the ideal learner to a more defined representation, we remove some of the guesswork from our design projects. We begin to understand what intrinsically motivates our learners to increase engagement, learning outcomes, productivity, and inclusivity for a diverse learner population. In short, learner personas and the human-centered learning experiences they provide help us design more meaningful projects based on the learners' day-to-day work and interests.

Learners in 3D

Sometimes colleagues challenge us to show the value of personas and to admit that, of course, they aren't a perfect solution. Using learner personas won't allow us to personalize every employee's learning experience, but they do help us to go far beyond traditional target audience analysis to understand learners in three dimensions rather than static two-dimensional data. Simply put, we can put ourselves in our audience's shoes.

With more information about learners' emotional lives, we can determine their pain points and greatest needs, see the bigger picture of their life experiences, and create more cohesive learning environments that cater to those needs. By identifying and understanding the *intrinsic* (or internal) elements that motivate learners and the *extrinsic* (or external) elements that motivate them, we can share the right content at the right time and place. We think this amounts to a huge win.

We should also note that tools based on artificial intelligence (AI), which are starting to influence the work of L&D professionals as we write this book, will allow us to leverage more and more personalization. We expect the combination of well-crafted learner personas and AI-based personalization of learning to help us serve everyone better in the future.

Create Effective Learner Personas

Learner personas have broad applicability across an organization. They are often developed in response to a specific project and revisited later, as needed, for other projects. A typical organization might create three to five personas (with this number increasing based on the size of the organization, its global footprint, or the number of business units). If you have too few personas, you will end up designing learning experiences with broad strokes and focusing on content instead of the learner. If you have too many personas in place, you may quickly overcomplicate your learning designs.

Too often, organizations jump straight to creating personas based on common wisdom, assumptions, or anecdotal feedback. We advocate for a thorough, research-based approach that includes four steps:
1. Align stakeholders and learners.
2. Gather information.
3. Analyze information.
4. Create learner personas.

The process sounds simple, but you should be aware that well-crafted personas take time, usually three or four months, depending on how many you create.

Step 1. Align Stakeholders and Learners

The most important step in creating personas is to identify which organizational business units need to be represented and who, within those units, should be included at the table as stakeholders. Aligning those stakeholders and getting their buy-in is crucial to success because they usually know the organization and learners well and can help determine the best methods for gathering information, including learner and manager interviews, surveys, observations, employee data, or a combination of these approaches.

Unfortunately, we have seen many projects fail during this early phase, mainly because stakeholders don't understand why the effort of creating personas is worthwhile.

Enlist Stakeholder Support

When it comes to setting up interviews, a variety of stakeholders (managers, executives, and relevant IT and HR players) can help you determine whether it's feasible to remove employees from their duties and, if so, for how long. You must ensure that managers are supportive of the initiative because their opposition can lead to a challenging uphill battle.

When you consult and align with stakeholders early on, you can secure their commitment to support your work and manage everyone's expectations throughout the process. Ideally, you will schedule two stakeholder meetings:

- **In the first meeting,** generate excitement, educate stakeholders about learner personas, and decide which personas to focus on.
- **In the second meeting,** discuss the information-gathering and communications processes.

It's important to make an impact with the first meeting. We generate excitement by introducing the concept of personas and highlighting all their benefits. For some stakeholders, personas will be new, and their value might not yet be understood. Drawing parallels to marketing's use of personas can help, because most of your stakeholders will understand and appreciate the concept of a buyer or customer persona. We encourage you to introduce the human-centered design concept in your first meeting. If your stakeholders want more information, refer them to helpful resources such as the Interaction Design Foundation and IDEO.

A practical example that showcases the transformative power of human-centric design and provides a terrific selling point is the work of Doug Dietz, who oversaw the redesign of an MRI scanner during his time at General Electric. (We recommend watching his talk at TEDx San Jose 2012, "Transforming Healthcare for Children and Their Families.") Dietz dedicated two years to revamping the machine to make it look sleeker and less intrusive and scary for patients. However, after observing his new machine's use in hospitals, he realized children were still terrified. In fact, 80 percent of all children undergoing the MRI procedure had to be sedated. Dietz had failed to consider the needs of *all* users, only designing the scanner from his perspective as an adult man.

Determined to rectify the situation, Dietz went back to the drawing board and created a more child-friendly environment. The pirate adventure MRI was born. Instead of a standard MRI scanner in a sterile room, Dietz imagined a pirate adventure. In his redesign, the MRI scanner represents a pirate ship with a railing and sails in the middle of the sea. The room is covered in bright colors and creates an atmosphere that directs children's attention away from the scary machine. As a result, the instances of sedation for children undergoing an MRI with this machine dropped below 8 percent.

Use this example to help stakeholders better understand why learner-centric design is crucial and how learner personas can support better learning design by putting the audience at the heart of everything we do.

Finally, we also suggest you showcase examples of learner personas and emphasize the creation process, which includes consulting with learners and their managers. Rather than diving deep into the nitty-gritty of time and effort, it's better to highlight the importance of personas at this stage. This approach makes it easier to gain buy-in over time.

Once stakeholders are on board with the idea of learner-centric design, it's time to discuss which personas to develop. Your focus in these discussions might focus on individual contributors or managers or whether to base personas on specific job roles or attitudes and aptitudes such as *achiever* or *supporter*. Here, it's helpful to segment the audience into groups first and then define more detailed persona characteristics for each group.

Segment Your Audience

Marketers often use five types of segmentation when dividing a larger audience into subsets of customers with common characteristics:

- **Demographic** is based on traits such as gender, age, level of education, or occupation.
- **Psychographic** is based on personalities and interests.
- **Geographic** is based on their location, which can include in-office and remote workers.
- **Behavioral** is based on their actions—what they do and don't do at work.
- **Firmographic** is based on the organization they work for (such as size, number of employees, revenue, or other characteristics).

Segmentation is a great way to enhance the focus of your marketing efforts and gain insights into several markets at the same time. It also allows marketers to delight customers (perhaps with a personalized holiday gift), which often results in better customer retention. In L&D, we can delight our learners by personalizing their experiences so they're only required to take the training they need due to our knowledge of their pre-existing knowledge.

Be sure to keep your segments broad enough. If they are too narrow, you run the risk of compiling data that is not statistically relevant. Segments should also be fluid, meaning they can change over time and are revisited regularly. And yes, this fluidity can make segmentation a time-consuming and costly process.

In L&D, the most common segments are job roles and geographic areas. We first identify what is already known about a segment and then list what we still need to learn. Table 2-1 offers an example of what an initial segmentation might look like.

Table 2-1. Learner Segments

Learner Segment	What We Know	What We Don't Know
New consultants	• They bring a range of skills and backgrounds. • They are comfortable with high-tech devices and learning solutions.	• How do they interact with other learner segments? • Are they interested in mentoring and coaching opportunities?
Mature consultants	• They are veterans of the industry. • They are less comfortable with high-tech devices and learning solutions.	• Are they open to new ways of learning? • Are they willing to change the way they work right now?

⚑ Terms You Should Know

Segmentation, Targeting, and Positioning
Segmentation refers to creating groups based on shared traits, such as geography or job roles. *Targeting* determines which segment you want to focus on—meaning that you are sharing specific information with a specific segment. And *positioning* is the act of developing tools and tactics to reach segments based on their preferences.

Discuss Information Gathering and Processing

During your second meeting with stakeholders, we recommend getting their buy-in about how to gather learner information. There are a few ways to do this:

- **One-on-one interviews and learner observations** are the best ways to achieve deep insights into learners' thoughts, emotions, and day-to-day experiences, but these methods take the most time.

- **Focus groups** can be another great option because you can talk to multiple people at the same time. However, learners may not feel as comfortable opening up in a group setting as they do in one-on-one conversations.
- **Surveys** are valuable, especially if stakeholders don't want to take employees off the clock for too long. But they don't allow you to ask follow-up questions.
- **Employee data** helps cement findings from interviews, observations, focus groups, or surveys. They build the backbone for a persona.

It's important to discuss the advantages and disadvantages of each option with stakeholders to make the best decision. After a decision has been made, designers and stakeholders need to determine which learners and managers will be involved in the process going forward and what questions to ask.

Follow Best Practices

In the data-gathering process for creating learner personas, it is best practice to include high and low performers to make sure a broad spectrum of knowledge, skills, and abilities is represented. As a rule, high performers will always be more engaged and willing to help compared with low performers. At the same time, high performers might motivate low performers to be part of the information-gathering process; they can act as ambassadors. It's also crucial to include multiple business lines and, if applicable, multiple geographies for the best outcomes. Of course, always mention that the responses are all anonymous and confidential. Let's look at a few other best practices in each category of data gathering.

Interviews and Focus Groups

In interviews and focus groups, keep questions broad and not restricted to learning-related topics. Remember that we want to create learner personas that encompass the learner as a whole. In human-centered design, we assume that there is a link between who our learners are outside work and who they are on the job every day. And if the organization is facing a specific challenge, you should address it head-on with a targeted question.

Questions in an interview or focus group might include:
- Can you describe your typical day for me?
- What are some of the challenges you face every day? Why are they challenges?
- What are some of the areas of your day-to-day work that delight you? Why?
- Does anything stand in the way of working to your full potential?
- What training opportunities have you had during your time with us?
- What else do you want to share today?

Surveys

In surveys, make sure your questions are similar to those we suggested for interviews. Don't ask more than 10 questions, so learners can easily complete the survey within 15 to 20 minutes. Ideally, you should create the survey on a platform that allows you to automatically collect all responses in a spreadsheet automatically, which will save you time later in the analysis phase. Set the stage for learners in the introductory text of the survey by giving them a high-level overview of the purpose of the survey and the time it will take to complete.

Observation

Observation is a great way to get deep insights into the day-to-day work of learners. Blue-collar jobs lend themselves much more to observation than white-collar jobs. You can easily join learners in blue-collar jobs at work to observe them throughout a full day of interactions. When it comes to white-collar workers, you will need to get managers involved. Managers can observe employees over multiple weeks and share feedback directly with you. When you or a manager sets out to observe learners, use a checklist to help standardize and streamline findings, particularly if several individuals will be observing. Develop the checklist after reviewing initial interviews, focus groups, or surveys. A tool such as a Likert-type scale can be helpful when combined with written notes.

Here is an example of a simple observation checklist that might be used for a sales position:
- Demographic and geographic employee information

- First area of focus: Customer greeting
- Second area of focus: Product presentation
- Third area of focus: Making the sale
- Fourth area of focus: Customer follow-up
- Other comments and observations

Employee Data

Employee data often provides additional insights about learners, but you'll need to discuss with stakeholders which data would be most beneficial. Your stakeholders can reach out to the appropriate people within the organization and pave the way for easy access to data later. Data sources could include demographic information from the HR department, usage data from the organization's intranet, or information from a messaging system such as Teams or Slack, a learning management system (LMS), or a learning experience platform (LXP). Annual employee pulse surveys, if available, can also be a valuable source of information. You will use the employee data during the analysis phase to augment findings from interviews, focus groups, or surveys and create a well-rounded learner persona.

Decide How to Communicate

After you've worked with stakeholders to plan the information-gathering process, you'll need to decide who will conduct interviews or focus groups, and, if applicable, who will distribute surveys, and who will be observing learners. Equipped with a list of names and decisions about the data collection approach, you can then communicate that information to managers.

Any communication with managers should come from the organization's leaders, who should explain the reasons for developing learner personas, what it means for managers and employees, and how they can support the effort. Managers should see that the initiative is driven and supported by those at the top. Communication should go out at least two weeks before the first interview, focus group, survey, or observation to allow managers to ask any questions they might have. This time will also allow you to address any concerns and bring the stakeholders back into the conversation as needed to help managers understand the importance of the approach.

As soon as you have the managers' buy-in, you can reach out to learners and invite them to participate in the interviews, focus group, or survey, or let them know about the observation sessions. The invitation should include the purpose of the interviews, focus group, survey, or observations, the questions you will ask, and a reminder that all interviews and observations will be kept confidential.

When Research Hits a Roadblock

Sometimes, despite our best efforts, we cannot convince an organization to let us create research-based learner personas. In this case, we have to take a step back and pivot to another approach.

Instead of spending time and effort gathering data, we bring stakeholders together for another meeting to go through a rapid persona creation exercise. During this collaborative session, we like to facilitate a conversation about the typical learner using the same questions we would have asked learners directly. Instead of getting the information from the learners, stakeholders assume the learners' point of view, and we create a rapid persona. This is, of course, less than ideal and can lead to misunderstandings like the one we shared at the beginning of this chapter. However, the exercise usually gets stakeholders in the mindset of focusing on the learner before the content. In our experience, stakeholders who have participated in a rapid persona exercise are more willing to spend time and money on research-based personas in the future.

Step 2. Gather Information

As noted, we consider learner and manager interviews and focus groups the best sources of information when creating personas. In some industries, observing learners can give us valuable insights as well. We also want to leverage any relevant employee data and analytics from HR or the IT department. We'll now go over a few details about each approach to information gathering.

Interviews and Focus Groups

We aim to interview 10 to 15 learners per persona to identify trends. For manager interviews, a sample size of five to eight is sufficient. We always conduct learner interviews first because this allows us to ask managers more specific questions based on findings from the learner interviews. The number of questions for each learner or manager should not exceed six. Always use the same initial questions, but you can ask different follow-up questions based on what learners and managers share.

Focus groups should have a maximum of five participants, should be scheduled for one hour, and include no more than 10 prepared questions. We often find that 30 minute one-on-one interviews yield better results because they allow for more honest answers. The choice of focus groups or one-on-one interviews will depend on the culture of the organization.

For both interviews and focus groups, a best practice is to have a separate notetaker in attendance. This allows the interviewer to focus on the interviewee, maintain eye contact, and read body language. When starting the interview, the interviewer should take a moment to introduce themself and the notetaker, talk about the reason for the meeting, and share again that all responses are confidential and will be handled anonymously.

All responses should be transcribed. The notetaker might want to add additional words for clarification in brackets or move learner answers to appropriate questions. Always spend time right after the interview cleaning up notes. Immediately begin collecting common themes and threads in a separate spreadsheet tab or document, which will make data analysis easier later. Many meeting tools now have AI functionality that allows you to automatically transcribe a meeting—a huge time saver that could replace the need for a notetaker in some cases.

Be aware that if employees get a chance to share insights about their work, the conversation can quickly turn negative. This is normal, but it is up to the interviewer to bring the conversation back on track and identify positive experiences as well.

We like to collect all learner responses in one spreadsheet, organizing the questions horizontally with individual learner responses vertically. This arrangement allows us to easily scan all answers for each question, identify trends, and spot differences. It not only streamlines our process but also ensures that the responses are well-organized and easily accessible. By simplifying data collection and organization, we can focus on what truly matters—drawing insights from people and creating solutions that resonate with the target audience.

Let's look at a use case to help us better understand how learner personas can make a difference. We will carry this particular example throughout the rest of the book as a way of illustrating the points we want to make in each chapter.

> **Background:** A national high-end kitchen design-and-build chain called LuxeKitchens saw a marked decline in their sales consultants' skills and performance over the course of a year. The company wanted to look at how to refresh its existing sales training program. The project started with learner interviews.
>
> Here's an excerpt of some of the responses:
>
> **Learner 1**
>
> *1. Describe your typical day.*
> My daily commute is 100 miles—so 50 miles there and back. I get in at 9 a.m. I'll take a look at leads, what we have in stock, and go over appointments. This cycle continues throughout the day unless there's specific training that needs to be done. I've been in this position for about a year. I came from an HR and payroll background and I use my skills from my previous job. My new job relates to my old career because I have to deal with customers and employees on a daily basis. I have to know how to talk to people with different personalities. Every customer has different wants and needs, and I have to be able to read them correctly. This job isn't just about making sales, it's about me helping customers find what they want. I don't consider myself to be a typical salesperson.
>
> *2. What are some of the challenges you face every day? Why?*
> As a sales consultant, our lack of inventory is a big challenge and it's frustrating to explain to customers why delivery might take longer than expected. The electronic sales guide is also a hurdle.

Create Learner Personas That Inspire | 41

Often, customers don't understand why we use our tablets when we talk to them. They like to see what their end product might look like, but they also don't have the patience to watch an entire video. It would be better if we could just email them some links, and then, after the sale is complete, send them a survey. Sometimes, we get bad ratings because customers feel like we wasted their time. That's frustrating.

3. What areas of your day-to-day work delight you? Why?
You know what my favorite part of the day is? Helping people who have made some not-so-great financial decisions buy a new kitchen. It's really satisfying to be able to share my knowledge and expertise with them and help them get back on track. It's a great feeling to provide that kind of assistance to a customer and help them live their life more successfully.

4. Does anything stand in the way of you giving your full potential at work?
I've noticed that sometimes I put limits or boundaries on myself without even trying to push them. It can be tough when external factors like a supply shortage limit me, but I try to remember that it's something outside my control. And sometimes, my family life can get in the way, and I have to prioritize them over work, but nothing specific comes to mind at the moment.

5. What else would you like to share?
When we're trying to help a customer design their new kitchen, the software often acts up and it can take up to five minutes or longer to resolve. Honestly, it makes me wonder if the organization still has some kinks to work out with the technology. I think it would be helpful if we could have a trainer from the organization come to the showroom again. Virtual training is great, but there's just something about having someone help us work through the issues in person that we're encountering in the field. It's like the difference between talking

to an expert for an hour on the phone versus having them in the showroom with us all day.

6. What training opportunities have you had during your time with us?
I've already taken all the new product training courses. However, I'm someone who values hands-on experience. So, whenever there's a new product, I like to get a feel for it. Now, when it comes to certification requirements, I have to be honest—some of them feel a bit repetitive to me. I mean, if there are major differences between brands, then I understand the need for a product test. But it seems like we're being tested on the same content every year. It would be awesome if we could have a bit more flexibility when it comes to required courses based on our tenure.

7. Outside work, when you need to learn something or find answers, what do you do? Describe the process for me.
If I ever need to find an answer, I've got a few options! I ask my amazing wife, who always seems to know where to look. Or, I turn to trusty old Google for some help. And of course, there's always YouTube—the perfect place to learn just about anything!

Learner 2

1. Describe your typical day.
I've been a sales consultant for almost eight years now, and I absolutely love my store. However, I feel like the organization doesn't appreciate the salespeople and focuses on the wrong things. Our training used to be all about the different brands and technology options, but now it's focused on demographics for marketing. While that's important, I don't think we're getting the training we need to actually sell kitchens, especially now that there are product shortages. I think it's important to have someone come to the showroom to train us, rather than just doing online training courses. It forces us to have conversations and really engage with the material.

The issue is that there's no incentive for us to be 100 percent certified. We're expected to be certified, but there's no reward or compensation for it. I don't think the organization is doing a good job of taking care of the people who are selling the brand. One frustrating thing is the surveys we receive from customers. They're terrible, and I feel like they're set up in a way that makes it impossible for us to get 100 percent. The wording is confusing and can be biased against us.

2. *What are some of the challenges you face every day? Why?*
Right now, we're dealing with a shortage of materials, which can lead to frustrated customers asking why we don't have certain products or brands and why their kitchens aren't arriving on time. It's a challenge, but we're doing our best to handle it. Another thing we're working on is promoting the organization's brand. It's very different than it was just a few years ago, and we have a lot of benefits over the competition. But we still get customers asking why they should choose our organization when they can get something else for less. It's our job to help them see the value in the brand. That being said, I haven't seen any specific training on how to communicate the brand to customers. While we have courses on the topic, they don't necessarily provide guidance on how to handle negative comments. If someone puts down the brand, I'm not sure what to say.

3. *What areas of your day-to-day work delight you? Why?*
One of the things I absolutely love about my job is when customers leave happy. It's such a great feeling to know that I was able to help someone find the kitchen they were looking for, especially if they initially thought it wasn't possible.

Let me tell you about this one customer I had who was looking for a kitchen with all the bells and whistles, smart electronics, you name it. He was an elderly man who wanted to surprise his wife. I took time to explain to him the different available options, and we ended up not adding the smart technologies after all, but that's OK. I remember he asked me if I could get mail at work, and I said yes. A few days later, I received a letter from him thanking me for taking the time to explain everything. He even included an origami creature made out of a $100 bill as a thank-you gesture! It really made my day. It's moments like these that make me realize how important it is to treat people with kindness and respect, even if they don't end up buying a kitchen from me. I try my best to put myself in their shoes and make sure they leave happy, and it's always rewarding when they appreciate what I do for them.

4. Does anything stand in the way of you giving your full potential at work?
The lack of inventory is tough on me and the team. Plus, having to deal with the clunky software while the customer sits with us is frustrating. Another thing that's been holding me back is the sales tracking system. It can be inaccurate, which can make it hard to reach my full potential. Sometimes it says I'm at 86 percent of my goal when I know I've gone through everything with my customers. And when the system is unavailable, it's tough to get customers to come back and go through everything with me. With all the new programs the organization has implemented, it feels like I'm constantly jumping through hoops just to earn my bonus. But I'm staying positive and doing my best to work through these challenges.

5. What else would you like to share?
I consider myself a hands-on learner, so I really appreciate having an instructor physically present at the showroom. While web-based training can be helpful, the 30-minute videos can be overwhelming with all the information packed in. Personally, I would love to have more opportunities for in-person training. Sitting in front of a computer for 30 minutes straight can be a bit dull.

6. What training opportunities have you had during your time with us?
Lately, the training has been mostly online, but I have to say, I really enjoyed the hands-on training we used to have with trainers who would demo the different features of each brand. We still have trainers come in occasionally, but it's not as often as I would like. Online training is usually easy, but I'm not sure how new employees can learn effectively just by taking tests. They really need hands-on experience.

One of the best training programs I ever participated in was when someone came in and talked to us about the challenges of installing the various brands. It really opened my eyes to what the customer experience is like after I sell them a kitchen. This type of hands-on experience is much more valuable than just searching for answers to questions. Plus, most of the time, the questions being tested aren't even the ones customers are asking.

I would love to have a tool that makes it easy to compare features across brands. It's difficult to do so now. The paper guides were the most helpful—they listed all the features and checked off which brand had each one.

7. Outside work, when you need to learn something or find answers, what do you do? Describe the process for me.
We have an awesome YouTube channel that I love to share with customers who want to learn more about installing and maintaining their new kitchens. It's a great resource if they forget something or if we don't cover it. Plus, who doesn't love a good visual aid? Whenever I need to look up something specific, I usually just do a quick Google search. Sometimes I end up on our organization's channel, but other times I find videos from other stores. If I ever figure out how to make videos myself, I'd love to upload them too! Fun fact: Before I worked here, I used to be a teacher and I actually made videos for my classes. I just need to figure out the YouTube part.

Surveys

If the only option to gather information from learners is through a survey, we suggest sending it to 20 to 25 people per learner persona. You won't get a 100 percent response, but you'll typically get 10 to 15 responses per persona. If the survey is set up correctly, the survey platform will automatically collect individual responses to each question. We usually go into the file and clean up some of the responses to ensure we understand what learners are sharing. If something is unclear in the responses, try to reach out to the learner for clarification.

Observations

We find that five to eight learner observations will complement learner interviews for each persona. You must establish the purpose of the observations to ensure that employees understand they will not be evaluated on their performance and that your focus is solely on identifying opportunities and pain points in the larger group. Sharing the observation checklist in advance and taking the time to explain the process and answer any questions is always helpful. And again, be sure to explain to employees that the observations and findings will be handled anonymously and confidentially.

When arriving at an employee's workplace, observers should introduce themselves and build rapport with any employees they observe. Keep in mind that it can be awkward for employees to be observed. Position observers close enough so they can truly see the learner's day-to-day work and interactions but far enough away that they don't skew results.

Observation findings should be collected in a central place, similar to the spreadsheet mentioned earlier, to more easily identify trends and similarities during the analysis phase. If multiple people are observing learners, we like to review all observation checklists before entering them into the central file. This creates consistency and makes data analysis much easier.

Employee Data

As we've mentioned already, employee data can come from various sources, which means it can also come in various forms. This lack of uniformity can be challenging. In the information-gathering stage, we focus on getting access to various systems and platforms (also a challenge!) and building relationships with the people who own these platforms. Downloading and saving reports is all we usually do at this stage.

Step 3. Analyze the Information

Whether we conduct interviews or focus groups, send out surveys, or observe employees' behaviors, we must combine our findings into a single source of truth and analyze them consistently. Sometimes, the amount of data we've collected can be overwhelming. That's why identifying trends and similarities is so essential. Through this process, we can effectively interpret the information and draw practical insights that will improve everyone's learning experience. Analysis is another task for which AI may become a huge time saver. AI tools can synthesize trends and similarities and lay down a baseline for creating learner personas.

Analyzing all the information you have collected and creating learner personas go hand-in-hand. When it comes to learner persona templates, there is no definitive right or wrong option, and there are multiple examples online that can serve as a starting point. Figure 2-1 shows a template that captures demographic information; what learners see, hear, do, think, and feel; their pain points; and their needs.

No matter which template you use, the most effective learner personas incorporate the emotional states of the learner and gather nonwork-related information. The needs and pain points of each persona should also be included.

Integrating the data you've gathered into a single persona template may appear overwhelming at first, but a systematic approach will simplify the process. By analyzing each question separately, you can classify responses into relevant categories and identify key themes. Consolidating similar responses into a single statement allows you to summarize the data effectively. Incorporating quotes can also add clarity to the findings. We recommend using AI tools to get started on these time-consuming processes.

Let's now return to our earlier example about the sales consultants at LuxeKitchens. We've created three examples of how we might transition from the responses in the spreadsheet to information presented in a template for the learner persona we have called Jordan, including quotes from learners and our summary analysis.

Figure 2-1. Learner Persona

Jordan Bark

Age: 26
Location: Nashville, TN
Tenure: 5 years
Role: Sales Consultant
Education: High School
Goal: Own his own franchise

Tech-savviness: High
Interests: Running and reading
Best time to learn: Late in the day
Can access training through: Any digital format
Other: He volunteers his time at a local charity

See
- Jordan sees a lack of inventory every day
- Jordan sees happy customers, but also disgruntled customers that aren't happy with delivery delays
- Jordan sees long, virtual trainings that don't meet his needs and are too long
- Jordan sees a buggy electronic sales guide
- Jordan sees a cumbersome certification program

Hear
- Jordan hears customers questioning the value of their brand
- Jordan hears customers complaining about delivery delays
- Jordan hears from satisfied customers after their kitchen has arrived
- Jordan hears his boss telling him about having to take the certification training
- Jordan hears from his coworkers that they miss in-person training

Do
- Jordan books meetings through email or over the phone, and takes walk-ins
- Jordan assesses customers' needs
- Jordan helps customers find their perfect high-end kitchen
- Jordan uses software while consulting customers on their new kitchens
- Jordan follows-up with customers on a regular basis

Think and Feel
- Jordan feels frustrated because of the lack of products
- Jordan loves helping customers, and he feels satisfied when customers leave happy
- Jordan thinks that in-person hands-on training is more valuable than online training
- Jordan feels challenged talking to difficult customers

Pain Points
- Because of product shortages, it's challenging for Jordan to explain to customers why deliveries are delayed, which affects his customer satisfaction scores
- Jordan doesn't know how to convey his organization's brand value to customers
- Jordan doesn't appreciate hour-long, online training sessions
- It's difficult for Jordan to have a seamless sales conversation when the electronic sales guide doesn't function properly
- The certification process is too cumbersome and doesn't teach Jordan the things he really needs to know about

Needs
- Jordan needs tools and tactics that allow him to overcome challenging customer conversations due to the shortage of products
- Jordan needs brand training to sell the value of the organization's brand to customers
- Jordan needs training that is shorter and in-person. He needs flexible training options that cater to his needs
- Jordan needs an electronic sales guide that has no bugs so he can delight his customers
- Jordan needs the certification requirements to be changed so his training and learning is relevant to him

Create Learner Personas That Inspire | 49

Example 1. What Learners See

When asked to describe their typical day, learner 1 said, "As a sales consultant, our lack of inventory is a big challenge, and it's frustrating to explain to customers why delivery might take longer than expected." Learner 2 said, "Right now, we're dealing with a shortage of materials, which can lead to frustrated customers asking why we don't have certain products or brands and why their kitchens aren't arriving on time. It's a challenge, but we're doing our best to handle it."

These comments show that our learners see a lack of inventory every day. We can summarize them under the *see* category as "Jordan sees a lack of inventory every day." Moreover, because the two learners both expressed some frustration, we can categorize their feedback under *think and feel* by stating, "Jordan feels frustrated by the lack of products."

Example 2. What Learners Think and Feel

When asked what areas of their day-to-day work delight them, learner 1 said, "You know what my favorite part of the day is? Helping people who have made some not-so-great financial decisions buy a new kitchen. It's really satisfying to be able to share my knowledge and expertise with them and help them get back on track. Being able to provide that kind of assistance to a customer and help them live their life more successfully is a great feeling."

Learner 2 said, "One of the things I absolutely love about my job is when customers leave happy. It's such a great feeling to know that I was able to help someone find the kitchen they were looking for, especially if they initially thought it wasn't possible."

Both learners express strong emotions in these two statements. It's clear they fit into the *think and feel* category, and we can condense them into the summary statement: "Jordan loves helping customers, and he feels satisfied when customers leave happy." In addition, the responses gave us insight into what drives and motivates Jordan, which is helping customers.

Now, we can answer Jordan's question: "How am I making a difference?" This speaks to the core of human-centered design and allows us to create relevance for him in our training.

Remember: To ensure accuracy in your analysis, it's essential to stay as close as possible to the learners' actual words and avoid personal interpretations. Once the emotional states have been completed, we can synthesize pain points and needs from each section.

Example 3. Learners' Pain Points and Needs

Based on our *see* and *think and feel* categories, we can identify Jordan's pain points and needs:

- **Pain point**—"Because of product shortages, it's challenging for Jordan to explain to customers why deliveries are delayed, which affects his customer satisfaction scores."
- **Need**—"Jordan needs tools and tactics that allow him to overcome challenging customer conversations due to the shortage of products."

As you develop your learner personas, you'll come across individual responses that deviate significantly from the norm. Depending on the substance and circumstances of each response, it may be appropriate to disregard the outlier responses or redirect them to other areas of the organization. Individual comments are generally not representative of your goal, which is to develop personas that represent the typical learner.

Integrate Various Types of Information

Now, we will integrate the insights gathered from our interviews and observations with qualitative and quantitative employee data that support our findings. If there are discrepancies between the information obtained from the interviews or observations and the data, further follow-up meetings can be arranged to investigate.

Some data is easier to digest than other data. When working with more challenging data, it can be helpful to collaborate with a colleague who has strong data literacy and technical abilities. This person will also come in handy when using AI tools for data analysis.

For example, the typical demographic data for our learner persona can be established using demographic HR information, such as work role, tenure, and education level. These details are often available in spreadsheets, and analyzing them with a pivot table can help identify trends, such as the most prevalent education level or geographic location. Alternatively, you can upload the spreadsheet to an AI tool to summarize the same information.

By looking at learner engagement data from communication platforms such as Microsoft Teams, Slack, or an LXP, it becomes possible to pinpoint where learners are spending their time. During interviews, learners may express enthusiasm about newly posted videos on the LXP, but by analyzing usage and engagement reports from the platform, you may discover that most learners disengage from the video at the midpoint. This information is significant for your learner persona because it suggests that their appreciation for the video may not be as genuine as they claimed or that the content quickly failed to meet their expectations because they already understand the subject matter. Either way, you can now go back to learners with additional questions to identify the cause of this discrepancy.

We know that detailed employee data isn't always easy to come by. What we've described here is an ideal situation; however, most of the time, we don't get our hands on any valuable data. The bottom line is that we have lots to do in the data and analytics realm in L&D to help us make data-driven decisions in the future.

Step 4. Create Learner Personas

Diversity and inclusivity are essential for creating a welcoming and supportive learning environment. That's why it's so important to ensure that our learner personas represent a diversity of backgrounds, ethnicities, abilities, and genders.

> **Don't Let Stereotypes Take Over**
>
> When creating personas, be aware of stereotypes and avoid them. Even when we try to heighten our awareness, stereotypes can still creep into our analysis because we all have unconscious biases. Let's talk about how to combat this issue.
>
> Personas are meant to represent typical learners, not assumptions based on preconceived notions. To help prevent stereotypes from infiltrating our personas, we can ask an external party—someone not involved in the creation process—to review the personas and look for any questionable language or stereotypes.

While it's natural to think of specific learners when creating personas, it's important not to replicate their traits exactly in any one persona. Using precise traits from learners we interview or observe can result in personas that are limited and not representative of the typical learner. Instead, we should try to take a holistic approach and consider the characteristics and needs of the whole group.

We shouldn't get bogged down in too many details. Personas are not meant to be exhaustive collections of every single learner's traits. They are meant to represent typical learners and serve as a guide for training design and development. We should focus on the key characteristics and needs that are relevant to the training program.

We want all our employees to identify with our personas, so it's worth taking a comprehensive look at the makeup of the entire organization rather than just the people we interact with daily. This will ensure that our personas accurately represent the learner base and that the learning content addresses the needs and experiences of all learners. We should strive to be creative and diverse with personas because they are the keys to crafting truly outstanding learning experiences.

Gender-Neutral and Ethnically Diverse Personas

Representation matters to learners and their organizations. When we work with our clients individually or present at conferences separately or together, we are often asked how to develop gender-neutral personas. Our approach is to always use some gender-neutral names (Jordan, Chris, Taylor, for example) and to use *they* and *them* as pronouns. It's not difficult to find images and photographs to help a gender-neutral persona come to life.

It's also important to use names that represent a diversity of cultures and ethnicities. So, rather than always choosing names such as John, Jane, Mary, or Joe, try using Amir, Priya, Ji-an, or Luis.

Review Personas With Stakeholders and Learners

To ensure that our personas resonate with stakeholders and learners, it's important to present them to both groups. Our goal is to create characters that accurately represent the people who will be using our learning materials.

First, we share personas with stakeholders to give them time to digest the information and ask any questions or raise concerns. We always provide as much information as possible without revealing the data source. Sometimes, stakeholders ask us to remove certain information if they think it casts their operations or people in a negative light. However, we believe it's important to highlight the risks of doing this. If we remove information shared by multiple learners, it distorts the reality of the learning experience. We often suggest rephrasing certain statements to soften their impact without losing sight of the underlying issue. Throughout the process, we remind stakeholders of the purpose of personas and why the organization embarked on the project in the first place; this often helps to alleviate their concerns.

Once the stakeholders approve the personas, it's time to ask learners to review them. We suggest that the key question learners should ask themselves is, "Can I see myself in this persona?" If learners ask to remove certain information because they think it could identify them, work with them to rephrase their comments. The goal is not to make anyone feel uncomfortable or vulnerable but to create personas that accurately reflect the learner's needs and goals.

When and How to Use Learner Personas

Let's revisit the example of our top-tier kitchen sales consultants. By pinpointing key pain points, the LuxeKitchens L&D team was able to revamp the training program with great success. In the analysis, we identified several pain points:
- Lack of communication skills
- Lack of ability to use software and tablets while working with customers
- Lack of interest in virtual training
- Length of training sessions

The revamped and revitalized training program placed the learners' passion for customers at the forefront. It emphasized practical, hands-on training in the showroom, with minimal digital pre- and post-work to maximize the learner's experience. To ensure success, the organization invested in a team of highly qualified facilitators who traveled to various locations across the country. The hands-on training was less formal, more action-oriented, and flexible, which gave sales consultants an opportunity to ask any questions that were top of mind.

This was a situation in which learner personas could not address every obstacle—especially because some didn't pertain to training. By taking a human-centered approach to design, however, we were able to create courses that resonated with employees more than traditional design methods.

It might go without saying, but after investing significant time and effort to create learner personas, it's essential to ensure they are used effectively. Avoid creating personas only to neglect them during the design process. We've seen many personas collecting dust in some virtual corner! We like to follow a few best practices at various stages of the design process. Let's review those now.

Design Thinking Sessions

Our favorite use of personas is during design thinking sessions. After all, the first step of that process is the empathize phase! Equipped with our personas, we define the specific challenges each persona is facing in the form of problem statements and how-might-we questions. These can easily be derived from the pain points and needs sections.

For example, take this problem statement: "Jordan feels overwhelmed every day because of product shortages. It's difficult for him to explain to customers why production is delayed, which results in negative customer satisfaction scores."

Now, let's reframe this statement in how-might-we questions:
- "How might we help Jordan have challenging conversations with customers?"
- "How might we help Jordan explain product shortages to customers in a simple manner?"

- "How might we help Jordan with additional insights into production schedules?"

In the ideate phase, we use the how-might-we questions to start developing solutions for our learners. There's no better way to create learner-centric experiences.

Ongoing or Transformational Projects

Creating personas is not a good use of time for short-term or one-time training requests, such as a two-hour session on new expense-reporting software. The time spent creating personas would exceed the time needed to develop the training. It's best to create personas for ongoing programs like onboarding or compliance training or large-scale transformational projects that have a broader influence on the organization. However, once the personas have been created, they can be easily applied to smaller projects as well.

The Program or Asset Level

When working on a larger project, personas can be applied at the program or asset level. For a longer learner journey that is part of a larger project, we can identify the entry and exit points for each persona. This allows us to consider how learners will interact with the training content and what they hope to get out of it. Next, we can consider which assets within the journey are important to each persona and when they'll need them. For example, some learners might benefit from videos, while others might prefer reading or interactive exercises. We need to determine the best way to deliver these assets based on each persona's needs and preferences.

When considering specific assets, we like to tailor the "What's in it for me?" message to speak directly to each persona, structure the content based on a learner's interests or existing knowledge, or use examples that resonate with each persona. This enables us to provide a high degree of flexibility for our target audience and to personalize the learning experience for each persona. Doing so will help make the training feel more targeted and relevant to each learner.

Let Personas Guide Delivery, Tone, and Voice

Personas help L&D professionals think about delivery mechanisms and how to engage learners. For example, if we have a persona who is a busy working parent, we might want to consider offering shorter, more bite-sized training modules they can easily fit into their schedule. On the other hand, if we have a persona who is highly tech-savvy, we might want to consider using more interactive and multimedia-based training methods.

But personas don't just inform our delivery methods; they help guide the tone and voice of the content. For a persona who is a recent college graduate, we use a more casual and conversational tone in training materials. On the other hand, we would tend to use a more formal, professional tone for a persona who is a senior executive with 25 years of experience.

> **Refer to Personas by Name**
> When we start to design new learning programs, we always try to refer to our personas by name to help them come to life. Select names that will resonate with you and stick! It also helps us build empathy when we ask ourselves, "What would Carlos do? How would Greta react to this?"

It's OK to reuse personas. In fact, when you've invested the time and effort to create a good persona, it is smart to use it whenever possible. But it's also important to review each one before using it for new designs. Sometimes, the organization's situation or needs change, strategic objectives evolve, or the program you are designing for has unique requirements. Take the time to ensure the personas reflect any essential changes in the organization.

Tools for Creating Learner Personas

A variety of tools can help you create personas. Each has advantages and disadvantages. Ultimately, the best tool will depend on your needs and preferences, as well as factors like budget, the level of collaboration, and the level of visual appeal. Let's look at a few options.

Pen and Paper

This simple, low-tech option lets you quickly sketch out personas by hand. The advantage of this method, other than being easy and quick, is that it allows for brainstorming and making changes on the fly. The disadvantage is that it can be hard to share and collaborate with others and may not be as visually appealing as other options.

Word Processing Programs

Many learning designers use word processing tools like Microsoft Word or Google Docs to create personas. The advantage of this method is that it's easy to share and collaborate with others, as well as revise and update. The disadvantage is that it may not be as visually appealing as some of the other options.

Online Persona Creation Tools

There are several online tools designed specifically for creating personas, including Xtensio, Userforge, and Hubspot's Make My Persona. These tools often include templates and prompts to help guide you through the process and create visually appealing personas. The advantage of these tools is that they are easy to use and create professional-looking personas. The disadvantage is that they may not offer as much flexibility as some of the other options.

Graphic Design Software

You can use graphic design software like Adobe Illustrator, PowerPoint, or Canva to create personas. The advantage of this method is that you can create visually appealing personas with a lot of flexibility. The disadvantage is that it may require a bit more time and effort to learn how to use these tools. It may also be harder to collaborate with others. PowerPoint is one of our favorite tools!

Whiteboarding Apps

Apps like Figjam, Miro, and Mural allow you to create and collaborate on personas in a virtual whiteboard environment. The advantage of this method is that it allows for easy collaboration with remote team members and provides a lot of flexibility for brainstorming and making changes. It's also a visually appealing option. The disadvantage is that, like graphic design software, it may take a bit of time to learn how to use the apps, and the user interface may not be as intuitive as some of the other options.

AI-Based Tools

At the time we're writing this book, AI-based tools for creating personas are still in the early stages of development. They do speed up the process of creating a usable template with some basic customer or learner demographics. However, because very few take a company's user or learner research into account, the output isn't realistic. If you use AI tools, ensure that they augment your existing research for the best outcomes and make sure to keep your employees' privacy in mind. Never upload confidential information.

Personas That Enhance Meaning for Learners

The use of learner personas has experienced a boom over the past few years. But sadly, it often ends up as a simple check-the-box exercise and isn't built into an organization's design DNA or given the time and respect it deserves. When used correctly, personas are incredibly valuable and allow us to enhance meaning in the workplace for our learners by identifying intrinsic and extrinsic motivators, specific needs, and pain points.

By collecting demographic information and exploring the emotional states of our typical learners, we can create personas that represent the unique characteristics of our target audience. These personas can then be used to guide the design of our learning content and experiences, ensuring they are tailored to meet the needs of our learners.

Using personas may not capture all the complexities of the target audience, but it can bring us much closer than a traditional target analysis. Personas also remind us to prioritize our learners' needs above our own content needs, leading to more relevant and engaging learning experiences.

While the process of creating learner personas can be time-consuming, it is well worth the effort, and it helps ensure that our learning content is relevant and engaging. We can train ourselves to become more aware of stereotypes and regularly revisit learner personas to ensure they're still aligned with any changes in our learners or our organization. Personas are the first step in any good design process and a critical step on the road to creating relevant experiences that resonate with our learners.

A Final Thought

Don't treat learner personas like just another item to tick off on your to-do list. The key to excellent learning design is to start with the learner, not the content. By crafting compelling learner personas, you're well on your way to creating epic experiences.

Activity 2-1. Learner-Centric Onboarding

Continuing with your onboarding program (or another program you have been working on), imagine your organization is now tasking you with designing a new learner-centric version. This is the perfect opportunity to create learner personas.

Objective
Quickly create a learner persona for your organization.

Steps
1. Think about the segments in your organization. What do you know about them? What don't you know about them? List as many elements as come to mind.
2. Identify three to five learner personas you want to create within one of your segments. We suggest picking the segment you know most about.
3. Create a learner persona template that represents your organization and learners. Make sure it includes demographic information; what they see, hear, do, think, and feel; and their pain points and needs.
4. Meet with a colleague and create at least one persona in an hour or less. Ideally, you want to validate the outcomes with your learners.

Chapter 3
Map Learner Journeys From Awareness to Action

> Focus on the journey, not the destination. Joy is found not in finishing an activity but in doing it.
> —Greg Anderson, wellness advocate and author

Think about the last time you bought something expensive. Was it a car, a new smartphone, a sofa? You probably remember a lot about the process of making that purchase. Maybe you started by researching options on the internet, moved on to product websites, and then explored brick-and-mortar stores. Perhaps you began by talking to friends or reading reviews on social media. Did your search for just the right product turn out to be easy and fun—or complicated and frustrating? As consumers, we can take a variety of paths and have a range of experiences before reaching our goal of buying the perfect TV or designer shoes. We can also have a range of experiences during our purchase and afterward. Memories of all those experiences—both good and bad—often affect our attitudes toward our next purchase.

Now, think about the journey your learners take when they interact with your learning experiences. What steps do they take to achieve the final objectives? Do they always achieve their goals? What happens when they're back on the job, putting into practice what they've learned? How do they feel about the journey?

Consider your most recent expensive purchase again. Marketers analyze your interactions with their products at specific touchpoints (search engines, shopping websites, brick-and-mortar stores, social media) to understand your customer journey. That journey includes everything from your first encounter with a brand to your postpurchase experience with the product. Marketers use digital and physical channels to connect with customers on an emotional level along these journeys, diving deep into their needs and perceptions and leveraging the data and insights they discover to improve the experience with a brand. In other words, marketers gather data to determine whether the touchpoints of each customer journey have led to the desired outcomes. They also use these insights to revise and optimize the journey in real time, which means that customer journeys are iterative and always changing.

In L&D, more often than not, we aren't designing iterative and always changing experiences. We usually design one-and-done resources without thinking about the shape of the overall learning experience. We don't analyze the first interactions our learners have with our learning solutions, and our focus in the postlearning experience is usually limited to sustainment or maintenance materials; in other words, it's performance support. Even when L&D professionals build a complex, multi-channel learning experience, examining learners' emotions about the experience is often an afterthought or simply ignored. Our job is to deliver training, achieve the desired outcome, and move on to the next thing as quickly as possible, right?

Marketers understand that the journey is as important as the outcome because without a positive experience many customers will never make it to the end to make a purchase. According to Aaron Agius (2024), 80 percent of customers consider their experience with a company to be as important as the quality of the product, and nearly 70 percent of online shoppers abandoned their carts in 2022. Do you know how many learners abandoned your training before they finished? How many considered it to be a positive, memorable experience?

Marketers view the engagement, the experience, and the result as the perfect trifecta. One can't exist without the others, and the buyer persona is always at the center of everything they do. If we want to make our learner journeys positive and memorable, L&D professionals should adopt customer journey principles that also focus on the engagement, the experience, and the result.

We often see colleagues begin designing a learner journey, but then they discover their organizations are still focused on one-time events and static training modules housed in an LMS. In other cases, the obstacle for designers is that their organization considers *curricula* or *learning paths* to be synonymous with *learner journeys*. In fact, learner journeys are much more complex than either traditional curricula or learning paths, both of which are collections of topics in a particular order with no emphasis on the experience itself.

We believe that organizations and L&D professionals need to shift toward ongoing learner-centric experiences that intertwine multiple digital and physical channels with expert communications and learner engagement, all while taking learners' emotions into account. If we make this shift in our thinking, we can gradually build knowledge and skills and improve performance. In this chapter, we'll discover that learner journeys, just like customer journeys, are iterative and allow us to react in the moment to our learners' emotions and perceptions, adjusting the experience to achieve what we need when we need it.

Customer Journey Versus Learner Journey

Our concept of a learner journey is adapted from the customer journey described by marketers, which includes all the touchpoints someone experiences when interacting with a brand or company. The sum of all the touchpoints equals the full customer experience, which ideally leads to customer loyalty (Kuehnl et al. 2019).

Customer journeys are always designed with a goal in mind: the purchase of a product or service. They are divided into three stages—prepurchase, purchase, and postpurchase—but can take many shapes and are often divided into more segments as needed. Consider Figure 3-1, which shows how one customer journey could be divided into phases. In this case, the prepurchase phase is divided into trigger and review; the purchase decision stands on its own; and the postpurchase phase includes engagement, relationship management, and renewal.

Figure 3-1. Phases of a Customer Journey.

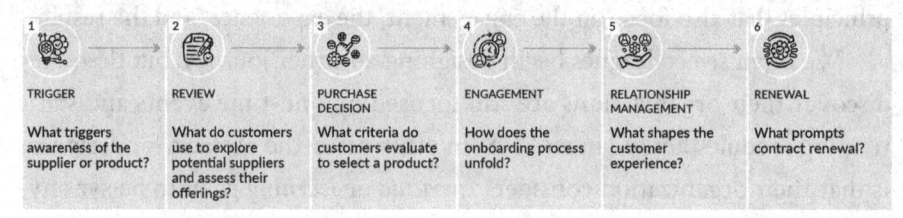

1 TRIGGER	2 REVIEW	3 PURCHASE DECISION	4 ENGAGEMENT	5 RELATIONSHIP MANAGEMENT	6 RENEWAL
What triggers awareness of the supplier or product?	What do customers use to explore potential suppliers and assess their offerings?	What criteria do customers evaluate to select a product?	How does the onboarding process unfold?	What shapes the customer experience?	What prompts contract renewal?

Source: Adapted from B2B International.

What about learner journeys? We describe a *learner journey* as an ongoing experience that offers relevant, valuable, and integrated interactions and touchpoints connected by a solid engagement and communication strategy to help learners achieve a particular goal. An effective learner journey will address how the learner feels, how they perceive the learning, and how learning leads to increased motivation. Like customer journeys, learner journeys can be divided into three phases: pretraining, training, and post-training (Figure 3-2).

Figure 3-2. Phases of a Learner Journey

Phase	Pretraining	Training				Post-Training
	Day 1	Week 1	Month 1	Month 2	Ongoing	Follow-Up

Before we examine a learner journey, let's look at how marketers define customer journeys.

Customer Journey Touchpoints, Interactions, and Channels

In marketing, a *touchpoint* is any connection point the customer has with your brand. This might include product demonstrations, the online checkout process, or a warranty return. An *interaction* is any activity a customer takes at a touchpoint, such as watching a product demonstration video, purchasing an item, or returning a product. And a *channel* is where the touchpoint and interaction take place. This might include brick-and-mortar stores or websites.

Each touchpoint is an opportunity for connection between the customer and the organization. Along the way, the customer might move from excitement to curiosity to doubt to confidence. Ideally, marketers see these behavior changes happen as customers advance through a journey.

Most customer journeys involve multiple channels, such as search engines, websites, social media, and brick-and-mortar stores. When marketers use multiple channels to engage customers, this is known as an *omnichannel strategy*.

Let's consider the customer journey of buying a new lawnmower. In the prepurchase phase, we see:

- **Touchpoint**—Product presentation
- **Interaction**—Research
- **Channel**—Website

Once the customer is ready to purchase (*touchpoint*), they go to the local hardware store (*channel*) to complete the purchase transaction (*interaction*). In the postpurchase phase, feedback provision is considered the touchpoint. The customer provides their feedback (*interaction*) via Google (*channel*). Figure 3-3 shows a graphic representation of a customer journey and includes lists of touchpoints in each phase.

▌Terms You Should Know

Customer Journey, Learner Journey, and Omnichannel

A *customer journey* is a multi-step process in which customers interact with a company or brand via touchpoints—usually to purchase a product or service—and the resulting experience they have during this process. We translate the customer journey concept into the world of L&D by designing blended *learner journeys* in which digital and physical channels engage learners over time, leading to improved performance.

Omnichannel refers to the creation of a seamless, consistent, and unified customer experience across various digital and physical channels. In L&D, we also need to align experiences across all our digital and physical channels to create a seamless experience. Whether a learner accesses an e-learning module or joins a live session, we should ensure that the information received is consistent and evokes positive emotions.

Each interaction and touchpoint in a learner journey provides an opportunity for connection between you and your learners. By viewing instructional design through the lens of a learner journey, we can analyze how learners

Figure 3-3. Customer Journey Phases and Touchpoints

	1 TRIGGER	2 REVIEW	3 PURCHASE DECISION	4 ENGAGEMENT	5 RELATIONSHIP MANAGEMENT	6 RENEWAL
GOAL	What triggers awareness of the supplier or product? Adopt the prospect's mindset and drive a call to action.	What do customers use to explore potential suppliers and assess their offerings? Meet the prospect's need for information.	What criteria do customers evaluate to select a product? Provide evidence of being the best fit (including a deep understanding of the prospect's needs).	How does the onboarding process unfold? Enable a seamless onboarding process.	What shapes the customer experience? Ensure the customer has the best experience possible.	What prompts contract renewal? Stay engaged with customers and drive renewal.
TOUCHPOINTS	• Direct mail • Email advertising • Word of mouth or customer referrals • Distributor reps, websites, or advertising • Retailer reps, websites, or advertising • Organic search results • Social media • Online advertising • Industry trade shows • Vendor-specific conferences • Print, TV, or radio advertising • Billboards • Sponsorship • Directories	• Brochures, catalogs, or spec sheets • Customer reviews and testimonials • Peer referrals • Third-party or expert reviews • Direct sales reps • Website • White papers • Webinars • Videos • Webcasts • Podcasts • Infographics • Distributor reps or websites • Retailer reps or websites • Professional associations or communities	• Case studies • Pitches or presentations • Deliverables • Best practices and accreditations • ROI data or tools • Awards • Testimonials	• Contract negotiation (pricing, terms, and conditions) • Invoicing • Stakeholder buy-in • Account management, communication, and support • Training	• Customer service and account management • Technical support • Ordering • Shipping and receiving • Performance mentoring • Market research • Dashboard or portal • Mobile apps • Customer events • User groups or communities • Hospitality and entertainment • Email communications • Direct mail • Webinars • Social media	• Account management or relations • Referral programs • Performance reviews • Contract negotiation (discounts and terms) • Hospitality and entertainment • Vendor-specific conferences • Newsletters • Infographics • Brochures and catalogs • Whitepapers • Webinars • Podcasts • Social media

Source: Adapted from B2B International.

interact with our training programs step-by-step across multiple touchpoints that exist in a blend of digital and physical channels. We also must take learners' emotions into account as they advance through the journey. They might feel unsure at the start before they gain confidence, or they might feel frustrated because they are having a difficult time learning new concepts.

A Sales Consultant's Learner Journey

Let's revisit our LuxeKitchens sales associates. Remember that the national chain of high-end kitchen retailers was seeing a decline in their sales consultants' skills and performance—and falling sales as a result. The company wanted to refresh its existing sales training program with the goal of increasing team members' sales numbers year over year.

If we want to identify the various touchpoints, interactions, and channels in a learner journey for LuxeKitchens sales consultants, it's helpful to start by listing the challenges they're facing and the things they need to know and do to increase sales. One challenge the consultants encounter is lead management, or the ability to communicate with prospective customers across various channels. Specifically, they struggle with tracking leads in the customer relationship management (CRM) system. Some of the things they need to master are phone skills, email etiquette, and CRM workflow. Here is how we would define some of the touchpoints, interactions, and channels for the LuxeKitchens learner journey:

- **Touchpoints.** The steps or tasks learners must complete to achieve a goal; for example, improving lead management by leveling up phone skills, email etiquette, and CRM workflow.
- **Interactions.** Actions learners take within a touchpoint; for example, watching a video, taking part in discussions, and reading emails.
- **Channels.** The place where the interaction takes place; for example, Microsoft Teams and the company's LMS.

Designing a Successful Learner Journey

Marketers understand a few essentials about customer journeys that we can take into consideration as we design the learner journey. First and foremost, a successful customer journey is centered on the customer. In other words, it is *human-centric*. Marketers consider touchpoints that are both within and beyond the customer's control, and they use what they've learned to create a consistent, cohesive design theme. Finally, to better understand who their customers are, marketers ensure that all decisions are data driven. We will now investigate each of these marketing success factors in more detail and then apply them to a learner journey.

Make the Design Human-Centric

Customer and learner journeys are rarely linear. Each person will take a slightly different path, skip some steps, and sometimes go backward or forward. No matter what their path looks like, a successful journey must put the customer (or learner) at the center, allowing them to move freely from one channel to the next while having the same experience, no matter which option they use (Palazón et al. 2023). A few guidelines can help us focus on a human-centric design, including staying flexible, creating relevance, and creating space for focus and reflection.

Stay Flexible

Flexibility helps us meet customers' and learners' expectations in an ever-changing world and ensure that they are aware of various channels, accomplish the same tasks, receive the same information, and experience the same feelings (Neslin 2020). We have to give customers and learners space to reflect, think, and make decisions—not an easy feat!

By putting customers at the center, marketers know they can create value through many interactions, rather than a single transaction. However, we must remember that there are two perspectives on value: how the company conceives value and how the customer perceives it. In a survey of 362 companies, 80 percent of senior executives said their companies provided excellent service. Only 8 percent of customers agreed! (Smith and Williams 2022). What is most important is creating value from the customer's or learner's perspective.

Create Relevance

Just as marketers put the customer at the center when they create customer journeys, L&D professionals must put the learner at the heart of learner journeys. Equipped with learner personas, we know what learners need and want, what they feel, and what their pain points are. This allows us to create valuable, proactive learning offerings that are personal and make a difference. We do this by engaging and exciting learners in new ways. When we do it right, we can get buy-in from audiences who initially weren't sure about, or aware of, our offerings.

One aspect of engaging and exciting learners is allowing them to navigate seamlessly across multiple touchpoints, experiencing the same emotions and receiving the same information as other learners, no matter how they access the experience. Returning to the human-centric tenet, each learner can have a slightly different experience, jumping ahead or going back to a previous touchpoint as needed. We engage learners by ensuring our messages are consistent across all interactions and channels, from face-to-face training to videos to performance support.

Create Space for Focus and Reflection

Marketers create space and time for customers to think about their products and make decisions. As L&D professionals, we have to remember to create space and time for learners to focus and reflect; otherwise, learning won't take place. We like to call these pauses *whitespace*. Learner journeys help us create whitespace because we don't look at the training we design as one-and-done events. We see our designs as continuous experiences connected through great communication strategies with ample room to focus and reflect.

Controlled Versus Noncontrolled Channels

Note: Marketers sometimes discuss touchpoints and channels interchangeably. To avoid confusion, we are using the word channel in this section.

As you can imagine, thanks to the sheer number of possible channels, it can be challenging for marketers to cut through the noise. On top of that, marketers struggle with the fact that there are brand-owned (controlled) channels, such as corporate websites or physical stores, as well as channels outside their control (noncontrolled), such as Google or Yelp. The number of channels is constantly increasing, making it more challenging to create a consistent and unified experience. You might wonder why marketers even worry about the noncontrolled channels. We have an answer for that.

Recent studies on omnichannel strategies show that the integration of various controlled and noncontrolled channels leads to higher customer engagement, which leads to higher purchase levels and positive word of mouth (Palazón et al. 2023). So, you see, not integrating noncontrolled channels isn't really an option. On the contrary, marketers have to manage controlled channels and integrate those they don't control through a cohesive brand theme across all touchpoints (thematic cohesion), a uniform design language (consistency), and personalization (context sensitivity) of the experience.

In L&D, just like in marketing, we have controlled channels and noncontrolled channels. Controlled channels are our LMS or LXP, SharePoint, and other in-house platforms. While these are still considered our go-to options, especially the LMS, our learners are used to getting information from myriad sources in their personal and professional lives. That is what they now expect from their training too—they want the option to augment information from controlled channels in any way they see fit.

Learners usually don't care where they get their information as long as it meets their needs at the moment and provides the right content at the right time and place. In the end, they are happy and satisfied and probably more engaged when they can use noncontrolled channels (such as YouTube or third-party websites that host webinars and podcasts) in addition to controlled channels.

Learners can also be great content curators, contributors, and moderators, and we have to tie those efforts into our own. For example, Google runs a training program they call "g2g," or "Googler-to-Googler," in which employees share their knowledge in a wide variety of fields. About 80 percent of the company's tracked training programs follow this model (Finelli 2023).

What would our learning brand be if it weren't for our learners? If we are successful in listening and integrating our learners and their preferences for various channels into our learning experiences, many of the channels that are out of our control right now might fold into the larger ecosystem and become much more controllable. The result? More learner engagement and a distinct learning culture that the organization can be proud of.

Ensure Consistency and Cohesion

Marketers strive to design thematically cohesive customer journeys with consistent touchpoints. To achieve this, they consider three aspects of their designs, all of which are valuable for learning designers as well: creating a common theme, developing a uniform design, and making all touchpoints responsive to learners' goals.

Create a Common Theme

Customers should be able to perceive a common brand theme and meaning across all controlled touchpoints. For example, a customer journey in the airline industry has common themes of travel and mobility. All touchpoints reinforce the same theme. In learning, this could translate to a variety of themes, depending on the topic of the learner journey. For example, in all LuxeKitchens training sessions, the facilitator reiterates the company's motto, "Designs for the heart of your family's home." Case studies and role plays involve challenges based on family scenarios to reinforce the theme of the family home. We would see the same theme across all deliverables.

Develop a Uniform Design

Customers appreciate uniform branding across all controlled touchpoints. In our airline example, customers expect to see the same corporate design across all touchpoints, such as the website, the ticketing counter, and the lounge.

As designers of learning experiences, we can implement this in many ways. The L&D team at LuxeKitchens, for example, could use the company's brand colors across all learning materials and communications. (This information is usually found in a style guide, which we will talk more about in chapter 6). They might go further and design the user interfaces for online training to mimic a kitchen planning tool, including icons representing an oven, refrigerator, sink, and so on. In-person training might take place in spaces that look like kitchen sales floors, and online training could include a branded LuxeKitchens backdrop.

Make All Touchpoints Responsive to Learners' Goals

Lastly, marketers emphasize the context sensitivity of controlled touchpoints, by reviewing how well touchpoints match their goals, situational context, and channel preferences (Kuehnl et al. 2019). For example, you can purchase flight tickets directly from the airline, through a third-party, or from a travel agent. LuxeKitchens sales associates are always on the move to the next customer, so the L&D team ensures that all learning modules and data visualizations are optimized for smartphones and tablets. However, if they come into the office to complete lessons and download data, the transition to a desktop computer is designed to be seamless.

Think about the last learning experience you designed. Did you ensure thematic cohesion across your learning and communication assets? Did you use a uniform design with consistent colors, fonts, and other elements? Was it clear that all deliverables fit into the same theme and nothing was out of place? No matter which deliverable your learners accessed and no matter how they accessed it, did they believe it represented your brand? Did you pay attention to *context sensitivity*—meaning that all learners received the same information across a learner journey, no matter which touchpoints they interacted with and no matter what they were trying to achieve?

Make Data-Driven Decisions

To make customer journeys truly successful, marketers use data—lots and lots of data! They collect it and design a journey around it.

Marketers keep track of customers' behaviors and habits throughout their journey, and they adjust the journey based on the data they gather. It's an ongoing process of capturing, analyzing, and adjusting. Marketers need to continuously make sure they're offering a valuable experience (from the customer's point of view) and measuring goal achievement, all while keeping customers engaged and happy.

Just like marketers leverage data throughout a customer journey, we can manage learner journeys and adjust them as needed based on real-time learner feedback and engagement. This allows us to optimize and improve at any point in time and make the journey even more engaging, relevant, and personal. There is no need to wait until the end anymore to make adjustments!

During LuxeKitchens training on lead management, for example, facilitators insert one-minute polls asking for learner feedback on specific questions one-third and two-thirds of the way through each lesson. In addition, the company uses data from digital learning materials, such as e-learning or videos, to ensure the content is resonating with the learners.

By focusing on a common theme, a uniform design, and context sensitivity, and then making good, data-driven decisions, we add real value to our designs, create meaning for our learners, and engage them emotionally.

Maps to Guide the Journey

It's time to take all this marketing knowledge and start mapping learner journeys. If we look at the marketer's toolbox, we see that they map customer journeys using their extensive analysis that gives them a realistic picture of the customer's perspective. Marketers outline and visualize the entire customer journey based on customer personas to identify gaps between customer expectations and actual experiences. They also look for areas to improve and ways to optimize the overall customer experience (Stipeche 2023). Figure 3-4 provides an example of what a customer journey map might look like.

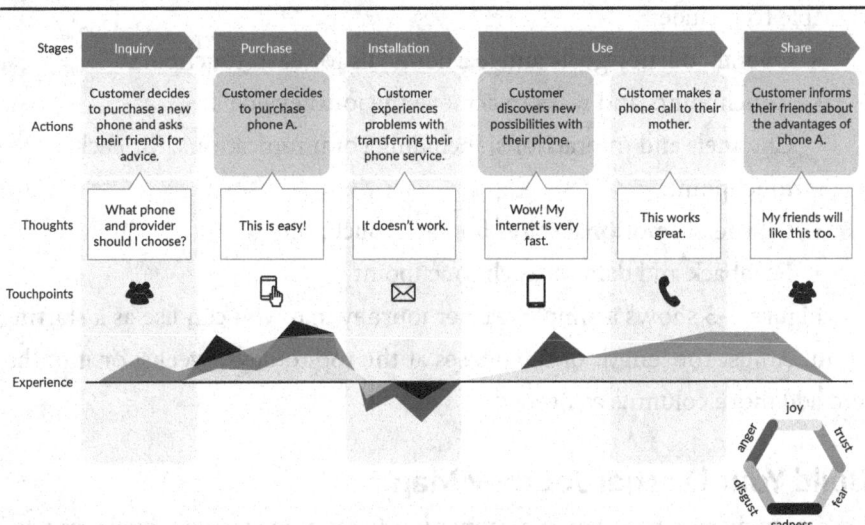

Figure 3-4. A Customer Journey Map

Stages	Inquiry	Purchase	Installation	Use		Share
Actions	Customer decides to purchase a new phone and asks their friends for advice.	Customer decides to purchase phone A.	Customer experiences problems with transferring their phone service.	Customer discovers new possibilities with their phone.	Customer makes a phone call to their mother.	Customer informs their friends about the advantages of phone A.
Thoughts	What phone and provider should I choose?	This is easy!	It doesn't work.	Wow! My internet is very fast.	This works great.	My friends will like this too.
Touchpoints	👥	📱	✉️	📱	📞	👥

Experience (emotion hexagon: joy, trust, fear, sadness, disgust, anger)

Source: Adapted from Customer Thermometer.

A learner journey map, in turn, provides a visual representation of the various touchpoints, interactions, and channels your learners experience while they engage with you and your brand—your learning offerings. The learner persona is the foundation of the learner journey, and we can use a variety of data points to outline the journey.

> ★ **Terms You Should Know**
>
> **Customer Journey Map and Learner Journey Map**
> A *customer journey map* is a visual representation of every touchpoint, interaction, and channel a customer has with a service, product, or brand. Translate this concept to L&D, and you will find that a *learner journey map* is a visual representation of the touchpoints, interactions, and channels learners experience with your learning offerings and your learning brand.

Create a Learner Journey Map

There are many ways to create a learner journey map and many elements that you should include. Start by looking carefully at your learners and your organization to decide which path to choose. Every situation is unique.

Over the years, Bianca has created learner journey maps for a variety of organizations and situations. She has found that these elements are always valuable to include:

- Overall journey goals and learner goals for each touchpoint
- Touchpoints and tasks to achieve the journey goals
- Channels and interactions, including communications, for each touchpoint
- Learners' emotional states for each touchpoint
- Feedback and data for each touchpoint

Figure 3-5 shows a simple learner journey map you can use as a starting point. Adjust the length of the phases at the top to days, weeks, or months, and add more columns as needed.

Build Your Learner Journey Map

Let's now discuss how you can transition from recognizing a business need to creating a learner journey map. We'll go back to LuxeKitchens at various

Figure 3-5. Learner Journey Map Template

Phase	Pretraining Day 1	Training Week 1	Month 1	Month 2	Ongoing	Post-Training Follow-Up
Learner Goals	Learner goals	Learner goals	Learner goals	Learner goals	Learner goals	Learner goals
Touchpoints	Touchpoints	Touchpoints	Touchpoints	Touchpoints	Touchpoints	Touchpoints
Channels and Interactions	Channels and interactions	Channels and interactions	Channels and interactions	Channels and interactions	Channels and interactions	Channels and interactions
Says or Asks	Learner says or asks . . .	Learner says or asks . . .	Learner says or asks . . .	Learner says or asks . . .	Learner says or asks . . .	Learner says or asks . . .
Feels or Thinks	Learner feels or thinks . . .	Learner feels or thinks . . .	Learner feels or thinks . . .	Learner feels or thinks . . .	Learner feels or thinks . . .	Learner feels or thinks . . .
Does	Learner does . . .	Learner does . . .	Learner does . . .	Learner does . . .	Learner does . . .	Learner does . . .
Feedback and Data	Feedback and data points	Feedback and data points	Feedback and data points	Feedback and data points	Feedback and data points	Feedback and data points

Learner Emotional State

Map Learner Journeys From Awareness to Action

points to provide examples. An (abbreviated) conversation between Karl, vice president of sales at LuxeKitchens, and Mei, the L&D pro, might go like this:

> "Hey there, Mei. I need a 30-minute e-learning module and a couple instructor-led training courses to get my team up to speed on some sales training, tools, techniques . . . that kind of stuff."
>
> "OK, Karl, we can help with that. But before we decide what we should deliver, can we take a step back?"
>
> "Sure, I guess so."
>
> "Great. Can you tell me a bit more about why you need this training right now? Has something changed recently? Is the team not performing, or are there any other challenges you can share with me?"
>
> "Well, I mean . . . the sales folks just don't do their jobs the way they should. I don't have time to babysit them all day long. I'm starting to think they don't actually know what they are supposed to do."
>
> "I see. How does that show up in their day-to-day? How did you become aware of this problem?"
>
> "I see it on a daily basis. A customer walks in, and the consultants don't get up. I overhear them on the phone and just roll my eyes when they ask questions. The usual stuff. But it didn't really hit me hard until I looked at last quarter's sales report. Our revenue is way, way down."

You've probably had those kinds of conversations. If we summarize it, we see that the business need is to increase sales numbers. That's our starting point. The workflow outlined in this chapter is based on Bianca's experience using processes she has developed over many years.

Goals

The foundation of every learner journey map is its goals, and there are two types: the overall journey goals and the learner goals.

Journey Goals

First, we need to set goals for the overall journey. These are driven by the business need and should be well aligned with your organization's business goals and strategic objectives. Ask yourself: "How will this learner journey affect our sales numbers, revenue, customer experience, and so on?"

When it comes to the overall journey goals, enlist the help of the organization's stakeholders to ensure your vision is in sync with their business goals and strategic objectives. Not only does this ensure you're aligned with various stakeholders and agree on the direction you want to take, but it also allows you to get their buy-in and excite them about the learner journey.

Start with a stakeholder engagement meeting. The main purpose should be to get to know one another, talk about the process ahead, and start thinking at a high level about where you want to take the training initiative. Follow up with an impact and clarity survey with five to eight questions, including:

- What current challenges would a new learner journey help solve?
- Why are you looking for a new approach to training now?
- What would happen if we didn't implement a new way of training?
- What industry changes are affecting our learners right now?
- What are you hoping a modern, actionable, and engaging training experience would achieve? What elements can you envision?
- What does success look like?

After analyzing the survey results, get everyone back together for a two-hour impact and clarity workshop to talk about trends you are already seeing. Use the information from the survey and the additional conversations during the workshop to create a three-pointed North Star:

- ⦿ Where do we want to go?
- ⦿ What's the vision?
- ⦿ What are the KPIs?

For the team at LuxeKitchens, the overall journey goal and KPI could be boosting kitchen sales across the company's different brands by 3 percent year over year.

Of course, these initial meetings don't always go smoothly. A company vice president once challenged Bianca about the process. He wasn't happy with the information she was presenting to the group, especially the answers about current challenges. She reminded him that she was merely the messenger and hadn't added personal bias to the survey responses. It turned out that many of the executives were not aware of some key challenges and didn't believe what they were hearing. After explaining the process again and ensuring the authenticity of the responses, Bianca was able to move forward. Eventually, the skeptical VP turned into a strong advocate for the entire program.

Learner Goals

A learner journey map also includes learner goals. These are comparable to the learner's learning and performance objectives and should be listed for every touchpoint in the journey. Each step needs a specific purpose, which is supplied by performance objectives. Ask yourself questions such as: "What will my learners be able to do differently after this touchpoint?"

In a learner journey map, each learner goal should align with the main journey goal. If they don't align, you will not see the desired results. Simply put, your journey goal is the collective result of all your performance objectives or learner goals. Bianca recommends first crafting your learner and performance goals and then verifying them with the business.

Touchpoints

With learner personas and journey goals in hand, it's time to start a series of learner journey map workshops. Invite all stakeholders from the initial engagement meeting, and ideally, ask learners to join too. This isn't always an option, but it's helpful to try.

> **Workshops: How Long?**
> If you are holding in-person workshops, a length of three hours, including two 15-minute breaks, usually works well. For virtual events, we advise sticking to two hours, including one 15-minute break.
>
> On average, use this as a guide:
>
> > 1 journey x 1 persona + 10 touchpoints (with multiple subtasks) =
> > 6 to 9 hours of workshops

Identify Touchpoints

During the first workshop, identify your touchpoints: What do learners need to know and do to achieve a specific goal? This process is similar to a task analysis, which you might be familiar with. Bianca recommends using a customer journey as a foundation because most organizations already have one mapped out. Just talk to your marketing or customer success teams. If you align the learner journey and the organization's customer journey, it's easier to get buy-in from stakeholders because you are building a learning experience around customer needs. In addition, the training will become more relevant for your learners and it will be easier to tie your data and measures to overall business goals and KPIs.

For LuxeKitchens sales consultants, we can now consider everything they need to know and do to ensure an outstanding customer experience and increase sales numbers. In this case, we might identify these touchpoints:

- Managing leads
- Discovering customer needs
- Showcasing kitchen designs
- Negotiating deals
- Delivering kitchens
- Following up after the sale

Write Problem Statements

Once all the touchpoints have been identified, we take a page out of the design thinking playbook and go back to the pain points and challenges we uncovered during the persona stage. We then write out a problem statement for each

touchpoint. Problem statements can take various forms, but it's often helpful to answer the five Ws:
- Who does the problem affect?
- What is the issue?
- When does the issue occur?
- Where is the issue occurring?
- Why is it important that we fix the problem?

For the LuxeKitchens sales consultants, we might first work on a problem statement related to the touchpoint of managing leads, which is often a challenging task. At LuxeKitchens, the systems aren't set up properly, leads come in from various sources, and consultants have to deal with walk-ins on top of everything else. The problem statement might be: "Jordan [*our learner persona from chapter 2*] feels anxious, but he's learned to ignore it for now. He lives in a small CRM world, focusing on the bare minimum. He's checking boxes so he can say, 'It's done.' But there are so many leads coming from diverse sources that they fall through the cracks daily."

We would use this problem statement to talk to stakeholders about the persona's feelings: "So, Jordan feels anxious; we know that already. But what else do you think he feels when he is continuously inundated with so many leads?"

This kind of question helps put the focus back on the learner and gets stakeholders to put themselves into the learner's shoes. Once they feel what the learner feels, we can move on to various how-might-we questions:

- How might we help Jordan deal with multiple leads during the day and get organized?
- How might we help Jordan reframe his negative emotions regarding lead management into positive ones?
- How might we help Jordan create customized experiences regardless of lead origin?

Depending on how much time you have with your organization's stakeholders, you can either collaborate with them to develop problem statements and how-might-we questions or prepare them beforehand. There should be one problem statement per touchpoint per persona and about three to five how-might-we questions per problem statement. You can see what this might look like in Figure 3-6.

Figure 3-6. Lead Management Example: Goals, Problem Statement, Emotional States, and How-Might-We Questions

Learner Goal	Use CRM efficiently to capture leads from various lead sources (including email, phone, and walk-ins).
Problem Statement	Jordan feels anxious, but he's learned to ignore it for now. He lives in a small CRM world, focusing on the bare minimum. He's checking boxes so he can say, "It's done." But there are so many leads coming from diverse sources that fall through the cracks.
Emotional State	Jordan feels overwhelmed, under pressure, less excited about work, annoyed, agitated, nervous, unsure, and concerned.
How-Might-We Questions	• How might we help him deal with multiple leads during the day and get organized? • How might we help him reframe his negative emotions regarding lead management into positive ones? • How might we help him create customized experiences regardless of lead origin?

The information in Figure 3-6 is much more detailed than in the learner journey map, but we have to take a slight detour to get to the channels, interactions, and communications of the learning experience. It's always worth the time and effort to leverage a design thinking approach before bringing all your findings back together in a journey map.

With these questions in mind, you and the workshop participants can identify the knowledge, skills, and abilities needed to complete each touchpoint (or individual task). Then, discuss the content needed at each step. Focus first on using content that already exists. Consider where you can repurpose content versus when you'll need to create content from scratch. We will talk more about content strategy and mapping in the next chapter.

Channels and Interactions

The next step in creating a learner journey map is *ideation*, which is when we brainstorm channels, interactions, and technologies that can help us engage with learners at each touchpoint. We also need to consider what works best for the content. In other words, it's time for high-level design.

In the case of LuxeKitchens, we may decide that phone skills are best practiced during a role-play exercise delivered through an AI-based role-play tool, but systems training can be done using simulations housed on the LMS.

You will probably want to use a mix of establishing channels and technologies, experimenting to find out how you can push the boundaries of each, and then propose a small number of new channels and technologies to help elevate the learning experience.

Prioritizing Elements

During ideation, you will create an extensive list of elements. The key is to ask stakeholders to vote and prioritize these items. Ensure that all decisions are aligned to the three points of your North Star so you can design the best possible learning experience aligned to business needs.

Keep it simple. Compare the importance and urgency of an element with its influence and potential rewards. Elements with high urgency and high impact should be the top priority. Those with low urgency and low impact should be eliminated (at least for the time being).

Another tool to help you prioritize is the How-Now-Wow Matrix (Figure 3-7). This matrix categorizes elements based on their originality (X-axis) and

Figure 3-7. How-Now-Wow Matrix

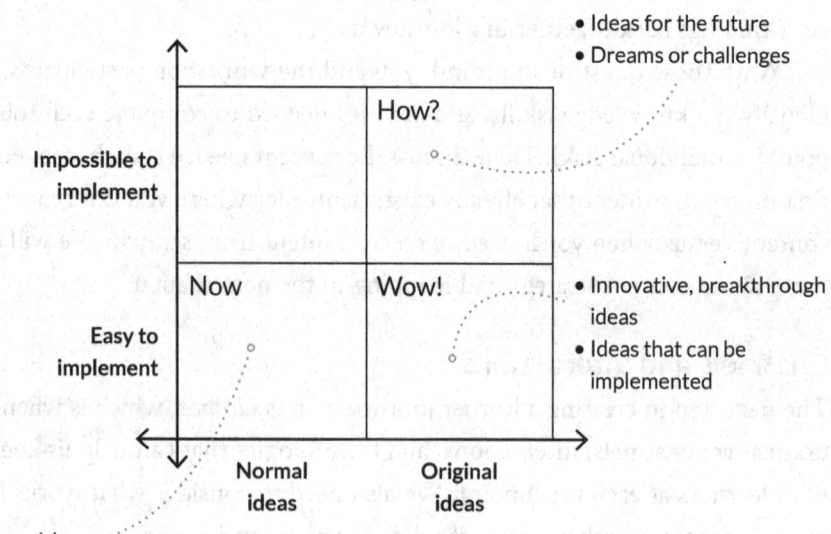

- Ideas for the future
- Dreams or challenges
- Innovative, breakthrough ideas
- Ideas that can be implemented
- Low risk
- High acceptability
- Existing examples

Source: Adapted from Game Storming.

ease of implementation (Y-axis). Ideas that aren't very innovative and are easy to implement fall into the lower left-hand quadrant and are considered "Now" ideas. "How" ideas sit in the top right-hand quadrant and are highly innovative but hard to implement. These are often saved for the future. In the bottom right-hand quadrant are the "Wow" ideas, which are both innovative and easy to implement. Those are the ones you want to go for! Unoriginal ideas that are difficult to implement go into the top left-hand corner and shouldn't be pursued (Game Storming 2011).

Feedback and Data

The last step in creating a successful learner journey map involves pinpointing feedback and data sources for each touchpoint. You'll find that metrics from the various platforms learners are using (such as LMSs, LXPs, Microsoft Teams, and CRMs) will be your go-to resources because they are easy to collect. We recommend using other kinds of data too, such as qualitative feedback via surveys. You can gain even more insight if you or other people observe the learners after their journey to gauge whether they can execute new tasks well.

Use Feedback to Make Adjustments

Following the launch of a learner journey, it's crucial to monitor engagement, collect feedback, and adjust your design as needed. That is the only way to identify gaps between your perception of what's working and what's *actually* working for your learners, so you can adapt to their needs. As we've mentioned already, the benefit of learner journeys is their adaptability.

For example, if you decided to use role-play exercises, you could leverage one of the many AI-based tools on the market designed for exactly that purpose. Not only would learners receive immediate feedback, but the tool would also collect data throughout the learning process and adjust scenarios accordingly, ensuring all participants get the most out of the experience. We will discuss data collection and analysis in more detail in chapter 9.

Figure 3-8 provides an example of what a completed lead management touchpoint for LuxeKitchens sales consultants might include.

When Bianca completes a workshop like the one we've described, she usually ends up with an unruly whiteboard with dozens and dozens of sticky notes—it's not nearly as organized as the example!

Figure 3-8. Lead Management Touchpoints for LuxeKitchens Sales Consultants

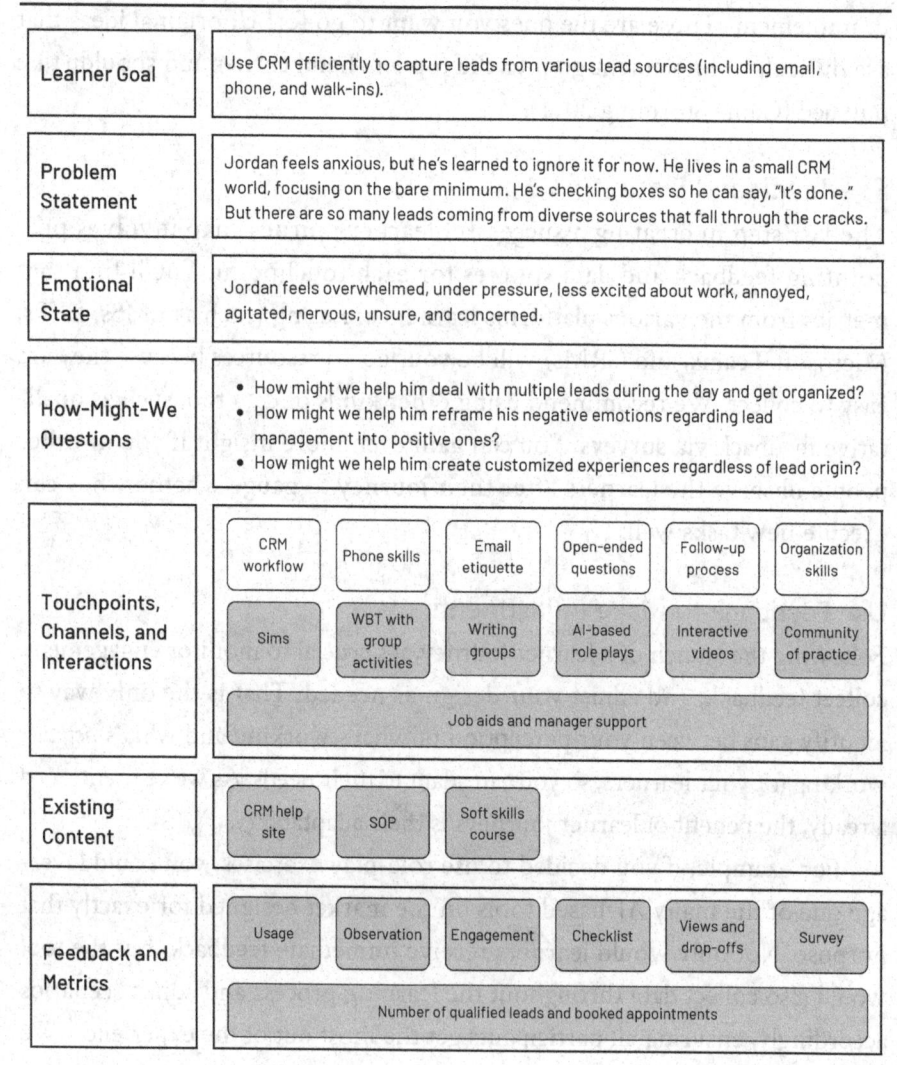

Learner Goal	Use CRM efficiently to capture leads from various lead sources (including email, phone, and walk-ins).
Problem Statement	Jordan feels anxious, but he's learned to ignore it for now. He lives in a small CRM world, focusing on the bare minimum. He's checking boxes so he can say, "It's done." But there are so many leads coming from diverse sources that fall through the cracks.
Emotional State	Jordan feels overwhelmed, under pressure, less excited about work, annoyed, agitated, nervous, unsure, and concerned.
How-Might-We Questions	• How might we help him deal with multiple leads during the day and get organized? • How might we help him reframe his negative emotions regarding lead management into positive ones? • How might we help him create customized experiences regardless of lead origin?
Touchpoints, Channels, and Interactions	CRM workflow · Phone skills · Email etiquette · Open-ended questions · Follow-up process · Organization skills Sims · WBT with group activities · Writing groups · AI-based role plays · Interactive videos · Community of practice Job aids and manager support
Existing Content	CRM help site · SOP · Soft skills course
Feedback and Metrics	Usage · Observation · Engagement · Checklist · Views and drop-offs · Survey Number of qualified leads and booked appointments

86 | Chapter 3

Completing the Map

At this point, the challenging work of making sense of all the information shared during the workshops begins. It's time to design a seamless and well-aligned learner journey that covers each section of the map in more detail. This is where you work in thematic cohesion, or a common brand theme, across the entire journey, as well as ensure consistency in terms of a uniform design language and context sensitivity. You need to ask yourself if all touchpoints and interactions are responsive and adaptive to learners' goals. We will touch on how to create a common brand theme and uniform design language in chapters 5 and 6.

Once your journey design is complete, Bianca recommends reconvening all stakeholders and learners to present your findings and gather feedback. Table 3-1 is an abbreviated version of what this feedback might look like.

Consider the Managers

Going back to our LuxeKitchens sales consultants again, we should also determine how the sales managers can support the sales consultants and what additional training the sales managers might need.

Start your learner journey workshop by thinking through all the elements sales consultants need to know and do differently. When you have a list, it's easy to translate that into what managers need to learn: everything the consultants do plus a level of managerial tasks, coaching, and mentoring. Having said that, sometimes it can make sense to work on two personas in parallel rather than one at a time during the same workshop.

Workshop Challenges and Solutions

Without fail, workshop participants will want to jump to solutions in the first five minutes. It's important to educate everyone on the concept of problem statements and how-might-we questions as part of the design thinking process. It's OK to acknowledge solutions that pop up during this phase, but you should gently remind everyone that, to stay learner-centric, you need to focus on challenges and pain points first.

Table 3-1. Learner Journey Map Feedback Excerpt

	Pretraining	Training	
	Week 1	Week 3	Week 5
Learner Goals	Buy in to the new sales curriculum	Use qualifying questions to uncover customer needs	Use expert communication skills to negotiate deals and deal with customer demands
Touchpoints	Create excitement • Get buy-in • Manage expectations	Discover customer needs • Ask open-ended questions • Product knowledge • Use relationship building skills	Negotiate deals • Be transparent • Demonstrate financial acumen • Navigate difficult conversations
Channels and Interactions	Join learning community on MS Teams	30-minute activity with an AI role-play tool to practice soft skills	• 30-minute vILT in Zoom to practice sales skills • 30-minute activities in AI role-play tool to practice negotiating with a demanding client
Says or Asks	"How will this training help me?"	"Are these AI role plays realistic?"	"This is hard."
Feels or Thinks	Overwhelmed and confused	Unsure	Lost
Does	Joins all learning activities while working in familiar ways	Uses more soft skills	Falls back into old ways of thinking
Feedback Data	MS Teams, email, and video analytics and manager observations	AI role-play tool analytics, manager observations, and number of qualified leads	Zoom and AI role-play tool analytics, manager observations, and lead conversion rate

Use humor in your workshops and gently push back on solutions if you aren't ready for them. Bianca always collects ideas in a separate section of the whiteboard, so nothing gets lost—which works most of the time!

You will soon discover that the wackiest ideas can make it into the final learning design. A few years ago, Bianca was working with an organization in the entertainment field. The team created a product training for their account executives (AEs), who were struggling with proposing the right product mix to customers, which often ended up in poorly written proposals.

One person in a workshop suggested, "Wouldn't it be great if we had a solution concierge? A tool that would allow AEs to enter the customer's objectives and KPIs, their geographical markets, and any other relevant information, and they would receive resources along the way to help them write proposals?"

Everyone laughed, but the idea got voted in as a "How" idea on the matrix. After the low-hanging fruit was taken care of, the organization built a custom application that did exactly what had been described. Unfortunately, this happened before AI tools arrived to make that whole process seamless!

When it comes to the actual ideation and solutioning, you will often get responses around delivery channels and technologies instead of the knowledge, skills, and abilities needed to complete a task. It's easy to write responses on sticky notes and put them in the appropriate section before returning to what the learners need to accomplish. Then, come back to technology and delivery channels later.

Before diving into the ideation stage, it's valuable to share current trends in the industry to allow everyone to dream big and think differently. Encourage participants to identify their wish list items rather than focusing on restrictions. For example, in an ideation session for LuxeKitchens, the participants might come up with this:

- **Problem statement.** Learners do not get the necessary face time with their managers, and trust is lacking.
- **How-might-we question.** How might we help learners build a better relationship with their managers?
- **"Dream big" solution (no restrictions).** Send them all to the happiest place on earth, Disneyland.
- **Adjustments to the idea (continuing ideation).** How might we create an environment in which learners and managers feel happy?

> **Workshop Best Practices**
>
> Follow these best practices in your workshops:
> - Set a time limit.
> - Stay on topic.
> - Defer judgment or criticism.
> - Encourage weird, wacky, and wild ideas.
> - Include people from outside the team.
> - Build on each other's ideas.
> - Be visual.
> - Have one conversation at a time.

More Helpful Tools

The learner journey map introduced earlier is just one of many options for designing your learner journeys. In this section, we share additional tools you might find helpful.

LX Canvas

Niels Floor created a fantastic tool called the LX Canvas. It covers many of the elements we have already talked about, but it also lists constraints and looks in more detail at the learners' environment. This is not a linear template, which can make the translation from the canvas to the actual learner journey with pretraining, training, and post-training a bit more challenging. Nevertheless, it's a fantastic tool with tutorials and courses you can join to learn more about the tool.

5 Moments of Need

Another valuable tool, often useful in combination with the learner journey map, is the 5 Moments of Need as defined by L&D professionals Bob Mosher and Conrad Gottfredson. The tool creates a beautiful journey in five steps:

1. Learn something for the first time.
2. Learn more about something.
3. Apply and refine what you have learned.
4. Adjust to change.
5. React to failure.

Within each of those steps, you can tie in the goals, touchpoints and interactions, learner emotional states, and, of course, data and feedback.

Marketing Funnel

We would be remiss if we didn't talk about the marketing funnel. There are different depictions of the funnel, but in essence, it includes these stages:

1. **Awareness.** Educate prospects about who you are.
2. **Consideration.** Prospects consider a product or service.
3. **Conversion.** Convince prospects to purchase the product or service.
4. **Loyalty.** Retain customers.
5. **Advocacy.** Turn customers into brand advocates.

Marketers use the marketing funnel to share content based on prospects' needs. For example, in the awareness stage, marketers educate prospective customers and show value, which means a blog post or a brief video might be better suited than sales-heavy content. In the consideration phase, marketers build deeper relationships by offering targeted, product-specific content. They know what prospects need because they read their digital body language.

When working through learner journeys, awareness of the funnel and how it is used in marketing can help us design experiences that excite and share the right content with our learners when they need it most. And, when a journey ends, we hope we have created advocates who help us spread the word about the amazing training offerings we have. It's a win-win.

> **L&D Funnel in Action**
>
> The funnel approach engages learners throughout the training initiative and delivers the right content at the right time.
>
> Consider this health and safety example:
> - **Awareness—Spark interest.** Use (dark) humor, short teaser videos, or intranet banners to raise awareness.
> - **Consideration—Entice learners about the importance of training.** Create personalized, department-focused training. Use dynamic content in landing pages or emails to tailor information. (We'll talk more about this in chapters 7 and 8.) Consult marketing for implementation.
> - **Conversion—Make learners true believers.** Conduct live webinars followed by online chats for discussion and suggestions on improving health and safety practices.

- **Loyalty and advocacy—Support behavior changes.** Support behavior change with performance support documents like infographics. Recognize and incentivize learners who become role models and advocates. Encourage peer and informal learning.

Gather data throughout each stage (such as video views, email click-through rates, and webinar engagement) to demonstrate participation and gain insights on engagement and content usability.

Making a Difference With Learner Journeys

Learner journeys are a valuable extension of learner-centric design and should be part of every L&D professional's toolkit. Instead of focusing on how content can be broken down into individual e-learning modules, we should focus on the whole learner journey—the holistic experience—and then overlay that experience with our content. If we focus on how individuals learn new information, change their behavior, and improve their performance, the possibilities are endless.

Each learner journey should have an overarching goal—made up of all individual learner performance goals—that is well-aligned with the organization's strategic goals and business objectives. Learner journeys are a game-changer for L&D professionals because they demonstrate that we speak the same language as the organization we are working with, and that we can draw a direct line between training and business outcomes. It's our way to have a seat at the table!

Learner journeys are successful if they have thematic cohesion, consistency of touchpoints, and context sensitivity. They need to allow the learner to seamlessly navigate multiple touchpoints, offering the same information no matter how a learner decides to interact with the experience. They are valuable to learners because they are explicitly designed *for* them and *with* them. The power of learner journeys lies in their data-driven nature and the fact that, as L&D professionals, we always consider learners' feedback to continually improve the experience. Furthermore, they allow us to improve learners' performance over time, gaining new skills along the way.

Journeys are also powerful because in preparing them we can bring stakeholders and learners together to collaboratively design an experience. No one is left out, and everyone understands why decisions are made, what needs to be covered, and how we can engage our learners and get the results we are aiming for.

What we've described in this chapter might seem like a time-consuming process, especially asking stakeholders to join various meetings and workshops. However, spending the time up front reduces the amount of future revisions because everyone is aligned from the start. Decisions aren't made in isolation, and the design develops over time. Just like with learner personas, not every project lends itself to a learner journey. Training programs with high visibility that span longer periods are best suited.

In effect, there is a journey within the journey, and your stakeholders will come to appreciate this process over time. Start with a smaller project that doesn't require too much time from your stakeholders to show them the value of collaborative time, as well as and how it can serve learners and, in the long run, the organization.

Learner journeys empower L&D professionals to go from designing one-time events to training over time, allowing for repetition, practice, and reflection. Throughout the process, we try to keep an awareness of the learner's emotions at the forefront. For us, journeys are about guidance, letting go of control, letting the learners explore what they need most, and being around to support those needs. It's all about forging connections, evoking emotions, and fostering behavioral changes.

A Final Thought

Learner journeys are an art and a powerful tool for creating engaging training that aligns with both business goals and learner needs. By embracing the power of learner journeys, you can transform your training programs from one-time events to ongoing, learner-focused growth experiences that inspire real change. To begin using learner journeys effectively and creatively, we, as L&D professionals, must step off our pedestals and invite learners to explore the possibilities that await us when we work and design together.

Activity 3-1. Map a Successful Learner Journey

Let's return to our learner-centric onboarding program (or another program you have been working on). You have already created your learner personas. Now, use one persona to build out the first week of the onboarding program. Leverage any of the templates provided in this chapter.

Objective
Map a high-level learner journey for an onboarding program or other initiative.

Steps
1. Identify the overall journey goal and individual learner goals for each touchpoint.
2. Identify touchpoints, interactions, and channels for the journey and think about how you can create awareness before the main training event. How will you sustain training after the event ends?
3. Align the touchpoints to your learners' emotional states.
4. Identify data and measures you could use to show the effectiveness of this journey.

Chapter 4
Maximize Learning With an Effective Content Strategy

> What I love about content is it has the power to change people's lives for a second or for a day or forever. Great content creates space for people to pause and reflect, and that space is where transformation happens.
> —Jolie Miller, content strategist, LinkedIn

It's Friday night. It's been a long week. You just got your favorite food out of the oven, opened a cold beverage, sat down in front of the TV, and started clicking through the library of your favorite streaming service. Thirty minutes, one cold meal, and a warm beverage later, you finally find something you really want to watch. Sound familiar?

The frustration you feel when you can't seem to find a TV show to fit your mood is how our learners often feel when they try to find content that's relevant to their needs. Just as content strategist Jolie Miller says in the chapter opener quote, L&D professionals need to create space for learners to pause and reflect. Instead, we tend to clutter up our LMSs and our learners' brains with too much stuff—much of which is not what they need. When we realize our content isn't working, our solution may be to add another technology platform, such as an LXP, to increase engagement and use of content. Newer technologies always claim to make searching and finding content easier, but we have yet to see a platform that made that wish come true.

Our frustrations aren't necessarily the platform's fault (although that's not unheard of). Sometimes, we don't categorize and tag content properly, or we find ourselves reacting to training requests without taking a moment to think. At other times, someone in our organization takes things into their own hands, creates a "training program," and just uploads it onto the LMS. Most of the time, our learners are frustrated by a combination of all these things. With the expansion of AI-based tools for content creation, this enormous, untagged, messy content pile is only going to get bigger.

Instead of adding more and more content and yet another new technology, we suggest taking a step back. The solution lies not in accumulating more content or adopting new platforms but in developing a robust *content strategy*. By focusing on relevance, organization, and accessibility, we can create a learning environment in which employees can easily find and engage with the content they need.

Unfortunately, content strategy, while central to effective learning and development, remains a mystery to many organizations. That's why, in this chapter, we want to consider what marketers can teach us.

From Confusion to Clarity

Marketers know how to use content strategically to turn confusion into clarity and results. We live in a world in which we are surrounded by marketing content—advertisements on TV and online, videos on TikTok and YouTube, posts on Facebook and Instagram, online magazines, newsletters, and websites. All these channels are trying to deliver the right message to the right people at the right time. Although no official research or validated statistics exist, some sources suggest we encounter about 100 ads per day (Anderson 2023). We create and consume content at an unrelenting pace, and each new technology only increases this rate. We expect the use of AI tools to expand the mountain of bad content to new heights.

So, how do marketers keep track of and control this massive crush of content? First, as we've already discussed, they put their audience at the center of everything they do. In addition, they dedicate people and resources to managing the content and technologies and making decisions that are aligned with organizational goals.

Enter, content strategy.

Talking About Content

Let's take a step back and talk about what content is. Several scholars have tried to define content in helpful ways. Giuseppe Getto and his colleagues (2023) define content as "useful information that an audience will consume." Ann Rockley and Charles Cooper (2012) coined the phrase *structured content*, which means that content is stripped of a specific generic format and simply stored in its basic form. Together with Scott Abel, Rockley and Cooper (2015) have also discussed *intelligent content*, or content that should be "modular, structured, reusable, and format-free, which allows content to be discoverable, reconfigurable, and adaptable."

For our purposes, *content* includes the written word, images, and other media, such as video and audio. When we ask people in our sessions what content means to them, they often say it means videos and e-learning modules. These are what we call *content types*. Some people say an LMS is content, but that is a *content channel*. Content is only the written words, images, and other media within those content types and channels.

You might wonder why these small distinctions matter, and this is a key point: When we look at content (the written word, images, and other media) as format-free, structured, and intelligent—as Rockley, Cooper, and Abel suggest—it changes the focus from content types (how we deliver the content) to the content itself (what we deliver). In short, instead of focusing on the how, we should focus on the *what* and make it relevant and valuable so we can deliver the right content at the right time to the right audience. In simpler terms, this approach encourages us to concentrate less on the format and more on the substance. The goal is to create content that is relevant and valuable to our audience. By doing so, we can ensure we're delivering the right information, to the right people, at the right time. This strategy helps us meet our audience's needs more effectively, regardless of how the content is ultimately presented or distributed.

Is this a familiar exchange? A business leader says, "I need a 30-minute e-learning module," and an L&D pro responds, "OK." Aside from the obvious fact that we should never respond to a request without further questions, the exchange points to a common problem: Stakeholders often focus only on *how* we deliver content. Their requests don't refer to what the learners need or what the business needs, let alone the influence an e-learning module is supposed to have on the organization. However, if we look at content as reusable and format-free, we can focus on learners' needs first, and then decide how we want to deliver content to different audiences to align with the business ask. For example, one learner group might receive a video, while another might prefer a simple PDF document, but the content would remain the same. Personalization and repurposing of content becomes a breeze if we distinguish between content, content types, and content channels. This helps us make learning relevant.

★ Terms You Should Know

Content, Content Types, Content Channels, and Content Strategy
Content refers to all useful information that your audience will consume, including written words, images, other media, and links. *Content types* are reusable containers for specific information that is useful to your audience. They have a common structure and purpose and include certain properties such as the title or name of the content, featured images, and metadata. In L&D, content types include videos and e-learning modules. Content types are consumed by your audience through *content channels* such as websites, blogs, or social media platforms. In L&D, a learner accesses a video (content type) through your LMS (content channel). In addition, a *content strategy* refers to the planning, creation, publication, and governance of useful, usable content. It's like a blueprint or inventory of your content.

Understanding Content Strategy

Let's now dive a bit deeper into the origins and importance of content strategy, which will allow us to use it to our favor in learning and development. *Content strategy* is a new name for something that has been around for centuries. In the 18th century, Benjamin Franklin created the persona of Poor Richard and used a storytelling approach to share relevant content about astrology, astronomy, the weather, proverbs, and more. He published and sold *Poor Richard's Almanack* as an ongoing book series, enticing readers to purchase the next volume and the next and the next. He knew that the content itself was the selling point, not the content channel.

Fast forward to the 21st century, and things have changed dramatically. Access to information comes through a wide variety of channels and technologies, and our content has to be adjusted to fit. Organizations, governments, educational institutions, and individuals create so much content we can no longer keep track of it. And think about our poor learners: How are they supposed to find any of it? At the same time, data inundates us, telling us what works and what doesn't. Somewhere around 2008, a new profession emerged within marketing to try to make sense of it all: the content strategist.

The goal of every marketer when creating a content strategy is to draw prospective customers into their marketing funnel and engage and nurture them, providing the right content at the right time and place to the right audience so they become loyal customers. It's not an easy task! Let's consider exactly how marketers go about this.

A content strategy must first ensure that content has a purpose and can answer the question: *Why do you want to publish this content?* In the previous example, your organization wants a learning product in the form of a 30-minute e-learning module. Their why needs to be aligned with the overall business goal to demonstrate the content's influence in the long run. Maybe that goal is to increase revenue year-over-year.

Second, a content strategy requires planning for the content your customers will need along different stages of the funnel. Third, it's about creating reusable content that's valuable and consistent in terms of the *how* and *what* so marketers can send it to different audiences with minimal tweaks. Fourth, it's about managing the publication and delivery of content throughout the entire funnel (the *where* and *when*). And fifth, it's about the governance of content, meaning maintaining and keeping it up to date. Last, a content strategy is about measuring how content performs. Above all, your content strategy is about people (the *who*) and how they consume content.

Now we've established that a content strategy is the blueprint that allows marketers to create high-quality content, but how do they cut through the noise to reach their audience? A content strategy is not only a plan for creating content; it's also a plan for distributing valuable, relevant, and consistent content to attract and retain a clearly defined audience and drive people to take action. Think about the last time you researched something on the internet, browsed various websites, and entered your email address into a form. Shortly after, you likely received emails from multiple organizations. You went back to some of their websites, browsed some more, and clicked some links; the next time you received an email, like magic, the content resonated better because it was more valuable and relevant to you. So, you go back to the website again. Rinse and repeat until you eventually purchase the product (take action).

Cutting through the noise isn't easy for marketers. Customers don't want to waste time finding answers to their questions, including their most common question: *Why should I care?* This is where a content strategy shines. A good content strategy allows marketers to ensure their content is seen and used because they plan for it to reach a specific audience at a certain time, to educate them if they are in the awareness stage of the funnel or to gently push them toward a purchase if they have moved on to the consideration phase. Marketers know that content needs to change based on where prospective customers are in the marketing funnel, and they act upon this knowledge at all times.

So, what does all this mean for L&D?

Content Strategy for L&D Pros

All your L&D content needs to have a purpose (the *why*) to drive learners to action, and you also need to measure its impact. To identify the why, return to your learner personas. You need to understand your learners' pain points, which you derive from learner persona research; this allows you to synthesize their needs.

To understand the actions you want learners to take, look at learner journeys. You will design the journey with the right mix of content, content types, and content channels to help address learners' pain points and keep them engaged. Each touchpoint of the journey drives learners to action. The sum of all these actions and their outcomes (learner goals) makes up your overall journey goals (organizational goals), which in turn allow you to measure the impact of your content. We just love it when things fall into place so neatly; don't you?

But what about the challenge of cutting through the noise? If you design your learning solutions around a persona and create journeys, you're still missing a content strategy that allows you to deliver relevant and valuable content at the right time and place to the right people. We know this is easier said than done.

If you are like most learning designers, you are already stretched thin. How are you supposed to take on the job of a content strategist on top of everything else? We are not suggesting that you do this, just that you start thinking like one.

Don't work in a silo. Collaborate with others in the organization to start working on a content strategy, and allow colleagues and learners into the fold when it comes to content creation. L&D doesn't have to own it all. On the contrary, we believe that L&D should become a mediator to help others create good content. When that happens, content is published when and where it is needed and in the preferred format, which could be anything from an email to a job aid to an elaborate e-learning module.

Benefits of a Good Content Strategy

Whether you're a marketer or a learning designer, a good content strategy is the only way to understand what content exists, what content should be created for your audience, and what content is no longer in use. It allows organizations to align content to their overall business goals and strategic objectives while putting the learner at the center of everything. This leads to reduced costs because you shift your focus to what's important and valuable to customers or learners and you produce only that content, which leads to higher engagement and motivation.

In L&D, our content strategy helps us understand what is most valuable to our learners based on our learner persona research; guides us in creating better, more personalized content; delivers that content at the right time; and supports our learners' behavior changes. In short, our content strategy guides us in the right direction by telling us which steps to take and when.

With the help of content strategies, we can also keep track of content consumption. This data tells us which content is in high demand and which has barely been touched, which in turn, helps us decide what content is no longer needed. Our rule: If no one has touched that video, e-learning module, or recorded webinar in over a year, no one is going to touch it tomorrow. Get rid of it!

As you assess the mountains of content, deciding what stays and what goes and planning for the future, you will start to align resources, processes, and technologies to get the most out of it. As you'll learn in the next section, a solid content strategy includes a governance structure that allows for regular maintenance and updates, so your content is always up to date. No more outdated screenshots or statistics, no more wrong information that's passed on to the learners. Again, all this should be a team effort—no more silos and no more duplication of work.

Finally, because everything and everyone is aligned, you should be able to achieve brand recognition across all the deliverables you create as an organization. This thematic and contextual consistency will excite and engage learners.

Content Strategy in Four Steps

Content strategy includes four distinct phases or steps: planning, creation, publication, and governance. Figure 4-1 illustrates each phase.

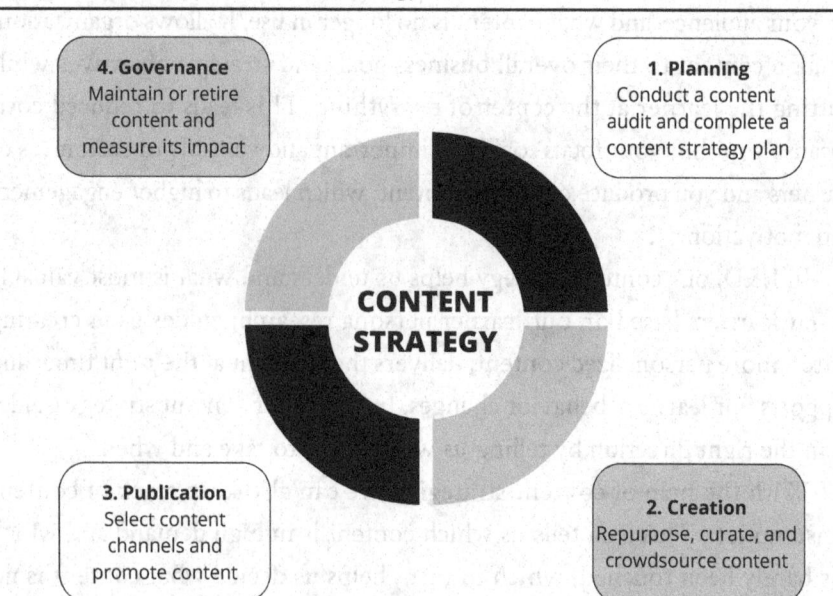

Figure 4-1. Creating Your Content Strategy

4. Governance
Maintain or retire content and measure its impact

1. Planning
Conduct a content audit and complete a content strategy plan

CONTENT STRATEGY

3. Publication
Select content channels and promote content

2. Creation
Repurpose, curate, and crowdsource content

It's helpful to ask yourself specific questions as you begin each stage.
- In the *planning phase*, ask:
  » What do you already have in place? This is known as a *content audit*.
  » How can you get organized, set goals, and begin to create content? This is your *content strategy plan*.
- In the *creation phase*, ask:
  » How can you use content that's already in place in new ways? This is known as *repurposing content*.
  » From what sources can you curate content to augment what you already have? This is known as *content curation*.
  » How can you leverage the power of your organization to create content? This is known as *crowdsourcing content*.
- In the *publication phase*, ask:
  » How can you best reach your audience? The answer will help you select content channels.
  » How can you let your learners know about new content? The answer will help you promote your content.
- In the *governance phase*, ask:
  » How do you update and maintain your content so it stays relevant? The answer can help determine not only how to maintain and update content but also when to retire certain content.
  » How do you know you content is effective? This can help you determine if your content has the desired impact.

We know that developing a content strategy can seem overwhelming. But as we break down the steps further, you will discover that you are already doing much of the work, which will help it seem more manageable. Let's dive in.

Phase 1. Planning

During this first crucial phase, you develop plans, templates, and guidelines that will later help you create your content. The planning phase begins with a content audit, in which you consider all of the content you have already produced and decide what's good, what's bad, and what's missing. Then you create a content strategy plan—a document outlining your goals, your target audience, and the types of content you'll be creating. These tasks take time, and it may seem like a lot of work to complete before you write your first word. But if you organize your thoughts and create a solid plan, it will save you a lot of time in the long run.

Conduct a Content Audit

When we ask a room of L&D professionals how many of them know exactly what content they have, where it is, and who is responsible for it, usually only one or two people raise their hands. This is a problem. When making basic decisions about your content, like where to focus your time and money, you need to know the answers to these questions. If you don't, it's time to do a thorough content audit.

Let's return to our friends at LuxeKitchens. Picture a bustling sales floor with phone lines ringing, the scent of freshly brewed coffee in the air, and people in sharp business attire talking animatedly. But something's amiss. The sales consultants keep frantically switching between windows on their computers, and phone conversations are stalling as they struggle to find the right resources. The employees of LuxeKitchens, a beacon in the industry, are entangled in a web of content. The sales consultants find an overwhelming number of documents, video tutorials, and guidelines when they do a simple search of the company's available content. The outcome is poor customer interactions, inefficient sales processes, and a decline in both customer satisfaction and revenue.

After recognizing the obstacles the sales consultants face, the company decides to move forward with a transformative change in its content strategy. The first step is to break down the challenges into two categories:

- A labyrinth of disjointed content repositories, leading to confusion and duplication of work
- Sales reps who cannot find crucial information, which affects their real-time conversations with customers

The next step for LuxeKitchens is doing a thorough content audit, which will allow them to create an inventory of the content, content types, and channels already in place.

For an L&D content audit, you will determine what content is still current and accurate. We suggest using a spreadsheet so you can work collaboratively with others. Start by recording these categories:

- **Name.** What is the content called?
- **Purpose (learning or performance objectives).** Why was this content created? What learning or performance goals does it support?
- **Target audience.** Who should receive this content?
- **Type and channel.** What type of content is it (an article, video, e-learning module)? How will you distribute it (LMS, website, social media)?
- **Creation and maintenance dates.** When was the content created? When should it be updated?
- **Metadata.** What are the search terms that people can use to find the content?
- **Location.** Where is the content stored?

Let's return to the sales training the LuxeKitchens team has been working on. After their L&D team identified the learner journey for the sales training and the corresponding content needed, the content audit revealed what they needed to create and what was already in existence. If you are involved in a large project such as this, try to perform a content audit for each training program, with content aligned to each step of the learner journey.

The example in Table 4-1 focuses on lead management training, specifically phone skills, which is part of the larger sales training program for our LuxeKitchens' sales consultants.

You can go into more detail than what you see in Table 4-1, but the more information you include in the spreadsheet, the harder it will be to manage. You'll find a content audit template you can download at TrainLikeAMarketer.com. Ask yourself what is most important to help your organization create and publish high-quality content. Always start small to avoid being overwhelmed.

After the content audit, you will have a long (potentially very, very long) list of content. The next step is to create a rubric to effectively assess all existing content (Getto et al. 2023). The categories in the rubric should align with your overall content goals. For example, if your organization is trying to make all content available through mobile devices, one criterion in the rubric could be: How easy is it to access the content on a mobile device?

Table 4-1. Content Audit Spreadsheet

Content Name	SOP—Phone Skills—Greeting	SOP—Phone Skills—Open Ended Questions	SOP—Phone Skills—Describing an Issue
Objectives	• Make customers feel welcome • Inform customers about their options	• Identify why customer is calling • Identify ways to help customer	• Manage customer expectations • Make customer feel heard
Target Audience	Sales representatives (new and experienced)	Sales representatives (new and experienced)	Sales representatives (new and experienced)
Content Types	• WBT with interactive videos • Job aids	• WBT with interactive videos • Role plays	• WBT with interactive videos • Videos
Content Channels	• LMS • MS Teams	• LMS • Team meetings	• LMS • Intranet • MS Teams
Creation Date	February 15, 2025	April 5, 2024	December 18, 2024
Maintenance Date	Annual	Annual	Annual
Metadata	Phone skills; greeting; welcome; lead management	Phone skills; open-ended questions; reason; lead management	Phone skills; issues; customer expectations; lead management
Location	SharePoint > Lead Management > Phone Skills	SharePoint > Lead Management > Phone Skills	SharePoint > Lead Management > Phone Skills

Some questions you can use to assess the effectiveness of content include:
- How often is content being accessed each week?
- How useful is this content to learners?
- How easy is it to find this content?

The bulk of your available content is often tied to mandatory training. Thus, you will be tempted to say it just needs to stay and rate it high in your rubric, but this is not always the best choice. Yes, you need the mandatory training, but if the content itself is not effective, you need to identify how to update and enhance it to align with your overall content goals. Consider each individual piece of content separately—don't look at your training offering for a particular program as a whole.

We often hear participants in workshops and conference sessions say that it's impossible to do a full content audit, especially for an organization with a long history and a lot of content. You may have come to that conclusion about your organization, and we agree that it can be daunting. Here's what we suggest: Instead of trying to review thousands of pieces of content all at once, start by adding new content to your content audit spreadsheet. Then, update the spreadsheet gradually every time you touch existing content. You may never be able to capture everything, but that's OK.

With the rubric in place, analyze your findings, and identify content gaps. More than 60 percent of very successful marketers conduct a content audit at least twice a year (Semrush 2023). Never get complacent!

Create a Content Strategy Plan

It's now time to augment your content audit spreadsheet with a written content strategy plan that will make creating content a breeze. The content strategy plan is like a template that allows everyone who creates content to follow the same guidelines. This ensures consistent, reusable content from the start. Typical elements of a content strategy plan include content goals, audience, content types, content channels, content models, and an editorial calendar.

Content goals are the first element of the plan and always need to be aligned with the audience. Ask how the content you are planning to create will help your audience. For example, if LuxeKitchens learned through data and feedback that its sales reps have a difficult time with a new feature in the CRM, one content goal could be to share relevant articles and videos with the reps to decrease the number of user errors related to this new feature. You might decide to share this content over the next two to four weeks. You would align each of your goals with the categories you have in your content audit rubric. After all, the elements of the rubric are aligned with your overall content goals already!

The audience is the second element of your content strategy plan. Who will consume your content? You probably guessed that this is where learner personas come back into play. Ensure that any content you want to create in the future aligns with your learners' pain points and needs. Share more background about your audience and link that to your learner personas.

Next, add content types to your plan. Share with everyone on your team how these content types should be created and saved so they are consistent and reusable. You already know which content types work best for your audience because you uncovered this information when you created the learner personas. Content types might include videos, infographics, articles, or e-books. As part of the content strategy plan, for example, you would identify how videos should be saved in a common format that allows for easy customization for any channel, so they will look great every time, no matter how someone edits them. (If you are still a bit fuzzy on the concept of content types, check out the 113 content types listed on the CoSchedule website at CoSchedule.com.)

Your plan should also include channels for delivering content. Again, you know this already because your learners have shared which channels work best for them. Use this information to create guidelines for your organization about which channels to focus on. In our learner journey workshops, we try to identify additional channels that create exceptional learning experiences. Ideally, you want to use channels that learners are already using as much as possible. We will talk about channels in more detail later in this chapter.

Content models are the next element in your content strategy plan. These are the specific requirements for each content type aligned with content goals and your audience. Let's say you identified that blog posts work especially well for your audience. A blog post is a content type that is made up of a heading, subheadings, a meta description, the body text, character limits, external links, and so on. Those are the specific attributes of a blog post, and the sum of those attributes is called a *content model*. Think of it as a checklist, template, or guidelines for various content types to ensure consistency. Content models are valuable because they help create, audit, and improve content (Getto et al. 2023). Another example of a content model is an e-learning module. In your content strategy plan, you can define what each e-learning module should include so that regardless of who in your organization created it, the learners have a similar experience.

Lastly, add an editorial calendar to your content strategy plan. This is a task list of what needs to be done, when, and by whom. In the calendar, you turn your goals into action steps, such as drafting content, editing content, or creating content models. Content creation might also be driven by seasonality in your business. For example, October is cybersecurity month, so you would probably want to align your goals and calendar accordingly. Make sure you look beyond the L&D team when it comes to assigning roles for content creation.

In our LuxeKitchens example, as the team worked through their content audit and content strategy plan, a simple but powerful insight emerged—most of the content sales consultants needed could be linked directly to the CRM they were already using. This "eureka" moment led to a significant shift in the L&D strategy and use of technology.

Phase 2. Creation

If you follow the planning steps precisely, your content will be usable, reusable, accessible, and consistent when you start to create it. Chapter 5 goes into more detail about how to write well, including how to find the right tone and voice. In this chapter, we'll focus more on the strategy behind content creation.

Not all gaps identified in the previous step have to be filled with content you create from scratch. On the contrary, purchasing, curating, repurposing, and flexing content should guide your content creation efforts. Creating something brand-new should be your last resort. Ask yourself: Does the content exist within the organization? Is it available via an open source? If yes, use it and curate it!

Next, ask yourself if the content exists "off the shelf." If the answer is yes, go out and purchase it. If off-the-shelf content doesn't work for you because you need more customization or it's too expensive, ask if there is another solution you could adapt to meet your content goals. If yes, flex, repurpose, and adapt existing or off-the-shelf content. Only build a solution from scratch if you can't answer any of the previous questions with a yes.

Now, we'll briefly explain content repurposing, content curation, and crowdsourced content to ensure you get the most out of your efforts without breaking the bank.

Repurpose

Repurposing content refers to reusing existing content but presenting it in a different format (Needle 2021). Repurposing content saves time and allows you to use content you know is performing well with learners in new, creative ways. This is one of the secrets to creating more engaging learning experiences. However, it's important to note that repurposing is not taking someone else's content and aligning it to your brand—that's stealing.

As long as it aligns with our audience's needs, flexing content can save time and money and lead to a successful content strategy. Here are a few examples of how you can repurpose content in L&D:

- Take an e-learning module and break it down into smaller, more digestible chunks. For example, you could create a series of short videos, podcasts, or blog posts, all on the same topic.
- Turn a webinar recording into a transcript or e-book. This way, learners can access the information at their own pace and in their preferred format.
- Take existing content and create new content types. For example, turn a blog post into a video or e-learning module.
- Transform the statistics you have shared in an e-book into an infographic.

We also like to call repurposing, *content atomization*, or the process of breaking down a large piece of content into smaller, reusable units. For example, Kapost, a software company, used one of its e-books to create 122 content assets, including an infographic, whitepapers, a video, unique landing pages, blog posts, outbound email campaigns, and social posts.

Not only does repurposing content save time, but it can also help personalize the learning experience for your learners. Not everyone wants to sit through a 20-minute e-learning module. By repurposing content into different formats, you can give learners the flexibility to choose the format that best suits their needs. Next time you're creating new content, consider how you can repurpose it in a variety of ways that might interest learners—they'll thank you for it.

Curate

Content curation is the art and science of finding and sharing the most valuable, relevant, and up-to-date content—even if it comes from outside sources. Curation can significantly reduce content development costs and time-to-delivery for training programs. By presenting curated content alongside original materials, you create a richer, more comprehensive learning experience that encourages critical thinking and a broader understanding of the topic. But it's important to do it right. You may wonder if *curation* is another word for *stealing*. It's not! The key difference is that if you use content created by someone else, you must always indicate the source and give credit for their work. You should also carefully integrate the curated content with your content for a seamless learning experience. Ideally, a learner shouldn't easily be able to tell the difference between your content and the content you've curated.

Content curation can be time-consuming, but it's often worthwhile because it ensures that your learners are exposed to a variety of high-quality content. Curation also allows L&D professionals to leverage external expertise to fill knowledge gaps and provide fresh perspectives.

To successfully curate and integrate someone else's content into your content strategy:

- Carefully vet all the sources you curate to make sure they are accurate and up to date.
- Tie the curated content into your content types and channels. For example, include their content in one of your blog posts, and include a link to the source at the end of the post.
- Align curated content to your content goals and your audience. For example, if your goal is to make all content easily accessible on mobile, you need to ensure that the curated content is responsive.
- Add context around each piece of content. Meaning, you can't just add a list of links to a topic. You need to write an introduction and body text, ensure that everything flows, and add a summary.
- Explain why you chose a specific piece of content and how it relates to your learning objectives.

Crowdsource

Imagine you could tap into an almost endless pool of knowledge and expertise to help you create content at almost no cost. We have good news for you, you can (and it's not about using AI). Your employees have insights, expertise, and, often, the motivation you need to create outstanding content. It's called *crowdsourcing* or *user-generated content*, and marketers have been using this technique for years. They ask the public for ideas and input, which allows them to create more diverse, helpful content at a much lower cost. If you have ever used the navigation app Waze, looked something up on Wikipedia, or found an image on Unsplash, you know the quality of crowdsourced content.

To leverage crowdsourced content in L&D, start by ideating the information you are looking for and how it should align with your overall goals. Next, get creative and promote your ask. It isn't enough to send out an email asking for help. Have some fun with this task. If your organization has an intranet page, create a banner to raise awareness or design and develop a short teaser video to excite employees about contributing to your project. Once you start receiving content, gather and sort through it to identify which suggestions work best. Use the rubric you created during the planning phase to objectively assess all submissions. When you have identified the best of the best ideas, revise them as needed and share them with the world.

The advantages of crowdsourcing are clear: low cost, high employee motivation, insights into more diverse areas of knowledge and expertise, maintenance of institutional knowledge, innovation, collaboration, and engagement. Yes, you'll need to exercise some oversight; you can't use crowdsourced content without reviewing and fact-checking it. Many educational technology platforms have a feature that can gather input from employees, including video uploads, and curated articles. Usually, an administrator can review and revise the submissions before they're made public.

We all know that two heads are better than one. Therefore, not only should L&D professionals crowdsource content, but we should also collaborate as much as possible. Your marketing department is an excellent source of content that you can reuse for learning purposes. Get planning meetings on the books with the marketing team and other colleagues with whom you want to collaborate. Set up regular status meetings and work through your content strategy plan, including your editorial calendar, together. Edit each other's work, fact-check it, and ensure all content aligns with your audience and your organizational goals. Ideally, you could also select learners to review and evaluate content before it is published to a wider audience. These collaborations can save you a lot of time and trouble down the road!

Finally, don't forget to leave space for unexpected requests, especially those that are backed up by data and show a real learner or organizational need. L&D professionals need to stay flexible and nimble while adhering to a solid content strategy plan. Also there are many new AI-driven tools at your disposal to help you create content. You might want to take a few of those for a test drive. However, always take the outputs of AI with a grain of salt—make sure they are accurate and add your personal and organizational voice.

Phase 3. Publication

Once L&D professionals have created relevant and valuable content, they often think that their job is done. All that's left is to upload the content to the LMS, right? Marketers know that publishing content isn't just about sharing it with the world; it's also about promoting that content and identifying the best channels for their audience. There is no one-size-fits-all solution. Marketers analyze their audience and where they are in their journeys and then align content and content channels with that audience's needs and preferences.

In creating your learning content, you will also want to consider your audience's needs and preferences during the publication phase. Make sure you have completed most or all of these steps before this phase: creating learner personas, mapping learner journeys, planning your content audit, and developing your content strategy.

The Right Content Channels for Your Audience

L&D professionals often consider only their organization's LMS as a content channel. In part, this is because of compliance requirements, but it's also because of inertia—"this is what we've always done." Why not try to innovate? If you need to track your content for compliance purposes, you can use other tools, such as Google Analytics or Microsoft Teams, which offer in-depth analytics. You can use Power Automate to automate and export reports and then import them back into your LMS. In this way, you can still meet any compliance requirements without relying on the LMS as your only content channel.

Sometimes, there's no need to track training at all. Instead, you can focus on measuring the behavior change resulting from your training as an indicator of your content's success. This is, ideally, what we should all be doing.

When marketers consider which channels to use, they think in terms of three main types of channels:

- **Owned channels** belong to the company or brand, such as landing pages, blog posts, social media accounts, and mobile apps.
- **Earned or shared channels** are external third-party channels that share content about a company or brand, such as shares, mentions, comments, or reviews.
- **Paid channels** are paid for by a company in exchange for promoting content, also known as pay-to-play, such as paid Google or social media ads and sponsored content in industry publications.

In the L&D world, we can see parallels to how marketers think. We can also divide our channels into three categories:

- **Owned channels** include proprietary, internally used technologies, such as a company intranet or knowledge management system, as well as physical facilities, such as common spaces, offices, and cubicles.
- **Shared channels** include the shares, likes, and comments on internally published content types.
- **Purchased channels** include LMS, LXP, Microsoft Teams, SharePoint, and other options from outside the organization.

The next time you think about where to publish your content as you work on your content strategy plan, keep the distinction among these types of channels in mind. There are many more exciting options in our world than the LMS.

Word on the Street: Let Learners Know About Your Training

As we've noted, the publication phase of your content strategy includes promoting your content. You have to create awareness so your audience knows what to look for in the first place. In our discussion of buyer and learner journeys, we briefly noted that creating awareness and engagement is crucial. Now, we will explore how you can create an adoption strategy that will help you do exactly that.

Adoption refers to an audience's acceptance of a new experience, which could be anything from a new assessment process to the release of a new week- or month-long training program to new technology implementations. The extent of your adoption strategy will differ based on the size of the learning experience.

An *adoption strategy* should build awareness, educate, and create curiosity by branding the experience, developing a communication plan, and creating a support system that delivers consistent messaging. This will help you entice people to adopt (try) and then continue to integrate (engage with) newly learned skills, knowledge, and abilities into their daily habits. We can divide adoption strategies into two distinct types: the rollout and communication strategy and the ambassador or champion strategy.

A defined rollout strategy aids in successfully implementing a change. It also helps to test and iterate your solution (experiences) so that adjustments and improvements can be made to ensure audience applicability and success. When considering and finessing a rollout strategy for any new experience—be it learning, training, or technology—it is crucial to identify your target audience, timeline, and competing risks. You also need to assess your organization's readiness for a proposed change and anchor the approach to your business strategy and culture. Focus on immediate and ongoing awareness, education, and action.

A rollout strategy can only be successful if accompanied by a solid communication strategy. When you start drafting your strategy, you should be able to answer these four questions:

- Who is sending the communication?
- How frequently should we "ping" learners?
- On what days and at what times should we communicate?
- When should managers and other stakeholders be included?

At this stage, the answers to those questions should already be clear, based on your learner personas, your learner journeys, and the content strategy plan. Just fill in the blanks for the specific training initiative you are working on. Start with a high-level communication strategy plan to better understand what should happen and when. That plan might look like Table 4-2.

Table 4-2. High-Level Communication Strategy Plan

Timing	Process	Owner
Intake process	• Initiative start and delivery date • High-level summary of initiative • Identify assets needed (email, banner, webinar)	Lara
5–6 months before launch	• Collaborative meeting between L&D and internal communication • Start to involve champions • Draft communication plan, including measures of success	Olaf
4 months before launch	• Start promotion of initiative	Lara

When your team and stakeholders have agreed upon the high-level milestones, it's time to dig into the details of the plan. Using our LuxeKitchens sales training example, we can create a communication plan that looks like Table 4-3. You'll find a template for this plan at TrainLikeAMarketer.com.

Table 4-3. Communication Plan

Phase	Phase 1. Pique curiosity	Phase 1. Pique curiosity	Phase 1. Pique curiosity
Communication	We Need You! Updated Sales Training	Are You Ready to Make a Difference?	What's Sales Got to Do With It?
Channel	Email and MS Teams	Email and MS Teams	Email and MS Teams
Key Message	Why behind new sales training and how leaders can support efforts	Why behind new sales training and role of ambassadors	Excite sales reps and get their buy-in for new sales training
CTA	Download info and share in team meetings and 1:1s	Join webinar	Watch teaser video
Audience	Leadership	Ambassadors	All sales
Owner	Lara	Lara	Lara
Timing	July 1	July 1	July 15
Measures of Success	Open rates, MS Teams, analytics, and downloads	Open rates, MS Teams, analytics, and webinar registration and attendance	Open rates, MS Teams, analytics, and video views

Over the years, Bianca has developed a five-phase approach to an adoption plan based on several change management models, which works well for L&D projects:

- **Phase 1.** Pique curiosity
- **Phase 2.** Experience it (Show it)
- **Phase 3.** Experience it (Try it)
- **Phase 4.** Embrace it
- **Phase 5.** Refresher

Let's apply this approach to the sales consultant training at LuxeKitchens (Table 4-4). Remember, our task is to refresh their sales training, which includes many new processes and approaches as well as mindset shifts. This is a huge disruption for the sales consultants, and without a solid adoption plan, the training program won't be successful.

Table 4-4. Five-Phase Adoption Plan

Phase	Timing	Adoption Support
1. Pique curiosity	3 months before implementation	Short-form content (such as teaser videos and flyers) containing high-level information about the new training content and how it will affect the day-to-day; initial email messages
2. Experience it (Show it)	2 months before implementation	5- to 15-minute recorded webinars starring business leaders who support the initiative and share the why behind the changes; show some samples of what's to come
3. Experience it (Try it)	1 month before implementation	Short simulations that engage sales reps and encourage them to try new approaches and processes in a safe environment; accompanied by MS Teams messages
4. Embrace it	During implementation	The bulk of the actual training program over multiple weeks (based on your learner journey map) is accompanied by regular messages on MS Teams or emails to remind sales reps about available resources
5. Refresher	Postimplementation (ongoing)	Ongoing communication reminders during town halls, in email newsletters, or on MS Teams to remind sales reps how to get help

An ambassador or champion strategy empowers early adopters and subject matter experts who act as ambassadors to incite organic growth and adoption. Ambassadors are not only passionate about what they do, but they are also excited to evangelize and help their peers get the most out of the new experiences. In addition, they:

- Help reduce the strain on the core project team and leadership and drive engagement throughout the community.
- Act as role models and advocates for the execution and adoption of your vision.
- Provide candid, constructive feedback to leadership and the core project team on adoption, risks, potential roadblocks, and emerging needs.
- Assist in engaging new members, providing guidance, and sharing best practices.
- Foster connections and remove barriers.
- Have a working knowledge of the learning experience, product, or service.
- Are empowered to guide, teach, and train their peers.
- Are given the space and time to promote and continue their own development and growth.
- Attend a regular cadence of ambassador meetings to share insights.

To recruit ambassadors, look for people within your organization who are willing to be evangelists on your behalf and share the same mindset about the culture you are trying to build. It's best to find people who are already involved with sharing training initiatives and are active on social media. If you have done a series of learner persona interviews, reconnect with those people to see if they want to become ambassadors. You will usually find a handful of people who are more than happy to support your project.

Once ambassadors are recruited, communicate your expectations and how their roles will affect the success of the new learning experience. The goal is to infuse the environment with energy and, through robust activities, engage the ambassadors daily for a minimum of five minutes to acclimate them and build their expertise and confidence. You might want to schedule a webinar to onboard them and complete a thorough walk-through of the activities to come. Demonstrate the processes and explain what the overall experience will be like. You could give them assignments such as scavenger hunts or reviewing and giving feedback on specific resources. Provide office hours to answer any questions. Ambassadors can be crucial to the success of an initiative, and their power and value shouldn't be underestimated.

Now that we have all the pieces of a successful adoption plan, we can see what a complete (but simplified) plan might look like for our sales training at LuxeKitchens (Table 4-5).

Table 4-5. Sales Consultant Training Adoption Plan Excerpt

	Phase 1: Pique Curiosity		Phase 2: Experience It (Show It)	
Timeline	July 1	July 15	August 1	August 15
Communication and change management (all)		What's Sales Got to Do With It?		Aren't You Curious?
Communication and change management (leadership)	We Need You!		Support New Sales Experience	
Communication and change management (ambassadors)	Are You Ready?		Experience New Sales Training	
Persona 1 training segment		Teaser video and flyer 1	Prerecorded webinar	WBT with video and example 1
Persona 2 training segment		Teaser video and flyer 2	Prerecorded webinar	WBT with video and example 2
Persona 3 training segment		Teaser video and flyer 3	Prerecorded webinar	WBT with video and example 3
Training development needs (What needs to happen in L&D before training can be launched?)	Design and develop assets for Phase 2		Design and develop assets for Phase 3	

Phase 4. Governance and Tracking Success

The last step in the content strategy process is to develop a way to keep your content up-to-date and relevant. This is called *content governance*. We know it sounds a bit boring, but governance is an essential step to ensure content consistency, strong messaging, and high-quality content. And, of course, you have to measure content success.

Governance

Unfortunately, more often than not, L&D professionals create content and rarely return to update it. The last step in developing a content strategy process takes us back to one of the first steps: the content audit. Your initial content audit isn't a one-and-done deal. On the contrary, it is crucial to revisit content regularly to ensure its accuracy. This is another reason it's so beneficial to have a single content repository from which you can make global updates and use content models as a foundation for your content strategy. You should also establish a cadence for updating your content strategy plan.

The good news is that if you have followed all the steps we've outlined as part of the content strategy process, you already have all the governance pieces in place. In other words, your governance model is the execution of your content strategy plan. The only thing left to do is continuously revisit your content strategy plan and ensure that everyone knows what their roles and responsibilities are.

Tracking and Measuring Content Success

We will spend more time on tracking and measuring success in chapter 9, but here, we want to highlight the essential elements for your content strategy plan.

Most marketers are savvy when it comes to tracking and measuring content success. According to Semrush (2023), 61 percent of marketers use social media engagement, and 52 percent use organic traffic as key metrics to measure content success. As L&D professionals, on the other hand, we hardly ever look at engagement rates, whether in a formal environment such as instructor-led training or virtual instructor-led training (smile sheets hardly count!) or an informal environment, such as engagement on Microsoft Teams. Instead, we focus on seat time and completion rates. Compare this with marketers, only 33 percent of whom consider time spent on a site as a worthwhile metric and only 27 percent of whom view conversion as a metric (Semrush 2023).

It's time for learning designers to look at different metrics and change how we think about tracking and measuring success. For example, the majority of marketers use Google Analytics and social media analytics tools to help determine content success (Semrush 2023). The L&D community has to get on that bandwagon and expand our reach. We also have to become more comfortable testing content with different audiences and learn to accept that things won't always work as planned. We need to keep adjusting our strategies and trying new approaches to reach our learners and deliver the right content at the right place and at the right time.

Returning to our sales consultants and the updated sales training for LuxeKitchens, an updated content strategy might lead to resolving many of the challenges we discussed at the beginning of this chapter:

- **Time saved.** Sales consultants dramatically reduce the time spent looking for information.
- **Increased engagement.** Content usage and completion rates soar.
- **Happy customers, more sales.** Satisfaction metrics and sales figures both climb.

How to Make Your Content Strategy Successful

Let's now consider what it takes to make your content strategy—and your organization—successful. According to Semrush (2023), 80 percent of very successful organizations have a documented content marketing strategy, compared with only 52 percent of unsuccessful organizations. And 66 percent of very successful companies have four or more content specialists compared with 32 percent of unsuccessful businesses. What about money spent on content marketing? Only 17 percent of very successful organizations spend less than $1,000 per month, compared with half of unsuccessful organizations. The numbers speak for themselves. It pays to have a content strategy in place.

We already know that the best strategies include a variety of content, content types, and content channels to personalize the learner' experience as much as possible, which can require a significant investment of people, time, and money. Many of the people reading this book are working for organizations that cannot afford a dedicated content specialist and can't spend $1,000 per month on content marketing. The good news is that there are three highly effective ways to make content strategies successful without a major investment:

1. Research your audience.
2. Improve the quality and value of your content.
3. Update and repurpose your content.

The most important element in the success of content strategies is audience research, according to almost half of strategists surveyed in 2023 (Semrush 2023). Understanding your target audience drives any solid content strategy. As L&D professionals, when we deeply research our learners and create learner personas, we better understand their challenges, pain points, needs, and goals, thus building a solid foundation for our content strategy.

In the same survey, 44 percent of marketers said that improving the quality and value of content is a crucial success factor (Semrush 2023). Your audience will identify high-quality content based on their needs, which brings us back full circle to the importance of audience research.

But even without extensive research, you can use common sense when it comes to your content. For example, customers and learners are both looking for authentic examples and case studies, a great user experience, consistent tone and voice, and original ideas. Don't disappoint them.

Your ultimate focus as an L&D professional designing content for employees should always be to create people-first content. Google's "Helpful Content Updates" is a great resource that will help you understand what this means (Google 2022). It includes a list of questions for marketers, which we've modified to fit the L&D realm:

- Do you have an intended audience for your learning offering that will find the content useful?
- Does your content demonstrate first-hand expertise and a depth of knowledge?
- Does your learning offering have a primary purpose or focus?
- After reading your content, will someone think they've learned enough about a topic to help achieve their goal?

- Will someone reading your content think they've had a satisfying experience?

Finally, a response that stands out in the Semrush (2023) report we've cited throughout this chapter is that 42 percent of marketers say that updating and repurposing content is crucial to success. With the expansion of AI tools, organizations will be creating more content in a shorter period, which is scary. This will likely lead to lower-quality content, which means our offerings need original content with a human touch to stand out. Originality and good quality content don't mean that you have to create everything from scratch. On the contrary, buying content or using AI prompts, is essential for augmenting content already in existence. The same holds true for repurposing long-form content. After all, why should we reinvent the wheel?

Tools and Examples

Many tools are available to make a content strategist's life easier. Although it's impossible to list them all here, we will provide an overview and a starting point for your own research. An essential toolkit would include the tools most of us use daily, including word processing tools (such as Microsoft Word, Google Docs, and Pages), presentation tools (such as Microsoft PowerPoint, Google Slides, and Keynote), and spreadsheet tools (such as Microsoft Excel, Google Sheets, and Numbers). Visual online collaboration, such as Mural or Miro, can make a content strategy come to life. Notion, Airtable, and Coda are great for versatile content organization and collaboration. Canva and Adobe Express are excellent tools for content creation and design. Trello, Asana, Wrike, and Jira are all helpful for tracking projects.

In addition to these tools, marketers also use a variety of authoring tools that allow content strategists to create deliverables in multiple formats. It's helpful to break the tools into four categories (Getto et al. 2023):

- **Authoring tools for structured content** allow content strategists to create structured content broken down into its basic components such as titles, body text, metadata, and so on. Structured authoring is great for large amounts of technical content across various channels. Tools include Adobe Framemaker and Oxygen.

- **Authoring tools for help content** allow content developers to create "help" content for a product or a service. Tools like Madcap Flare and Adobe RoboHelp can manage thousands of pages of help content.
- **API and developer documentation tools** allow marketers to create technical content that explains how an application runs. This is also known as "docs as code" and is highly technical. Tools such as Sphinx and Swagger support content strategists in completing this common task.
- **All-in-one tools** allow content strategists to accomplish all the tasks described here and more. Digital Asset Management Systems (DAM) fall into this category, and examples include Author-It and Adobe Experience Manager. These systems can become a repository for all your digital content, which will make it easier to make global content updates and support a consistent structure to store content.
- **Content management systems (CMSs)**, such as WordPress or Drupal, allow content strategists to create content more easily, keep it structured and organized, and maintain it regularly (Getto et al. 2023).

File Naming Conventions

Structured file naming conventions enable organizations to work more efficiently and make content easily accessible. While they primarily benefit L&D professionals, they ultimately enhance the experience for learners as well. File naming conventions provide a systematic approach to naming files, making it easier to find and retrieve content. These conventions foster consistency across files, which is especially important when multiple individuals are involved in content creation. Furthermore, when teams within an organization collaborate on content development, the company can achieve even greater effectiveness and efficiency.

While you may not have any of these specific tools or the budget to purchase them, many LMSs and LXPs have similar functions and can act as central repositories for your content. Talk to your IT team or software representative to find out which features are available in the systems you already have and be sure to consider them when you purchase a new system. The right tools can make your life much easier.

However, the best new software won't make a difference unless you include a structured file-naming convention in your content strategy plan. We'd rather work with a solid content strategy plan using simple, existing collaborative tools than the latest and greatest technology with no strategy driving its use.

An Investment in the Future

If you don't have a good content strategy in place, no technology in the world will fix the problem, and you will never be able to create relevant, valuable content for your learners. Planning a content strategy and putting all the necessary resources in place before you write the actual content can seem daunting—or even like a waste of time. We empathize with that feeling. However, we also know from years of experience that investing in planning before you create and publish content will save hours and hours of work down the road. A quick fix in the moment won't benefit your L&D team or your organization in the long run, but an investment in your content strategy will.

By the time you start thinking about your content strategy, you have already researched your audience and laid out the best possible learner journeys for them. As part of the learner journey planning process, you listed the content that's important to make the journey come to life. You likely have many of the pieces already in place, although they might be out of sight. To find all the pieces you need, become an advocate for content strategy within your organization. Start small, learn, fail, and try again.

A Final Thought

You can inspire your learners by offering the right content at the right time and the right place. It will look like magic to them! The extra effort you put into setting up a content strategy upfront will be worth it if the result is that you motivate your employees and encourage them to be more productive. Start small and build your strategy over time to achieve the best outcomes.

Activity 4-1. Create a Content Strategy

Choose one element from your onboarding program (or another program you have been working on) and initiate a content audit for the assets that are part of that initiative. When you have completed the audit, create a content strategy to keep the training program up to date.

Objective
Create a high-level content strategy.

Steps
1. Identify categories you want to capture in your content audit and build a spreadsheet using those categories. Connect with others in your organization to solicit their contributions.
2. Collaborate to complete the content audit spreadsheet.
3. Augment the content audit spreadsheet with a content strategy that covers the planning, creation, publication, and governance phases.
4. During the content creation phase, identify content that you can repurpose, curate, and crowdsource.

Chapter 5
Captivate Learners With Writing That Clicks!

> Make it simple. Make it memorable. Make it inviting to look at. Make it fun to read.
> —Leo Burnett, American advertising executive

Alex, an experienced L&D manager at LuxeKitchens, took pride in their team's work. Everyone spent countless hours designing and developing learning content for the sales consultants, trying to ensure every detail was perfect. This time, however, as Alex stared at dismal course completion rates, a sinking feeling settled in their stomach. Despite the designers' best efforts, learners were not engaging with the content. All of their carefully crafted modules sat almost untouched, gathering virtual dust.

Alex knew something had to change, but the path forward remained elusive. The soft glow of the laptop screen illuminated their tired face as they scrolled through social media feeds one evening. Suddenly, an advertisement for hiking boots caught their eye. The rugged beauty of the mountains in the photos was a stark contrast to their current surroundings. The website was a masterclass in digital marketing. Alex's finger hovered over the images, drawn in by the family-owned company's story unfolding with each click, and they imagined conquering mountain trails. Images of sunlit peaks and smiling hikers tugged at their heartstrings, but most powerful were the headlines that promised adventure and self-discovery. Alex nodded along, absorbing the key information.

As Alex finished paying for their new boots, a spark of professional inspiration struck. The marketing copy that had so effectively captured their attention and motivated them to make a purchase could be the key to solving the engagement issues the team had been grappling with at work. The simplicity and emotional appeal of the words on the boot company's website stood in stark contrast to the dense, technical content the team had been producing. Maybe the marketing principles at play could be adapted to improve their L&D work.

Alex called a team meeting the next day and set out to reimagine their approach to sales consultant courses by analyzing and then deploying the principles in the boot ad. The approach could be summed up succinctly as:

- Keep it **simple**.
- Keep it **useful**.
- Keep it emotionally **resonant**.
- Make it **easy to skim**.

Within a few months, the LuxeKitchens team had overhauled a short series of courses, first combining knowledge gleaned from developing their learner personas with an improved content strategy, and then taking a whole new approach to writing the content. The results were impressive. Learners not only completed the courses at a higher-than-normal rate, but they also wrote glowing evaluations of their experiences—and, most importantly, performed better at their jobs.

Capturing learners' attention and motivating them to change their behavior is critical to our success as L&D professionals. By adopting well-established marketing strategies to make our writing simple, useful, resonant, and easy to skim, we can transform our content from mundane to irresistible.

While we recognize the importance of depth and complexity in a great deal of training content, we shouldn't pursue those goals at the expense of accessible and compelling learning content. The writing strategies we'll discuss in this chapter speak to the ways people think, as we discussed in chapter 1, and can help us create instructional designs that educate, engage, and motivate.

The SURE Principles

To help align our writing with the way our learners think, we can use the four core SURE principles to guide us: Keep all communication simple, useful, resonant, and easy to skim (Table 5-1).

Table 5-1. The SURE Principles for Writing Content

Simple	Useful	Resonant	Easy to Skim
Learners crave simple, clear information for efficient learning, making readability key in L&D.	Ditch generic content and write for learners' problems—just like marketers target customer needs for better engagement.	Emotional learning content creates lasting influence by connecting with hearts and minds, not just facts.	Busy learners skim, so create skimmable content with clear headings, short chunks, and visuals to boost learning.

Simple Prose Is Powerful

Most of us crave simplicity—we want information that's easy to digest and remember. This preference for simplicity isn't just a matter of convenience; it's deeply rooted in our thinking. When information is presented in a clear, concise, and accessible manner, our brains can process it more efficiently, reducing cognitive load and freeing mental resources for deeper learning and retention. Remember that cognitive load is the mental effort required to understand, recall, and use information.

In the context of L&D, simplicity is beneficial for effective learning, with the caveat that the optimal level of simplicity or complexity varies depending on the content and the learner's prior knowledge. Generally, when content is accessible and easy to read, learners can absorb, retain, and apply new knowledge more quickly and effectively. Conversely, content that is overly complex or convoluted can lead to cognitive overload, disengagement, and poor learning outcomes. In other words, readability is a proxy for ease of learning (Johnson and Kress 1972).

So, how can L&D professionals ensure that their content is simple and accessible enough to engage learners? One key metric, as we've just noted, is *readability*, which refers to the ease with which a reader can understand a written text and encompasses factors such as word choice, sentence structure, and overall clarity of expression. Readability tests, such as the Flesch-Kincaid

Grade Level Test and the Flesch Reading Ease Test, quantitatively measure a text's readability. The Flesch-Kincaid test, for example, calculates readability based on sentence length and syllable count, producing a score between 0 and 100. Higher scores indicate greater readability, while lower scores mean the text may be too complex for the average reader (Table 5-2).

Table 5-2. The Flesch Grade Level Scale

Score	Readability	Grade Level
90–100	Very easy	5th grade or below
80–90	Easy	6th–8th grade
70–80	Fairly easy	9th–12th grade
60–70	Standard	College
50–60	Fairly difficult	College graduate
30–50	Difficult	Professional or graduate-level
30 or below	Very difficult	Technical or legal writing

Source: Adapted from How to Write Plain English by Rudolf Franz Flesch.

Rudolf Flesch, the test's co-creator, designed the formula in the 1970s. Here are some average Flesch-Kincaid readability scores for different categories of writing, from most to least readable:

- Comics: 92
- Consumer ads: 82
- *Time* magazine: 52
- *Harvard Business Review*: 43
- A standard insurance policy: 10

According to a 2013 National Center for Education Statistics study, the average US adult reads at a seventh- or eighth-grade level. When you write your content at this level, it helps ensure that it is engaging and more people understand it. Improved readability often means shorter sentences, simpler words, and clearer structure, which also makes your content more accessible to those who are neurodivergent—for example, learners who have dyslexia or attention deficit hyperactivity disorder (ADHD)—and helps with screen reader integration (Toonen 2024). When you focus on readability and accessibility, you create content that works for all. This isn't about "dumbing down" your material; it's about making it as accessible as possible to the largest number of learners. After all, the most profound ideas and complex theories are useless if people can't understand them. The key is to find the right balance of simplicity and depth.

Three Strategies for Simplifying Your Writing

Achieving simplicity in your writing is a skill that can be developed with practice and intentionality. Try to employ these strategies to make your learning content more readable and engaging.

1. Use Short Words and Sentences

One of the most effective ways to improve the readability of your content is to opt for short, simple words and sentences wherever possible. As the renowned writer George Orwell once advised, never use a long word where a short one will do. While it may be tempting to use complex or obscure vocabulary to convey your expertise, simpler language is usually more effective in getting your message across.

When you use long, complicated words, you place an extra cognitive burden on your readers. They have to slow down, decipher the meaning, and then reintegrate that understanding into the larger context of the text. This can be mentally taxing and disruptive to the flow of learning. In contrast, simpler words allow for quick, seamless processing, keeping learners engaged and focused on the content.

The same principle applies to sentence structure. Long, convoluted sentences with multiple clauses can be difficult to parse, requiring learners to simultaneously hold several ideas in their working memory. Breaking these into shorter, more digestible sentences can significantly enhance readability and comprehension. For example:

> **Original**
> The integration of role-playing scenarios in our training curriculum augments the sales team's capacity to navigate complex client objections and elucidate the value proposition of our premium products.

> **Simplified**
> We use role-play in training to help you:
> - Handle tough questions from clients.
> - Explain why our high-end products are worth the price.
> - Feel more confident in sales situations.

The original sentence has a Flesch Reading Ease Score of 23 (very difficult), but the simplified version has a score of 84 (very easy). Now consider another example:

> **Original**
> The assimilation of product knowledge pertaining to our premium appliance line necessitates a comprehensive understanding of cutting-edge culinary technology and its practical applications in high-end kitchen environments.
>
> **Simplified**
> To sell our top-tier appliances we'll:
> - Learn about the latest cooking tech.
> - Understand how it works in luxury kitchens.
> - Practice explaining these benefits to customers.

The original sentence has a Flesch Reading Ease Score of 16.3 (very difficult), while the simplified version has a score of 80.9 (easy).

2. Use Active Voice Instead of Passive Voice

Another way to make your writing more engaging and easier to understand is to use active voice rather than passive voice. In active voice, the subject of the sentence performs the action, creating more direct and dynamic prose. Passive voice, on the other hand, can make your writing lifeless, too wordy, and less engaging. Consider the difference between these two sentences:

> **Passive**
> The decision to raise prices was met with strong backlash from consumers.

> **Active**
> Consumers strongly opposed the decision to raise prices.

The active voice sentence is concise, forceful, and easier to grasp. It focuses on the actors (consumers) and their response, rather than on the abstract concept of a decision being met with backlash. Pro tip: If you're not sure whether your sentence is active or passive, try to insert "by zombies" after the verb. If you can do that easily, you're in passive voice!

3. Avoid Jargon and Buzzwords

Jargon and buzzwords refer to specialized vocabulary terms that people within a particular field or industry use. While they can serve as shorthand for those in the know, they can be alienating and confusing for readers unfamiliar with the terminology. Remember that the audience for your training content may come from diverse backgrounds and may not share your level of expertise. Using too much jargon can exclude some learners, undermining the goal of effective learning.

Instead of academic, business, or other types of jargon, use plain, straightforward language. If you need to use technical terms, define them clearly and provide context to help the learners integrate it into their existing knowledge frameworks. To illustrate these principles in action, let's look at an example of how we can simplify a piece of learning content.

> **Original**
> Our brain's reward system (also known as the mesolimbic system), is made up of many areas, including the nucleus accumbens and ventral tegmental area. The reward system shows increased activity when exposed to novel and stimulating experiences (Henley 2021; Fuentes-Claramonte et al. 2015).
>
> **Revised**
> Our brains like new and exciting things.

Readability Tools

Simplifying your writing requires practice, feedback, and repetition. Fortunately, you can use many different tools to assess and improve the readability of your content:

- **Microsoft Word** has a built-in readability statistics feature that provides a snapshot of your document's readability each time you run a spell check. The statistics include metrics like the Flesch-Kincaid Grade Level scale and the Flesch Reading Ease score. You can quickly see your readability statistics from the Home tab by selecting Editor and then going to Document Stats. In addition, you can use Microsoft's Accessibility Checker to make your content more readable for people with disabilities. This feature also works in Outlook, Excel, and PowerPoint.
- **The Hemingway App** is a dedicated readability tools that offers a more comprehensive analysis. This browser-based tool color-codes your text to highlight complex sentences, passive voice, and other readability issues. It also provides an overall readability grade and concrete suggestions for simplifying your prose, making it a valuable resource for writers looking to improve the accessibility of their content.
- **Grammarly**—a popular and easy-to-use AI-powered writing assistant— offers readability scores and suggestions as part of its premium service. While primarily known as a grammar and spelling checker, Grammarly's readability features can help identify many opportunities to streamline and improve your writing.
- **Other AI-based writing tools**—including Jasper.ai, Copy.ai, Rytr, and ProWritingAid—use advanced language models to analyze and optimize text for readability and other factors. Popular AI-based chatbots, such as ChatGPT and Claude, can help you organize and simplify your writing. You can even tell chatbots specifically what kind of audience you are writing for and the tone or academic level you prefer. By providing alternative word choices, suggestions for rephrasing, and even complete rewrites, AI assistants can be powerful allies in your quest for simplicity.

It's worth noting that no readability tools are perfect, but in combination with human input, they can dramatically improve your ability to reach a diverse group of learners.

The original sentence, while informative, is denser and more technical. Specialized vocabulary (such as *nucleus accumbens* and *ventral tegmental area*) may be unfamiliar and intimidating to some readers. The structure of the first sentence is also fairly complex.

The revised sentence is simple. It conveys the essential idea that our brains enjoy novelty in plain, accessible terms. The clause about parts of the physical brain is not essential to the main point, so it was deleted. The result is a sentence that is easy to read, understand, and remember—precisely the qualities we aim for in effective learning content.

Simplicity, the first SURE principle, can help manage cognitive load in learning. By presenting information clearly and concisely, we can reduce demands on working memory, allowing learners to focus on core concepts. However, simplicity doesn't mean eliminating all challenges—learning is inherently difficult. The goal is to remove extraneous complexity while maintaining the necessary cognitive engagement for effective learning.

Useful Content Sparks Engagement

In the world of L&D, creating content that is useful and relevant to your learners is paramount. Just as the best marketers focus on solving their customers' problems, effective L&D professionals must develop learning experiences that are relevant to their audience's needs and interests. This aligns with the cognitive process known as *elaborative encoding*, which suggests that linking new information to existing knowledge not only facilitates learning and retention but also enhances emotional engagement. This process taps into our brain's inherent craving for context and meaningful connections.

For example, instead of creating a generic training program called "Introduction to Leadership," a better option might be to design a course called, "Overcoming Leadership Challenges: Strategies for New Managers." By focusing on challenges that new managers face, the latter title is more likely to grab learners' attention and inspire them to engage with the content.

Three Strategies to Craft More Engaging Content

To create useful content that learners will notice, remember, and act on, consider these strategies:

1. **Get to know your learners.** Find out what they need, want, and struggle with. This helps you make content that really matters to them. (Personas are great for this purpose!)
2. **Align your content with business needs so that learners can use what they learn right away.** When content is more immediately relevant to their needs, people are more likely to use it.
3. **Use data to guide what you create and improve your content.** Look at readability scores, click-through rates, page views, course completions, and learner feedback and ratings to make content that works well for your specific learners.

When learners encounter material that is immediately useful, they transition from passive consumers to active participants in their own learning experiences. Useful content acts like a treasure map, inspiring learners to keep searching for more information. It creates a cycle where learning leads to doing, and doing leads to more learning. This ongoing process fuels growth and development. When we create useful and relevant content, we once again tap into our natural drive for engagement, retention, and real-world impact.

Resonance Taps Into Learners' Emotions

Creating content that resonates emotionally with learners is just as crucial as ensuring its usefulness and simplicity. By tapping into the power of emotions with this third SURE principle, we can design learning experiences that captivate, inspire, and drive lasting change.

You may remember Subaru's popular and highly effective 2014 ad campaign and its emotional tagline: *They lived.* The television commercial showcased the car's safety features through a series of emotionally charged vignettes instead of just listing facts and figures about crash test ratings. The image of a totaled vehicle, along with various observers who report that the people in the crash survived, packs an emotional punch, making viewers feel deeply invested. We think about our own loved ones and imagine, "What if?" Logic is important, but emotions drive action. Tap into your audience's feelings to make your message truly resonate.

Imagine applying this same principle to designing a safe driving training program for LuxeKitchens's delivery team. Instead of simply presenting slides filled with safety statistics and highway regulations, your program could open with a powerful narrative about the real-life consequences of distracted or reckless driving. It might feature testimonials from employees who have been affected by accidents or use vivid images to illustrate potential dangers on the road—images that would resonate with everyone who is participating.

By creating an emotional connection between your audience and the content, this type of training is far more likely to engage learners, stick in their minds, and influence their behavior behind the wheel.

Research consistently supports the effectiveness of emotionally resonant content in learning. The emotional enhancement effect on memory, which has been documented in numerous studies, suggests that people recall information associated with positive or negative emotions more easily and accurately than content not linked to emotional arousal (Mayer and Brünken 2006). Emotionally engaging content can potentially stimulate deeper encoding, which may allow learners to form more meaningful connections between new and existing knowledge.

Four Strategies for Content That Resonates Emotionally

To create learning content that speaks to the heart as well as the mind, consider the following strategies:

1. **Use vivid language and imagery.** Help learners visualize the concepts you're teaching. Paint a picture in their minds with descriptive language and metaphors. In the safe driving example, you might describe the screech of tires, the smell of burning rubber, or the heart-stopping jolt of a sudden impact.
2. **Tell stories.** Harness the power of narrative to engage learners' emotions. Share real-life case studies and anecdotes illustrating your key points. For instance, the safe driving training facilitator could tell a story about an employee who avoided a serious accident by following specific driving protocols discussed in the training.
3. **Appeal to emotions.** Consider what feelings you want to evoke in learners. Do you want them to feel inspired, motivated, or empowered? Craft your content accordingly. In the context of safe driving, you might appeal to learners' sense of responsibility, their

desire to protect themselves and others, or their commitment to returning home safely to their loved ones.
4. **Inform, entertain, and educate.** Blend facts, stories, and human insights to create a rich, multidimensional learning experience. Keep your content fresh, engaging, and emotionally compelling. Use a mix of media (including videos, interactive scenarios, and personal anecdotes) to maintain learners' interest and emotional investment.

By infusing strong emotions into your learning materials, you'll create content that resonates on a deeper level. You'll also forge powerful connections that enhance retention, recall, and application, ultimately driving real behavior change (Zak 2014). In the case of safe driving training, this could translate into fewer accidents, reduced liability, and, most importantly, saved lives. By making the training content emotionally compelling, you're not just sharing knowledge; you're influencing hearts and minds and creating real-world impact. When you design a learning program, no matter the topic, remember: It's not just about the facts; it's about the *feelings* too. When you tap into the power of emotional resonance, you create truly effective learning experiences.

Skimmable Content Is Easy to Absorb and Apply

People rarely have the time or inclination to read training materials from start to finish. Instead, they skim the content, searching for the most relevant and valuable information. Skimming engages emotions and provides information immediately, activating our preference for immediate rewards. As L&D professionals, we must adapt to this reality by creating content that is concise, skimmable, and easy to navigate. This allows learners to grasp the main points without reading every word, quickly identify key concepts, absorb essential information, and apply their new knowledge to real-world situations right away.

Four Ways to Make Learning Content More Skimmable

Follow a few best practices to make the content of your training programs easy to skim:
1. **Use clear, descriptive subheadings to organize your content into logical sections.** This will help learners understand the structure of the material and locate the information they need.

2. **Break up long paragraphs into shorter, more digestible chunks.** Aim for paragraphs of three to four sentences and use bullet points or numbered lists to present related ideas or steps in a process.
3. **Highlight key terms, definitions, and takeaways using bold text, italics, or color coding.** This draws learners' attention to the most important information and reinforces the knowledge.
4. **Include visual aids, such as images, charts, and diagrams.** Visuals break up the text and offer alternative ways of digesting information. We will dive deep into the power of visual aids in the next chapter.

Research shows that how we format text makes a big difference in how well people learn. When text includes short paragraphs, bullet points, and clear headings, readers remember and understand more (Hartley and Trueman 1983). Studies have found that these formatting tools help readers find what they need quickly. In fact, readers work with well-formatted text up to 124 percent more effectively than with plain blocks of text (Nielsen 1997). Other research confirms that clear, well-organized writing helps readers better understand and use what they learn (Mayer et al. 1996).

To illustrate the impact of skimmable formatting, let's look at a before-and-after example drawing on our LuxeKitchens case study. Figure 5-1 shows two versions of an install guide for smart refrigerators. The "before" is filled with dense text, while the "after" is styled using bulleted lists.

As you can see, the shorter, skimmable version is much easier to scan and understand quickly. The information is presented clearly and concisely using subheadings and bullet points to facilitate action-oriented reading. Readability scores confirm that the revised content is now more accessible and engaging for a broader range of learners.

Skimmable writing lets the reader see the lay of the land before diving into specifics. It's a great way to learn efficiently, especially for busy people or anyone who needs to grasp information quickly.

By making your learning content skimmable, you'll not only improve comprehension and retention, but you'll also create a more enjoyable and effective learning experience. Keep your training materials concise, organized, and easy to navigate, and your learners will thank you.

Figure 5-1. Writing Skimmable Content: Before and After

Smart Refrigerator Installation

Welcome to the training manual for installing our state-of-the-art smart refrigerators. These refrigerators are equipped with the latest technology, including touch-screen controls, voice-activated features, and energy-efficient systems. This manual aims to provide you with comprehensive instructions to ensure a successful installation.

Safety is of utmost importance. Before starting the installation, make sure to turn off all electrical connections related to the appliance. Always wear safety gear, including gloves and goggles, to protect yourself from any accidental injuries.

For this installation, you will need a variety of tools. These include a screwdriver set, a level, a tape measure, a power drill, and wire strippers. Ensure that you have all these tools available before you begin the installation process.

The installation process is quite detailed and requires careful attention. Start by unboxing the refrigerator and inspecting it for any damages. Then, move it to the installation site and make sure the area is clean and level. Connect the electrical and water supply following the schematics provided. Secure the refrigerator in its place and attach any additional accessories like water filters or ice makers. Finally, turn on the appliance and run a series of tests to ensure it is functioning as expected.

If you encounter any issues during the installation, consult this section for troubleshooting tips. Common problems include incorrect electrical connections, water leakage, and software issues. Make sure to double-check all connections and settings if you encounter any problems.

Installing a smart refrigerator is a complex task that requires a high level of skill and attention to detail. This manual has aimed to provide you with all the necessary information to complete this task successfully. Thank you for your attention and good luck with your installation.

LUXE Kitchens

Smart Refrigerator Installation

Steps for installing the LuxeKitchens high-tech fridge with voice controls, touch controls, and eco-modes

Safety:
- Electricals. Turn off all related connections.
- Gear. Gloves and goggles are mandatory.

Tools:
- Screwdriver set
- Level
- Tape measure
- Drill
- Wire strippers

Steps:
1. Unbox and inspect. Check for damage right away.
2. Site prep. Clean and level area.
3. Electrical and water. Follow schematics for connections.
4. Secure and accessorize. Lock fridge in place and add filters or ice maker.
5. Test run. Confirm all systems go.

Troubleshooting:
- Electrical. Recheck all connections.
- Water. Look for leaks and tighten fittings.
- Software. Reset settings if needed.

Double-check everything, and you're good to go.

From Attention to Action

In the marketing world, two crucial elements bookend the journey from capturing attention to driving action: a compelling headline and a strong call to action (CTA). For L&D professionals, embracing these two essentials can be transformative.

For example, when Mike was a new community manager at Articulate, he was eager to make his mark. He spent hours crafting what he believed to be an insightful blog post on instructional design. Proud of his work, he emailed it to his boss, hoping for some helpful feedback. Instead, he received a reply that ended up reshaping his whole approach to content creation.

His boss pointed out two critical issues. First, the title was forgettable. A headline is like a first impression, he explained; if it doesn't grab attention, even the most brilliant content may go unread. Second, unlike every other Articulate blog post, Mike's lacked a CTA. His boss explained that while Mike had provided great information, he hadn't told the readers what to do with it. Without a clear CTA, there was no bridge between learning and doing.

> ⭐ **Terms You Should Know**
>
> **Call to Action**
> In marketing, a *call to action* (CTA) is a clear and concise message that instructs the audience to take a specific next step. It's essentially a prompt designed to get a desired response.

Chastened but motivated, Mike revisited the article. He brainstormed attention-grabbing titles and came up with one much more compelling than the original. He added a clear directive as the CTA, encouraging readers to download a free instructional design checklist to help them start applying the principles immediately. When Articulate published the revised version, the response was immediate and positive. Readership went up, downloads skyrocketed, and the community buzzed with discussions about implementing the principles.

That experience taught Mike that in L&D, as in marketing, capturing attention with a compelling headline and driving action with a strong CTA are crucial. Great content isn't enough; you need to get people to engage with it and then guide them toward action.

Compelling Titles

The headline is your most powerful weapon in the fierce battle for learners' attention. It's the first impression of your course or training program—the hook that draws learners in and convinces them that your content is worth their time. A compelling headline can make the difference between a learning resource that gets ignored and one that sparks curiosity, engagement, and action.

To craft headlines that truly resonate with your audience, you need to understand a little about the psychology behind what makes people engage or click to view the next slide or read the next piece of content. Effective headline techniques tap into some of our innate desires and motivations. A few of the most essential techniques include using specificity, action-oriented language, audience pain points, numbers or data, and emotion.

Specificity

Vague, generic titles like "Leadership Skills Training" don't provide a clear idea of what learners will gain from engaging with the content. Try something more specific and benefits-driven, like "Unlock Your Leadership Potential: Five Proven Strategies for Inspiring Your Team." This title promises a specific outcome (inspiring your team) and provides a concrete road map (five proven strategies).

Action-Oriented Language

Verbs such as *unlock*, *discover*, *master*, and *transform* are dynamic and create a feeling of boundless potential. They suggest that learners can actively improve their skills and knowledge by engaging with the information you're sharing. For example, the headline "Discover the Secrets of Effective Communication" is more compelling than "Effective Communication Techniques."

Audience Pain Points

Put yourself in your learners' shoes and consider the challenges they face, their goals, and what motivates them. Craft headlines that speak directly to these needs and aspirations. For instance, if you're creating content for new managers, a headline like "From Rookie to Rockstar: Navigating the First 90 Days as a New Manager" would probably resonate more than a more generic headline like "Management 101."

Numbers and Data

As we've already discussed, our brains are drawn to specificity. Numbers and data points usually suggest a clear, quantifiable benefit. A headline such as "Boost Your Productivity by 30 Percent With These Seven Simple Hacks" or "The Five-Step Framework for Effective Decision Making" can give learners a tangible sense of what they'll gain from your content.

Emotion

While L&D content should always be professional and credible, that doesn't mean it has to be dry or dull. Emotional triggers like curiosity, excitement, or even a hint of fear or fear of missing out (FOMO) can be powerful motivators. A headline such as "Are You Making These Five Common Leadership Mistakes?" will tap into learners' fear of falling short while also sparking curiosity about what those common mistakes might be.

Of course, crafting the perfect headline often takes time and iteration. Don't be afraid to brainstorm multiple options, get feedback from colleagues or learners, and test different variations to see what resonates best with your audience. Tools such as Sharethrough's Headline Analyzer or CoSchedule's Headline Studio can provide data-driven insights and suggestions for optimizing the titles and headings in your learning content. (Try out these tools using Activity 5-2 at the end of this chapter.)

Keeping your audience front and center is always the key to writing compelling headlines. What do they need? What do they want? What will spark their interest and motivate them to engage? By answering these questions and leveraging proven psychological principles, you can create headlines that don't just inform but also intrigue, inspire, and drive action.

Strong Calls to Action

If your headline is the spark that ignites interest, your CTA is the fuel that propels your learners forward. It's the strategic endpoint of your content, the signpost that directs learners toward a desired action or outcome. Whether it's enrolling in a course, downloading a resource, or applying a new skill on the job, a strong CTA is essential for transforming passive engagement into active participation.

Choose the Right Words

To create CTAs that truly motivate and inspire action, it's essential to understand four key elements that make them effective:

- **Action oriented.** They use strong verbs that leave no room for doubt about the desired response. Instead of writing "Learn More" at the bottom of your course's homepage, try "Enroll Now" or "Download Today."
- **Specific.** They clearly state what the audience should do next. "Sign Up for Our Negotiation Skills Masterclass" is much more specific than "Explore Our Courses."

- **Benefit driven.** They highlight the value proposition of taking the action. "Boost Your Productivity with Our Time Management Toolkit" emphasizes the benefit of improved productivity.
- **Visually prominent.** They stand out from the surrounding content, often using buttons or contrasting colors to draw the eye and encourage clicks.

The dull, default registration page in Figure 5-2 has a generic title, cluttered design, and lacks crucial details about the webinar's value. Now, compare that to the webinar registration page in Figure 5-3, which features a compelling and specific title that promises clear value, a clean and visually appealing layout with ample white space, and concise, informative content about the webinar's benefits. This layout is much more likely to attract a learner's attention. The simplified registration form, prominent CTA button, and inclusion of speaker information further reduce barriers to signing up.

In addition to these essential characteristics, a few more techniques will help you create CTAs that spark immediate interest and drive action:

- **Create a sense of urgency.** People who think that they might miss a valuable opportunity if they don't act quickly are more likely to take the desired action. You can create urgency by using time-sensitive language like "Enroll Before Friday and Save 20 Percent!" or "Limited Spots Available: Secure Your Seat Now!"
- **Personalize the CTA.** By tailoring your language to the target audience's specific needs, goals, and challenges, you can create a sense of relevance and personal connection that motivates action. For example, a CTA like "Advance Your Career: Join Our Leadership Bootcamp for Women in Tech" would probably be more effective for its specific audience than a generic call to "Sign Up Now." In fact, research by HubSpot found that personalized CTAs perform more than 200 percent better than more generic CTAs, underscoring the power of targeted messaging (Nielsen Norman Group 2008).

The generic CTAs in Table 5-3 are bland and could apply to any course or any audience. The more personalized CTAs, on the other hand, speak directly to specific learners and are much more likely to result in action. Remember, our brains tend to focus first on what they perceive as directly pertinent to us.

Figure 5-2. A Generic Zoom Meeting Registration Page

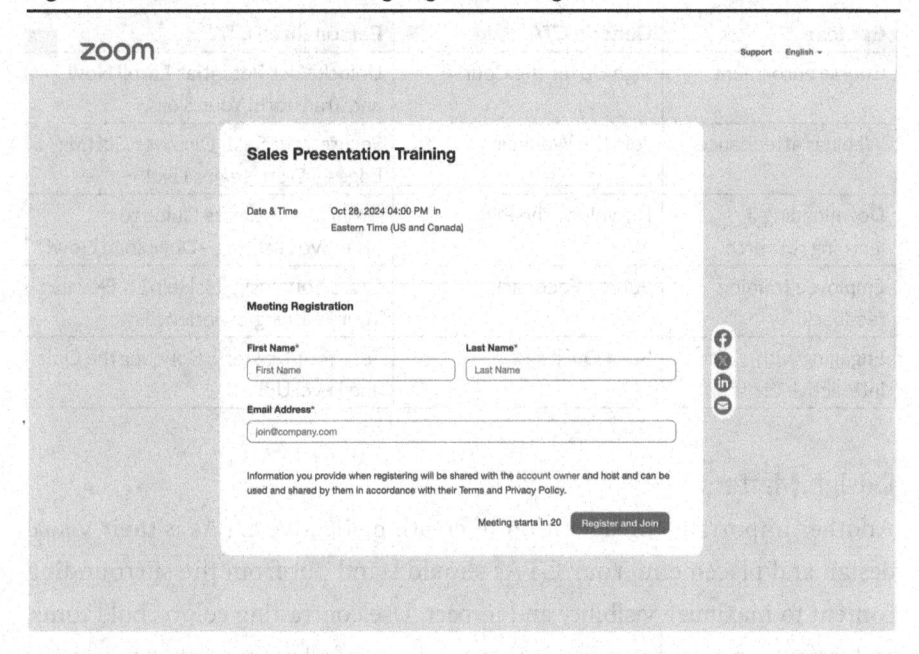

Figure 5-3. A Detailed Webinar Registration Page Example

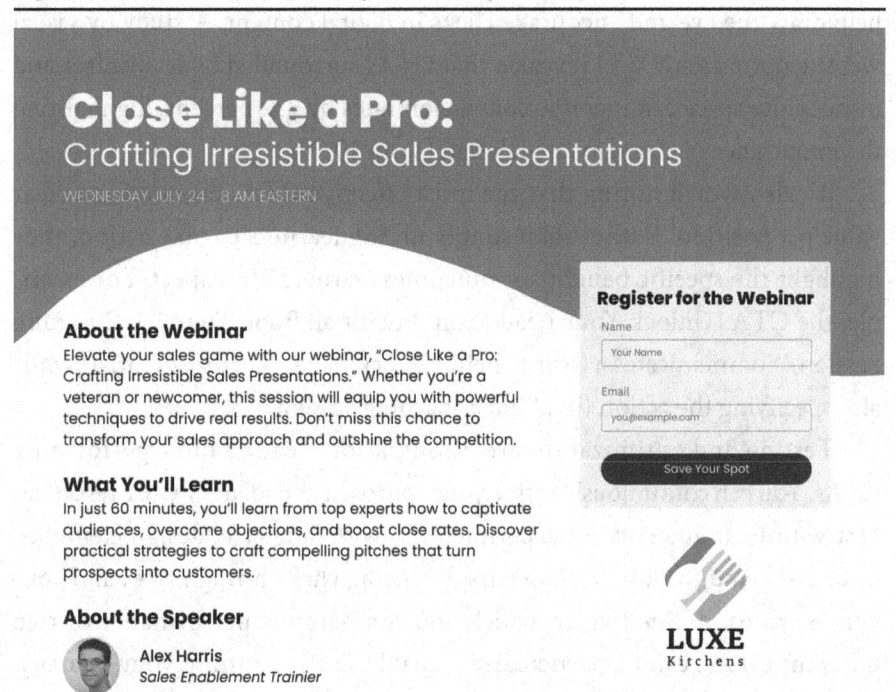

Captivate Learners With Writing That Clicks! | 145

Table 5-3. CTAs Before and After

Context	Generic CTA	Personalized CTA
Course enrollment	Sign Up for the Course	Unlock Your Potential: Enroll Now and Transform Your Skills
Webinar attendance	Join the Webinar	Secure Your Seat: Discover Cutting-Edge L&D Strategies Live!
Downloading a learning resource	Download the PDF	Grab Your Ultimate Guide to Effective Learning—Download Now!
Employee training feedback	Submit Feedback	Share Your Insights: Help Us Elevate Your Learning Experience
Engaging with interactive content	Start Quiz	Test Your Mastery: Conquer the Quiz and Level Up!

Design Matters

Another important consideration in creating effective CTAs is their visual design and placement. Your CTAs should stand out from the surrounding content to maximize visibility and impact. Use contrasting colors, bold fonts, and strategic placement, such as above the fold of a brochure or at the end of a section of digital content. Visually appealing buttons and banners can also help draw the eye and encourage clicks in digital content. A study by visual website optimizer VWO revealed that CTAs surrounded by less clutter and more white space can increase conversion rates by 232 percent, highlighting the importance of clean, focused design (Vora 2023).

It's also worth noting that the most effective CTAs often offer a clear value proposition. Rather than simply urging learners to take action, they highlight the specific benefits or outcomes learners can expect. For example, the CTA "Unlock Your Leadership Potential: Book Your 1:1 Coaching Session," communicates a clear benefit (unlocking leadership potential) while also specifying the action (booking a coaching session).

Testing and optimization are essential for creating high-performing CTAs. You can continuously refine your approach and identify what resonates best with your audience by experimenting with language, design elements, placement, and tracking key metrics, including click-through rates and conversion rates. *A/B testing*, in which you compare the performance of two different CTAs, can be particularly valuable for fine-tuning your strategy. We'll discuss A/B testing further in chapter 6.

Ultimately, the key to creating strong a CTA is keeping the learner's perspective in mind. What do they need? What do they want? What will motivate them to take the next step? By crafting CTAs that are action-oriented, specific, benefit-driven, and visually prominent, you can drive engagement, boost conversions, and help your audience translate learning into action.

Writing to Captivate and Inspire Learners

Throughout this chapter, we've explored the transformative power of good writing. By applying marketing principles and strategies that resonate with the way we think, L&D professionals can create content that not only informs but also engages, motivates, and inspires.

From crafting headlines that spark curiosity to designing CTAs that drive learners to take the next step, the secrets of effective writing are at your fingertips. By embracing the SURE principles (simple, useful, resonant, and easy to skim), you can transform your learning content from boring to brilliant.

Remember, the key to captivating your audience begins with understanding their needs, challenges, and aspirations, ideally through learner personas and a carefully crafted content strategy. Conduct thorough research, align your content with business objectives, and leverage data-driven insights to create learning experiences that are not only relevant but also highly effective.

Finally, as you embark on your journey to revolutionize your L&D writing, keep the power of emotions at the forefront of your mind. Tap into the human craving for stories, metaphors, and vivid imagery to forge deep connections with your learners. By making your content emotionally resonant, you'll create learning experiences that stick, inspiring real change and growth.

So, are you ready to become a master of captivating content? Embrace the art and science of powerful writing and watch as your engagement rates soar and your learners thrive.

A Final Thought

In every presentation or workshop Mike presents about what L&D can and should "steal" from marketing, he always asks what people would most like to steal. His favorite answer among thousands he's heard is "efficiency of messaging."

The essence of great instructional design is learning distilled to its most efficient form. Great writing should aspire for this same type of efficiency. There's no better field to look to for inspiration than marketing because its messages must be clear, concise, and attention-grabbing. And marketers have to write in a way that makes people want to do something.

Anyone who designs learning content has to do the same thing.

Activity 5-1. Put Simplicity Into Practice

Improving readability in L&D programs clears the path to knowledge, boosting comprehension and engagement while making content accessible to diverse learners. This efficiency saves time, improves retention, and ultimately leads to better learning outcomes and a more effective L&D strategy.

Objective
Put simplicity principles into practice, try this exercise to simplify and clarify existing educational materials, ideally from the program you have been using for all activities throughout this book.

Steps
1. Take a piece of your existing learning content (start with a paragraph or short section).
2. Run the content through a readability tool like the Hemingway App or Microsoft Word's readability statistics.
3. Note the current readability score and grade level.
4. Identify areas where the language or structure could be simplified. Look for long sentences, complex words, passive voice, and jargon.
5. Rewrite the content, applying the strategies discussed in this chapter. Aim for shorter sentences, simpler vocabulary, active voice, and clear, jargon-free language.
6. Run the revised content through the readability tool and note the new scores.
7. Reflect on the changes you made. Is the content more readable? Does it still convey the essential information? How might these changes influence learner engagement and comprehension?

By regularly practicing this kind of intentional simplification, you can develop your skills as a writer and create learning content that is more accessible, engaging, and effective.

Activity 5-2. The Headline Analyzer: Marketing's Secret Weapon for Effective Titles

A headline analyzer is a tool that evaluates the effectiveness of a headline in terms of clarity, creativity, and overall impact. It can help you identify areas for improvement and suggest alternative options that may perform better. In this activity, you'll use a free online headline analyzer to assess the titles of your recent L&D materials. You'll enter your current titles, analyze the results, and then brainstorm ways to improve each one based on the feedback provided.

Objective

Use an online headline analyzer tool to rewrite and optimize your current titles and headlines (ideally from the program you have been using for all activities throughout this book) so they're more effective and engaging.

Steps

1. **Prepare.** List several headlines you've used for your courses or other learning materials in a document for reference. In your web browser, open the headline analyzing tool of your choice. (Two of our favorites are produced by Sharethrough and CoSchedule.)
2. **Analyze.** Type your headlines into the tool, get a score for each, and review the feedback.
3. **Improve.** The analyzer will provide tips for how to improve. Use them to write new versions of your headlines. Aim for a higher score!
4. **Continue.** Repeat the process with all your titles and headlines. By the end of this process, you should not only have more effective headlines, but also have an increased awareness of what constitutes a strong headline. Happy headline crafting!

Activity 5-3. Evaluate Your Current CTAs

Objective
Improve your content's calls to action. (Use the program you have been using for all activities throughout this book if possible.)

Materials
Samples of your existing learning content with CTAs (course descriptions, promotional emails, or instructional videos), a CTA Evaluation Rubric (provided on the next page), a digital tool for writing and testing CTAs (such as CoSchedule Headline Analyzer, ChatGPT, or Claude).

Steps
1. **Gather content.** Find examples of CTAs from your materials (or places where a CTA should be used but isn't).
2. **Rate your CTAs.** Use the scoring sheet on the next page to rate each CTA individually.
3. **Rewrite CTAs.** Apply the principles discussed in this chapter and create or rewrite new, better CTAs.

After trying your hand at rewriting, recruit some AI-powered assistance. Try this prompt with ChatGPT, Claude, or a similar tool: "Please act as a Conversion Rate Optimization (CRO) specialist to help me create a compelling call to action (CTA) for my content. The goal is to [*your goal here*]. The target audience is [*target audience*]. The tone should be [*tone*], and the CTA should convey a sense of urgency and benefit. What are some effective CTAs that can achieve this goal?"

For example, you might say: "Please act as a Conversion Rate Optimization (CRO) Specialist and provide compelling call to action (CTA) suggestions for an upcoming webinar titled 'The Future of Remote Work.' The goal is to encourage sign-ups from HR professionals and team leaders who are adapting to remote work. Use a professional yet inviting tone and ensure each CTA conveys a sense of urgency and benefit to the audience."

CTA Evaluation Rubric

Use the following scale to rate each CTA from 1 to 5 (1 = weak; 5 = very strong)

Action Oriented
Does the CTA use strong, clear verbs? (*Start Now* vs. *Learn More*)
1   2   3   4   5

Specific
How clear is the CTA about what action learners should take? (Download the Guide)
1   2   3   4   5

Benefit Driven
Does the CTA clearly state the benefit of taking the action? (Unlock Your Potential)
1   2   3   4   5

Visual Prominence
How visually compelling is the CTA? Does it stand out?
1   2   3   4   5

Personalization
Is the CTA tailored to the audience?
1   2   3   4   5

Urgency
Does the CTA create a sense of urgency?
1   2   3   4   5

CTA Effectiveness Score

Total the scores for a maximum of 30 points.
- 25–30: Great CTA!
- 15–24: Good, but there's room for improvement
- Below 15: Needs significant rework

Chapter 6
Leverage Visuals for Maximum Impact

> We live in a visual age. If your content isn't visually compelling, it's like whispering in a crowded room.
> —Don Draper, fictional TV ad executive

Ayo, a veteran L&D professional, had always relied on traditional, text-heavy training materials. Despite her best efforts, she noticed that her learners had seemed disengaged recently and struggled to retain the information she presented. Frustrated, Ayo attended a marketing conference recommended by a colleague, hoping to gain some fresh insights.

At the conference, she immediately noticed the visual differences between the marketers' presentations and her own. The slides were stunning, with bold images, clear headlines, and minimal text. They captured the attention of everyone in the room and communicated messages with clarity and impact.

Ayo made a point of meeting some of the presenters and asking them about their approach to communicating and persuading audiences.

"It's getting tougher to grab attention in today's fast-paced, information-rich world," one of them admitted. "But we know that people process visual information faster than text and that visuals have a direct line to customers' emotions, so graphics, images, and video are our most powerful tools for engagement and persuasion. I'm selling ideas and trying to influence people's behavior," he added. "The best way to do that is to create an emotional connection. I also want to simplify complex information. I find both of those things are easier when I use strong visual elements."

Ayo left the conference wondering if she and her L&D colleagues should think more in terms of selling ideas instead of delivering content. She decided to try transferring the techniques she'd learned to some of her training materials, starting with simplifying the designs of slides, handouts, and worksheets to make the information easier to digest. She worked to establish clear visual hierarchies and added more compelling images—including people's faces—designed to connect with learners emotionally.

Almost immediately, Ayo noticed an improvement in learner engagement and retention, with more people actively participating in her revised programs. "The new visuals helped me understand our supply chain process in ways I never could before," said John from operations. Lisa from HR added, "Ayo's new approach made our compliance training not just bearable but actually engaging. I never thought I'd say that about a mandatory course!" During a quarterly review, Ayo's manager publicly praised her innovative approach: "Since implementing these new visual learning techniques, we've seen an increase in knowledge retention rates and a reduction in time-to-competency for new hires."

Going forward, Ayo and her team made powerful visuals a permanent part of their strategy.

In this chapter, we'll explore ways we can leverage the powerful effects of visuals in our designs to create maximum impact and maximum learning.

Attention-Grabbing Messages

L&D professionals face the same challenges as marketers—information overload, short attention spans, and perpetual noise and distractions inside and outside the workplace. Like marketers, we need to find ways to engage our audiences, convey complex information, and drive behavior change. Because the human brain processes visual information faster than it processes text, visuals can grab attention, evoke emotions, and communicate complex messages quickly and memorably (Potter et al. 2014; Borkin et al.

2016). By strategically incorporating more powerful visuals in our L&D content, we can create learning experiences that not only inform but also inspire and motivate.

To illustrate the difference between a typical instructional designer's approach to visuals and a marketer's approach, let's consider a hypothetical example. Imagine you're a restaurant manager on a mission to convince customers to try a new menu item. Your whole marketing department is out sick, so you decide to give this challenge to your L&D department instead of hiring an advertising firm. Unfortunately, the L&D design team produces a billboard like the one in Figure 6-1.

Figure 6-1. One L&D Team's Take on Selling Hamburgers

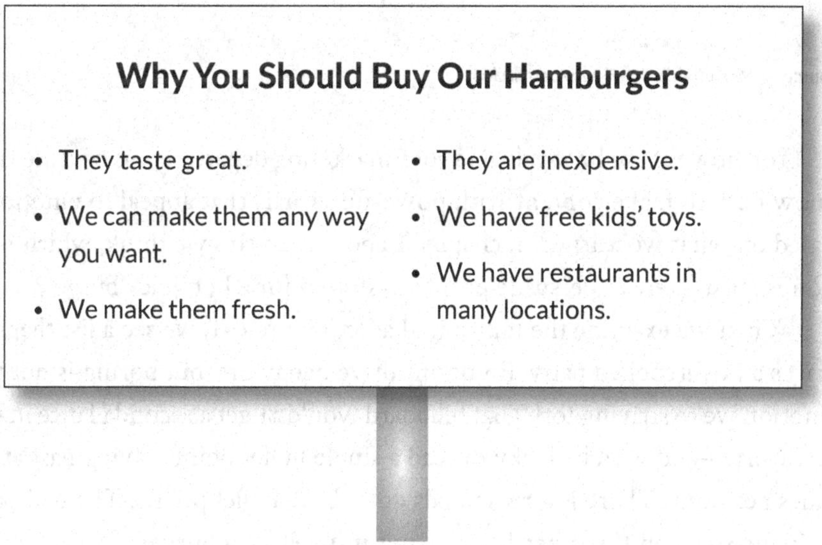

Why You Should Buy Our Hamburgers

- They taste great.
- We can make them any way you want.
- We make them fresh.
- They are inexpensive.
- We have free kids' toys.
- We have restaurants in many locations.

Yes, we've exaggerated the dullness to make a point, but the truth is, even the best L&D professionals can default to dry, text-heavy content that bores rather than engages. Logic (in the form of bullet-point facts) usually isn't the most persuasive tool. This billboard simply won't convince many customers to give a new menu item a try.

Now, let's imagine the marketing team has returned and you've given this challenge back to them. The result might be something you see in Figure 6-2.

Figure 6-2. Billboard Selling McDonald's Angus Third-Pounders

Source: © McDonald's. Used with permission.

You now realize how valuable your marketing department is because they know how to make content with powerful visuals that appeal to emotions. Based on what we learned in chapter 1 about the ways we think, which version is most likely to persuade people to stop in for a hot, juicy burger?

When we examine the uninspired ad in Figure 6-1, we see a list that's as dry as an overcooked patty. Emotions drive behaviors, but boring is not the emotion we're striving for! That billboard wouldn't get a second glance in the real world—and we'd be lucky to read a single bullet point driving past at 55 miles per hour. There is a reason ads don't have bullet points. The billboard in Figure 6-2, on the other hand, is not just selling a burger—it's selling an experience. It's lean on words but heavy on impact, serving up a psychological feast with the evocative phrase "meat perfection" and the large, enticing image of the burger. If you were viewing the image in color, you would see that the burger itself is multi-colored, and the background is bright red.

Let's look at the many marketing principles at work here:

- **Emotional appeal.** The photo of a juicy cheeseburger stirs up hunger and craving through its vivid imagery and bold claim of "perfection." The appeal is visceral.

- **Sensory engagement.** The fact that the image of the burger is so large and vivid that we can count individual sesame seeds on the bun and see onions and cheese glistening engages our senses. We can almost smell the smokiness, taste the juiciness, and feel the texture of the bun in our hands.
- **Simplicity.** The message is concise. Unlike the bullet-pointed memo in Figure 6-1, we see a single, instantly understandable sentence that's also a clever play on words.
- **Value proposition.** This principle recognizes that in advertising, especially when viewers have limited time, the first impression is crucial. By presenting a visually appealing image and a confident, simple message, the ad aims to trigger a positive, instinctive response, positioning a hamburger not just as food but as an experience of perfection that transcends practical concerns like cost or other attributes.
- **Brand consistency.** The decades-long history of ad campaigns and repeated exposure of audiences to McDonald's iconic "golden arches" logo immediately associates the second billboard with a well-established brand identity that invokes familiarity and trust.

What lessons can we learn from the "meat perfection" example if we want to transform cerebral, text-based content into a more effective message?

1. Start with a stunning visual.
2. Distill the message down to a short, compelling essence.

Ayo took both those lessons to heart in transforming her approach to learning design. But something one of the speakers at the marketing conference told her became her L&D team's guiding principle going forward: *People don't buy products; they buy better versions of themselves.* Always try to appeal to their aspirations.

In the learning experiences we create, we need to take that lesson to heart, too. The participants in our learning experiences are not there only to acquire knowledge; they also want to become better versions of themselves; we are in the perfect position to fulfill that desire.

The Science of Visual Communication

As L&D professionals, we know that understanding the science behind visual communication is crucial for creating engaging and effective learning experiences. By learning more about the psychology of attention and the principles of effective visual design, we can unlock the full potential of visuals in our work.

Creating Powerful Visuals

Research has consistently shown that the human brain is wired to process visual information faster and more efficiently than text. Studies suggest that we can process images in as little as 13 milliseconds and that visuals are processed faster than text-based or verbal information (Potter et al. 2014; Scharf 2017). This ability is rooted in our evolutionary history, for the majority of which quick visual processing—including recognizing threats and identifying food—was crucial for survival.

You can easily see for yourself that we process text and images at different speeds by looking at the two representations of the same information in Figure 6-3.

Figure 6-3. Text-Based Versus Visual Description

Text Description	Visual Description
A circle is a two-dimensional shape consisting of all the points in a plane that are at a constant distance (known as the radius) from a fixed point (called the center). The diameter, which passes through the center and ends at two points on the circle's boundary, is twice the radius.	◯

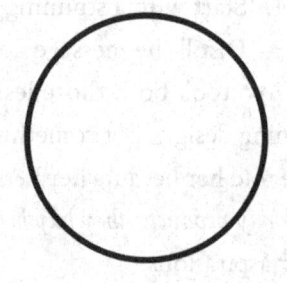

It's not just speed that makes visuals so effective; it's also the fact that images can engage our emotions so directly. As we've already noted, visual images such as photos, videos, and illustrations can evoke powerful emotional responses, which then play a crucial role in memory retention and decision making. Marketing professionals have long understood how to create emotional connections with their audience and drive behavior change with the careful use of visual images. Just recall the dramatic image of a wrecked car in the Subaru ad mentioned in chapter 5.

One of the fundamental principles at play when we process visual images is the *picture superiority effect*, which means that people tend to remember images more clearly and effectively than words (Paivio and Caspo 1973). When we look at an image, our brains create a mental representation that includes the visual details as well as any associated emotions and context. This multisensory encoding helps the information stick in our long-term memories.

The question for us, as L&D professionals, is how we can more effectively harness the power of the picture superiority effect. One way is to use compelling visuals to capture and hold learners' attention and direct their focus to the most important information. In the next sections, we'll discuss some of the best ways to do that.

Visual Hierarchy

The first thing we need to understand is the *visual hierarchy* principle, which is all about arranging visual elements to guide the viewer's attention. By using contrasting colors, sizes, and positions of elements on a page or screen, designers can create a clear path for the eye to follow, highlighting key points and minimizing distractions.

Marketing offers plenty of examples of visual hierarchy in action. Look at any well-designed advertisement or website, and you'll notice a clear focal point, strategic use of white space, and thoughtful placement of text and images. These design choices aren't just aesthetically pleasing; they serve the practical purpose of directing attention and conveying information effectively. We'll discuss visual hierarchy in more detail later in this chapter.

Apple's website is a masterclass in visual hierarchy (Figure 6-4). The company uses large, bold headlines to grab attention, followed by high-quality images and concise text. The judicious use of white space ensures that the primary message stands out, and the CTA buttons are strategically placed and clearly visible.

Figure 6-4. Visual Hierarchy on Apple's Website

Cognitive Load

Another important consideration in visual communication is limiting cognitive load. Our working memory can only handle a limited amount of information at a time, so it's essential to be strategic about what we include. The best designs are simple, stripping away extraneous details to focus on the core message. Often, a single powerful image can convey even a complex idea much more efficiently than a block of text.

Infographics help limit cognitive load by combining simple visuals, brief text, and clear organization to make complex data easier to understand at a glance. They're a staple in the marketing world and can be just as effective in L&D when we need to convey complicated learning content so learners can grasp it more easily and quickly.

Consider the mental effort involved in parsing the vital information from the lengthy text-based document on the left in Figure 6-5. The infographic on the right provides the same content, but spotlights key points and makes them easier to find and remember.

Figure 6-5. Two Versions of a LuxeKitchens Employee Policy

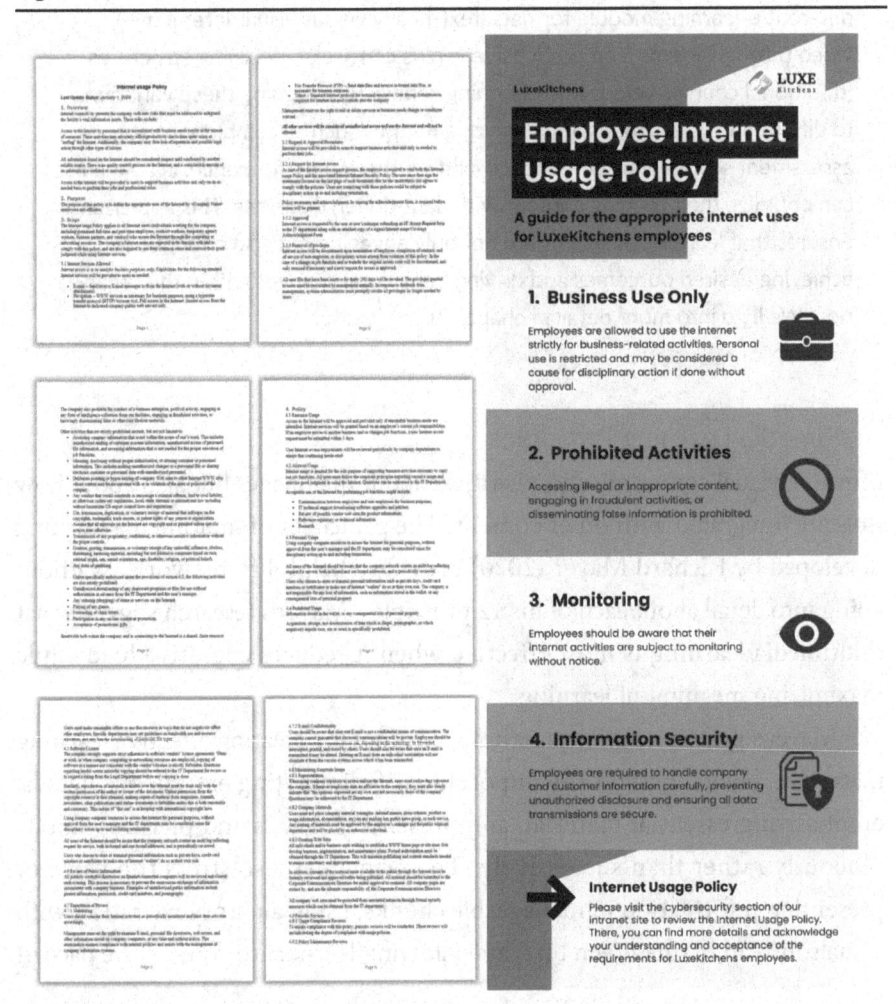

Wall-of-text documents obscure important ideas, unlike infographics, which highlight them.

> **Using A/B Testing to Improve Visuals**
>
> As highlighted in chapter 2 on learner personas, understanding your audience's specific needs and preferences is crucial when designing visuals for learning. Marketing teams often use A/B testing to refine their visuals. This involves presenting two or more design variations to different audience segments and measuring their performance. By analyzing these results, marketers can make data-driven choices and optimize visual elements for maximum impact.
>
> Adopt similar testing to enhance your content. For example, you can compare different e-learning module formats (text-heavy versus visual-interactive), video tutorial lengths (comprehensive versus concise), or learning structures (traditional courses versus microlearning series). By assigning these variations to different learner groups and analyzing metrics such as completion rates, assessment scores, learner feedback, and on-the-job performance, L&D teams can optimize their training content with data-driven decisions. This approach ensures that learning programs are not only engaging but also effective in achieving desired outcomes and driving behavioral changes within the organization. We'll go into more detail in chapter 8.

Multimedia Learning Principles

Effective visual communication isn't just about the images but also about how they are integrated with other content. The principles of multimedia learning developed by Richard Mayer (2020) provide a helpful framework. Without going into detail about each of his 12 principles, Mayer's research suggests that multimedia learning is most effective when it reduces cognitive load while maximizing meaningful learning.

Mayer's principles offer practical guidelines for creating effective learning materials. They highlight the importance of eliminating extraneous details, emphasizing essential material, and presenting words and pictures simultaneously rather than successively. The principles also stress the value of presenting information in manageable chunks, using auditory narration with visuals instead of on-screen text, and allowing learners to control the pace of their learning. By considering aspects such as spatial and temporal contiguity, coherence, and personalization, instructional designers and educators can create learning experiences that not only capture attention but also facilitate deeper understanding and better retention of information.

These principles are particularly relevant today, when multimedia learning is increasingly prevalent. They provide a scientific basis for leveraging technology and diverse media formats in ways that enhance rather than hinder learning. Whether designing e-learning modules, educational videos, or interactive presentations, Mayer's principles offer a robust framework for creating engaging and effective learning materials. Ultimately, they remind us that effective visual communication in learning is not just about making content look appealing but about strategically designing multimedia elements to align with cognitive processes, leading to more meaningful and lasting learning outcomes. This might mean using images to illustrate complex concepts, providing visual cues to highlight important information, or including interactive elements to engage learners.

As you incorporate visuals into your L&D programs, remember that effective visual communication is both an art and a science. It requires an understanding of how we process visual information and a creative eye for design. By combining these approaches, you can create learning experiences that not only inform but also inspire and engage.

Design Rules and Strategies

How can we practically use all we know about the power of visual communication? In our work as L&D professionals, we can adopt some key design rules and strategies that marketers use regularly.

One thing we know is that people tend to look for patterns and familiar shapes, colors, and movements, which helps us make decisions fast. For example, when we see faces or any images in high contrast, they grab our attention. Consider how road signs, like those shown in Figure 6-6, demonstrate masterful design, conveying crucial information at a glance. Through the strategic use of high contrast, size, symbols, and layout hierarchy, these signs communicate directions, destinations, highway numbers, and exit details to enable drivers to make quick decisions while maintaining focus on the road ahead.

Figure 6-6. Simple, High-Contrast Signs Convey Information Quickly

While we can't cover all the marketing design strategies, we can discuss a few essential points related to how our learners' think when they view the materials we share in person and in remote learning experiences. Understanding a few basic rules can help us make well-informed design choices, significantly improve the effectiveness of our presentations, and enhance learner engagement and retention.

Techniques That Tell Us Where to Look

According to Larry Jordan (2020), six compositional techniques—movement, focus, contrast, brightness, size, and proximity—determine where someone looks first in an image. Let's explore them in more detail.

Movement

We are hard-wired for many things, including detecting and focusing on motion, a trait that probably evolved as a survival mechanism. Even in static images, the illusion of movement can be powerful. Imagine a photograph of a speeding train. The contrast between a blurred train and a crisp, unmoving background of trees and sky creates a dynamic sense of motion, engaging our eyes and minds.

In the L&D context, we can harness this natural inclination to pay attention to movement to enhance engagement and comprehension by incorporating:

- **Animated GIFs** can break down complex procedures into easily digestible, step-by-step visual instructions. Their subtle motion draws attention and helps learners follow along seamlessly.
- **Motion graphics** can illustrate intricate concepts or data trends over time. The fluid movement can make abstract ideas more tangible and help learners visualize changes or processes that occur over extended periods.
- **Subtle animations** in slide transitions or content reveals guide the learner's attention from one key point to the next and create a natural flow of information.
- **Interactive simulations** allow learners to manipulate elements and see immediate cause-and-effect relationships. Active engagement through movement reinforces learning and improves retention.

Focus

When an image lacks movement, our eyes naturally gravitate toward the sharpest area of focus. We assume that the clearest element is the most important or relevant. Consider a photograph of a crowd in which one individual stands out in sharp detail while others remain out-of-focus blurs. Our attention is immediately drawn to the clearly defined person, illustrating the power of focus in visual composition. In the context of learning and development, we can leverage this principle of focus to direct attention, emphasize key information, and enhance comprehension.

There are several ways to apply this technique in training:

- **Selective blurring** in images or diagrams can highlight specific areas or components. For instance, in a technical schematic, keep the relevant part in sharp focus while slightly blurring the surrounding elements. This technique guides the learner's eye to the most crucial information without removing contextual details.
- **Spotlighting in videos** helps draw attention to key elements or speakers. This could involve slightly dimming the background while keeping the important area well-lit or using a subtle vignette effect to frame the focal point. Spotlighting is particularly effective in software tutorials or when demonstrating physical processes.

- **Progressive disclosure** is useful for breaking down complex diagrams or processes by using a series of images to progressively bring different elements into focus. This can help break down complex information into more digestible parts, guiding the learner through a logical sequence of focal points.

Contrast

Within a sharply focused image, our eyes are naturally drawn to elements that stand out from their surroundings. This visual phenomenon, known as *contrast*, can occur through variations in color, brightness, shape, or texture. Consider a jigsaw puzzle in which one piece is a vibrant red in a sea of blue pieces; your attention is immediately captured by the contrasting element. This principle of contrast is a powerful tool in visual communication, particularly in L&D contexts. In training and educational settings, we can leverage contrast to highlight important information, differentiate between concepts, and guide learners' attention.

Here are several effective ways to apply contrast in your learning materials:

- **Before-and-after comparisons** can employ contrasting visuals to illustrate the impact of learning or process improvements. Present "before" scenarios in muted colors or grayscale and "after" scenarios in vibrant colors. This stark contrast helps learners quickly grasp the positive outcomes of implementing new knowledge or procedures.
- **Typographic emphasis**, such as contrasting fonts or text sizes, to emphasize key takeaways or important statistics. For example, present main points in a bold, large font while using a standard, smaller font for supporting details. This creates a clear visual hierarchy, helping learners identify and remember crucial information.
- **Process improvement visualization** can create visual comparisons between old and new processes to highlight improvements or changes. Use contrasting colors or styles to represent different stages or methods, making it easy for learners to identify modifications and enhancements.
- **Interactive elements** will stand out more in e-learning and other digital content if you use contrasting colors. For instance,

make clickable buttons a color that contrasts with the background, intuitively guiding learners on how to interact with the content.

Remember that although contrast is a powerful tool, it should be used judiciously. Overuse of contrast can lead to visual clutter and cognitive overload. The goal is to guide the learner's attention to the most important elements, not to create a visually chaotic environment.

Brightness

In static images where all elements are equally sharp, our eyes are naturally drawn to the brightest areas. For instance, in a photograph of a dimly lit room, a face illuminated by a shaft of light immediately captures our attention. In learning contexts, we can harness brightness to guide attention, emphasize key information, and enhance overall comprehension.

Here are several ways to apply this technique in your learning design:

- **Highlight key performance indicators** in dashboards or reports using bright colors. This technique immediately draws the learner's eye to the most important metrics, facilitating a quick understanding of complex data sets. For example, use a bright yellow or vibrant green to highlight positive trends or achieved targets.
- **Focus attention in digital content** by employing a "dim the lights" effect in e-learning modules and other digital content. This involves slightly darkening the screen while keeping the crucial information brightly lit. This technique is particularly effective when introducing new concepts or emphasizing key takeaways.
- **Guide learners through sequential steps** by brightening each step as it's discussed. This technique is especially useful in software tutorials or when explaining complex procedures.
- **Create interactive hotspots** in digital learning materials that brighten when hovered over or clicked. This not only draws attention to interactive elements but also provides immediate visual feedback, enhancing engagement and navigation.

When applying these techniques, it's crucial to maintain a balance. Brightness is an effective attention-grabbing tool, but overuse can lead to visual fatigue or distraction. Try to guide the learner's attention smoothly without creating a visually overwhelming experience.

Size

As you might expect, size plays a crucial role in directing attention and conveying importance. Larger elements naturally dominate our field of vision and are instinctively perceived as more significant than smaller ones. In instructional settings, we can harness the power of size to guide focus, establish hierarchies, and emphasize key information.

Here are two ways to apply this technique in your learning materials:

1. **Highlight key information in graphics** by making significant data points larger. For example, in a slide showing market share, depict companies with larger shares using bigger icons. This visual hierarchy helps learners quickly grasp the relative importance and relationships between data points.
2. **Use interactive elements** in e-learning modules and other digital content. Make important clickable elements or buttons larger than less crucial ones. This not only draws attention but also improves user experience by making key interactions more prominent.

While size is a powerful technique for guiding attention, as with all the other techniques we've discussed, it's important to use it judiciously. An overabundance of large elements can lead to visual clutter. The goal is to create a clear visual hierarchy that guides the learner through the material in a logical and meaningful way.

Figure 6-7 demonstrates how size can be an especially powerful tool to establish a focal point and guide the viewer's attention in text-based content. Large, bold text will act like a signpost, helping learners find the important information they're looking for quickly. Varying the text size boosts reading speed and understanding and helps learners avoid information overload. When designing learning materials, use larger fonts for main concepts or chapter titles, medium sizes for subtopics, and smaller sizes for supporting details. This creates a clear visual hierarchy that helps learners understand the structure of the information.

Figure 6-7. Text Size as a Design Technique

YOU WILL READ THIS FIRST.

At some point you might come back and read this...or you might not.

And then you'll read this line next.

Curious for all the details? This text might be your destination. Dense with light-weight font, tight lines, and small size, it demands the most effort. Uncaptivating intros lead many to skip walls of text like this. Visual hierarchy is key to grab attention and make your message stand out.

You'll probably read this before the paragraph text.

Proximity

Finally, if all other factors are equal, our eyes will be drawn to the elements closest to us, and we will perceive them to be more relevant or important. In a learning environment, you might use this technique in a few ways:

- **Highlight key concepts** by placing the most important information at the center or top of your layout, with supporting details clustered nearby. This central positioning draws the eye and emphasizes crucial points. For instance, in a slide about photosynthesis, put the main concept in the center, with related processes radiating outward.
- **Organize information** by grouping related information in mind maps or concept diagrams. Placing associated ideas or concepts near one another creates visual clusters that learners can easily identify and remember. This technique helps learners build mental models and understand relationships between different pieces of information.
- **Enhance user interface design** in e-learning courses or digital learning materials by grouping related controls or information. For instance, place the "next" button near the end of the content and the "help" button consistently in one corner. This makes navigation more intuitive and reduces cognitive load.

By thoughtfully applying the principle of proximity in your learning materials, you can create more intuitive, organized, and effective educational experiences, potentially improving comprehension and retention.

Layer Multiple Techniques

For greater visual impact in any learning experience, consider layering several of the techniques we've discussed. In a recent project to help people spot fake phishing emails, Mike created the image in Figure 6-8. It shows how eye-catching techniques can work together. The bright email stands out clearly against the blurred, darkened background. The contrast of white highlighted words makes important info easy to spot. Bigger things like the "report phishing" button grab your attention. These methods team up to guide your eyes and create a clear path for your eyes to follow. It makes the important parts stand out more than others.

Figure 6-8. A Visual From Mike's Course on the Dangers of Phishing Emails

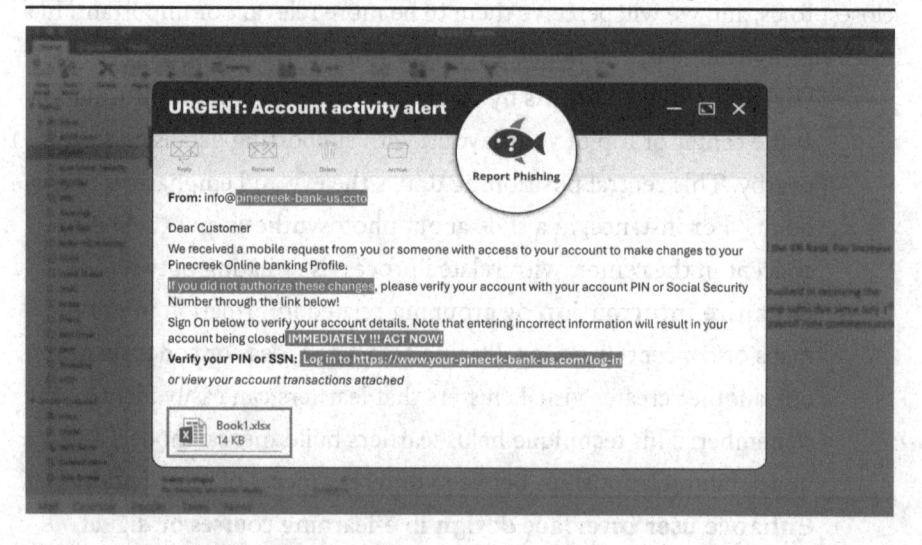

The Impact of the Human Face

Marketers understand how to use the human face (and often animal faces) to grab attention. As social creatures, we respond to other people's faces, particularly those that display strong emotions. We have dedicated neural circuits for processing facial expressions and we tend to see faces everywhere, even in inanimate objects (Ungerleider and Mishkin 1982). This tendency has important design implications. In learning design, for example, faces can direct attention to key content.

First, let's consider an example from the marketing world, and then we'll apply what we learn to L&D. Usability specialist James Breeze (2018) used eye-tracking technology to observe viewers' interaction with the advertisements in Figure 6-9 (the darker a spot is, the longer people looked at that part of the image). When the baby faced viewers directly in the image on the left, they fixated solely on the face and neglected the ad's message. In the image on the right, the baby is looking at the advertisement's headline, which emphasizes a key quality of the product. This simple change shifted the viewers' attention so both the baby and the ad copy were focal points.

Figure 6-9. A Baby's Face Shifts Viewers' Attention

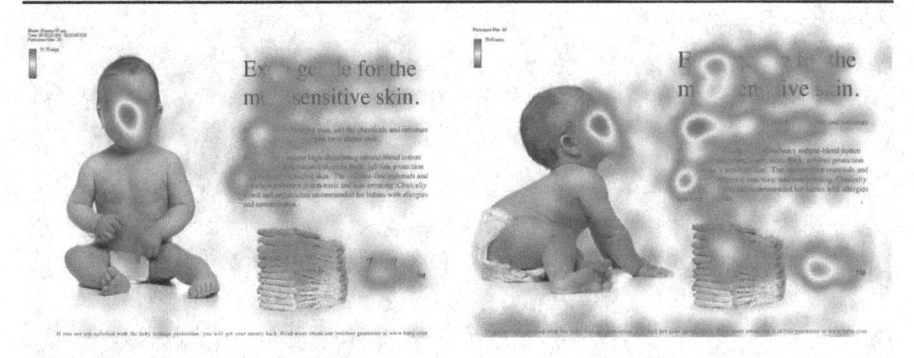

Source: James Breeze. Used with permission.

This comparison of two almost identical images illustrates the tendency of viewers to follow the gaze of others in photographs. In your own learning content, you can take advantage of this tendency by strategically positioning people in your images to direct the viewer's attention to key elements or messages. For example, you could include an image of an employee looking at a new product or an important safety sign to subtly guide the learner's focus to that critical information.

Always look for ways you can include human or animal faces in your learning content. A smiling person can convey a sense of achievement and satisfaction, or an image of a concerned manager can underscore the critical importance of a compliance training module. The best approach is often to

A/B test two versions of an image—one with a human face and one without—to see which connects more strongly with learners.

In an identity theft course, for example, Mike employed a visually striking "shady character" to leverage our innate attraction to faces and make the content more engaging and memorable for learners (Figure 6-10).

Figure 6-10. A Visual From Mike's E-Learning Course on Identity Theft

The Rule of Thirds

In addition to the design techniques discussed so far in this chapter, another design "secret" we swear by is the Rule of Thirds. This concept says that an image is more interesting and dynamic if you place the primary subject in specific areas of a page or screen—the areas toward which our eyes naturally gravitate.

To understand how this works, look at the graphic in Figure 6-11. Take any image and draw imaginary lines that divide the frame into thirds, both horizontally and vertically—like a tic-tac-toe board. The intersections where those lines cross are "points of interest" to which our eyes will naturally travel.

If key parts of the image are placed at those points, they will stand out. In addition, viewers will have to expend less effort to understand the image because they've been given a road map to the most critical information.

Figure 6-11. The Rule of Thirds

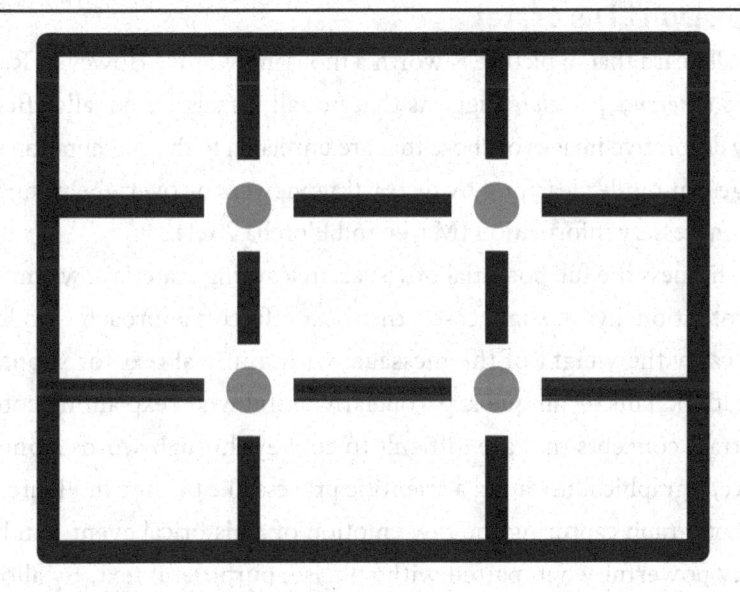

Try this with a photo or illustration you use in a training experience. Draw a grid like the one in Figure 6-11 over the image and move it around. The lines and intersections of this grid serve as strategic points where you can place key elements. In the example in Figure 6-12, placing the woman's face at a point of interest on the grid creates a more engaging and visually pleasing image than putting her face in the center of the frame.

Figure 6-12. Applying the Rule of Thirds to a Photo

Leverage Visuals for Maximum Impact | 173

Applying the Rule of Thirds to images improves information processing by guiding viewers' gaze, aiding in recognition of the main subject and narrative, and reducing cognitive load (Koliska and Oh 2023). This reduces mental effort and makes the message clearer.

Design, Don't Decorate!

We've all heard that "a picture is worth a thousand words." However, Richard Mayer's *coherence principle* suggests that not all visuals are equally effective. Merely decorative images or those that are unrelated to the presentation's core message can hinder learning by distracting viewers or overwhelming them with unnecessary information (Mayer and Fiorella 2021).

To harness the full potential of visuals in learning materials, we must use them intentionally. In some cases, the most effective approach is to let the image carry the weight of the message, with minimal text for support or clarification. This technique is particularly useful when explaining complex or abstract concepts that are difficult to convey through words alone. For instance, a graphic illustrating a scientific process like the one in Figure 6-13, or a photograph capturing the raw emotion of a historical event, can be incredibly powerful when paired with concise, purposeful text. By allowing the image to serve as a comprehensive summary and using text to guide the learner's understanding, designers can create learning experiences that are both engaging and effective.

The key to success in any learning design is finding the right balance between visuals and text, ensuring each element serves a clear purpose and contributes to the overall learning objective. By combining compelling visuals with focused, concise text, designers can unlock the full potential of both, fostering deeper understanding and longer-lasting retention for learners.

How to Maximize the Impact of Your Visuals

We like to think of visual design as the first handshake of any learning content, and as such, we need to make it count. Good visual design does so much more than make our slides look pretty. It packs a punch, shaping how we react to what we see in any learning experience. Our initial reactions to a design can make or break our judgment of the relevance, credibility, and ease of use of the learning content.

Figure 6-13. Simplified Illustration of Earth's Water Cycle

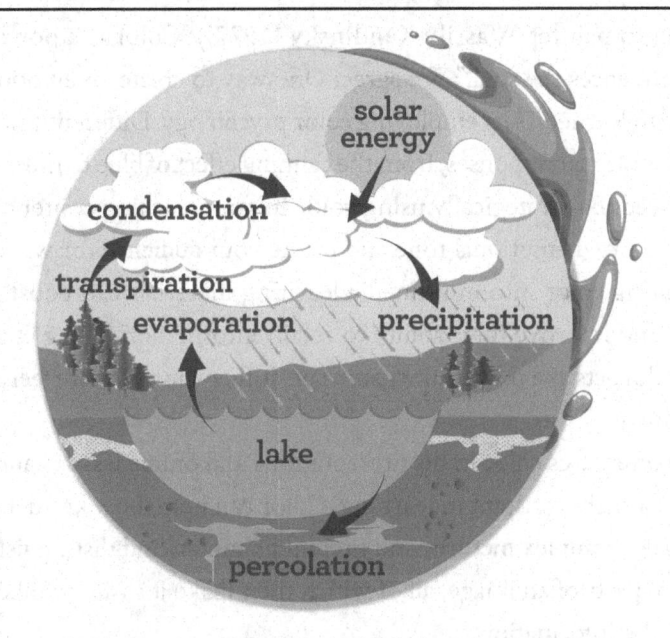

Source: Southwest Florida Water Management District. Used with permission.

Our brains make subconscious judgments incredibly quickly—in as little as 17 to 50 milliseconds (Lindgaard et al. 2006; Tuch et al. 2012). For comparison, it takes about 100 to 400 milliseconds to blink your eye. This means that we must always try to make a strong first impression on our audience. Most learners are forgiving of minor flaws in well-designed content, but poorly designed materials create an immediate negative impression (Raita and Oulasvirta 2011). A good first impression can even last throughout an entire experience. This "halo effect" can override later problems because early vibes have such an enduring impact (Soper 2014).

By prioritizing simple, familiar, and visually appealing designs that adhere to established marketing conventions, we can capture our learners' attention, connect with them emotionally, and foster a positive experience from the first second of interaction. The emotional connections, as we know, are especially important. Marketing conventions that will maximize initial visual impact include color, human-centered images, humor and surprise, simplicity, consistency, and flexibility.

Color

According to painter Wassily Kandinsky (1977), "Color is a power which directly influences the soul." We agree! One way to create an emotional connection with learners is by employing color psychology. Different colors evoke different emotional responses, from the calming effect of blue to the energizing impact of red. By strategically using color in your learning content, you can create the desired emotional tone and prime your audience for what's ahead. Incorporating color into multimedia learning materials can boost learners' emotions and improve their ability to retain information (Tyng et al. 2019). Overall, color acts as a powerful sensory cue, influencing how we feel and what we remember.

Mike often uses color in his presentations and online lessons and considers it to be a silent assistant in learning. Color can help show key details more clearly, make complex pictures and graphics simpler, and distinguish among a variety of parts of an image, all of which then make it easier to take in, sort, and recall the information.

Human-Centered Images

Imagine a training module in which every image feels like a mirror, reflecting the diverse faces and experiences of your learners. Strategically chosen images of real people in authentic situations can transform a learning experience, creating deep emotional connections and enhancing engagement.

Consider a corporate ethics training course. While generic stock photos of handshakes and office buildings might technically illustrate the content, they will fail to resonate. If that same course featured candid images of ordinary employees from various departments facing ethical dilemmas, learners could see themselves and their colleagues in the material, triggering a stronger emotional response and improved retention. Groundbreaking research in the 1990s identified the fusiform face area (FFA), which is a region in the typical human brain that responds strongly to human faces. When we encounter faces in learning materials, the FFA reacts, intensifying our engagement with the content (Kanwisher et al. 1997).

The implications of this research are significant for instructional design in several ways:

- **Attention.** Human faces naturally draw and hold learners' focus, and this effect can be enhanced by using especially expressive faces to convey emotions relevant to your learning content.
- **Emotional connection.** Seeing relatable individuals creates empathy and personal investment in the material, and incorporating diverse faces that reflect the learners' community can level up that investment.
- **Memory.** The heightened brain activity associated with facial recognition can improve information recall, as can pairing faces with names, roles, or key concepts.
- **Application.** When learners see people who look like themselves successfully applying new skills, it boosts their confidence in doing the same—this concept is called *self-modeling*.

To leverage these benefits, consider these strategies:

- Use photos of real employees or students rather than models when possible—but only after obtaining their permission.
- Ensure diversity in your imagery to represent your entire learning audience.
- Choose images that depict realistic scenarios relevant to your content.
- Pair key concepts with photos of people demonstrating or reacting to those ideas.

By thoughtfully incorporating human-centered images, you create learning experiences that don't just inform; they resonate.

Humor and Surprise

We can foster emotional connections through the use of humor, surprise, or playful provocation. Think about how many viral marketing campaigns feature unexpected or humorous elements that catch people's attention and get them talking. While humor may not be appropriate for all L&D content, finding ways to delight and engage learners' expressions of joy, amusement, or surprise can make your content more memorable and effective.

Imagine a safety training module that uses an image of someone in a hyper-realistic illustration of the company's warehouse trying to hoist an elephant above his head to show improper lifting techniques. This unexpected image might make people laugh and help them remember the lesson. When we encounter something funny in learning materials, it triggers the release of feel-good chemicals called endorphins in our brains. Endorphins can help us pay attention and remember information better. It's like our brain is saying, "Hey, this is interesting! Let's remember this!"

However, what's funny to one person might not be amusing to someone else. Try to use universally relatable, light-hearted visuals that will make learning fun for everyone.

Simplicity

Of course, creating emotional resonance doesn't mean sacrificing clarity or professionalism. The best marketing visuals strike a balance between sparking an emotional reaction and communicating key information clearly and effectively. The crucial principle, as discussed in chapter 5, is simplicity.

The most effective marketing visuals are often the simplest; they have a clear focal point, minimal clutter, and a straightforward message. By stripping away extraneous details, you make it easy for the viewers to grasp your core idea quickly. For L&D professionals, simplicity is about cognitive efficiency. Every element should serve to support your learning objectives. Anything that doesn't contribute to those objectives is visual noise.

One way to achieve simplicity is through the use of visual hierarchy, as discussed earlier in this chapter. By giving the most important elements the greatest visual weight and prominence, you can guide learners' attention to key takeaways. This could mean using larger fonts for headlines, brighter colors for key data points, or more prominent placement for the central image.

Small Chunks

Another way to achieve simplicity is by breaking complex information into smaller, more manageable chunks. This is where infographics and data visualization can be helpful. By presenting information in a clear, visually organized way, these techniques make it easier for learners to process and retain complex ideas.

Striving for simplicity doesn't mean dumbing things down or stripping away all nuance and detail. Instead, it's about presenting information in the clearest, most concise way possible while maintaining the necessary depth. The best visuals find a balance between simplicity and substance.

Consistency

Another fundamental principle marketers use to create effective visuals is consistency, which is similar to the topic of uniform design we discussed in chapter 3. Consistent visual branding helps create a cohesive, recognizable, and trustworthy image. Think about how easily you recognize major brands' logos, color schemes, and visual styles—whether it's the Nike Swoosh, the Disney castle, or the Apple apple. That's the power of visual consistency.

In L&D, visual consistency across your learning materials—from the color palette and font choices to the style of illustrations and photography—all help create a unified, professional look and feel. This consistency makes it easier for learners to navigate and engage with the content, and it reinforces the credibility and authority of the information.

Consistency doesn't mean that every visual component needs to look the same. Instead, it's about creating a cohesive visual language that links all your learning content. This can be achieved by using templates, style guides, and design systems that help ensure visual uniformity while still allowing for flexibility and creativity. And branding isn't just for external audiences; it's equally crucial for internal training organizations. A strong, consistent brand for your learning and development initiatives reinforces the value of training within the company, enhances credibility, and creates a sense of professionalism that can boost engagement and participation.

⚑ Terms You Should Know

Style Guide
In marketing, a *style guide* is a road map for how your content should be presented, ensuring consistency across all channels. It goes deeper than just grammar and formatting by focusing on building a consistent and recognizable identity across all channels. This typically includes establishing a color palette, defining a limited set of fonts you'll use, and outlining the styles of images that best represent your brand.

Flexibility

As you can see, L&D professionals can draw a wealth of inspiration from the marketing world and learn proven strategies to create effective visuals that make a lasting impact. By understanding and applying all these conventions, you can take your visual communication to the next level. But remember, none of these conventions and techniques are rigid rules. Instead, consider them to be flexible guidelines you can adapt to your needs.

The most effective visuals are always tailored to your unique audience, content, and goals. Find the balance and combinations that work for your learners.

> **Creating Powerful Learning Visuals: Essential Questions**
> By continually asking questions and experimenting with different visual techniques, you'll develop a powerful toolkit for creating your own learning visuals to drive behavior change.
> - Who is your audience, and what visual style will resonate with them?
> - What story can you tell through your visuals to make the content more engaging and memorable?
> - How can you create an emotional connection that will make learning more effective?
> - Have you struck the right balance between simplicity and substance in your visual design?

A World of Potential Learning in Visuals

By mastering some essential techniques of visually presenting information to learners and embracing a marketing mindset, instructional designers can unlock a world of potential and create more effective learning experiences that captivate, educate, and inspire.

Before we can truly master these techniques, however, we must first understand and apply fundamental principles of visual perception, simplifying complex information and strategically using visuals to support learning objectives. Remember these essential points:

- The brain processes visuals faster than text alone.
- Visuals operate with a direct line to our emotions, which aids memory retention and decision making.

- Effective visuals can capture learners' attention, minimize cognitive load, and create clear visual hierarchies.
- Multimedia learning, when visuals and words are combined effectively, can significantly enhance comprehension and engagement.
- Research and user testing can help optimize visuals for a specific audience. By continually testing and refining our programs, we can unlock the full potential of visually enriched learning materials and create experiences that truly resonate with our audience.

As you embark on your journey to create visually compelling learning content, start by understanding your audience's needs and preferences, and then use the power of visuals to create an emotional connection, guide attention, facilitate understanding, and create content that truly makes a difference.

A Final Thought

Visual design isn't just about aesthetics; as Edward Tufte famously said, "Good design is clear thinking made visible." For L&D professionals, this means we can use design strategically to illuminate, simplify, and amplify our messages, ensuring they support clear thinking for our audiences.

We believe that good visual design has the potential to create transformative learning experiences, helping us dissect complex concepts, ignite curiosity, and motivate action. We aspire to design experiences that inform and empower learners to see information through a new lens and help them reach the potential to which they aspire when they join a course or training program.

Let clarity and results be your guiding stars as you craft learning experiences that make a real difference.

Activity 6-1. Rule of Thirds Practice

Objective
Enhance your understanding of the Rule of Thirds composition technique to craft visually engaging images that enhance learning experiences.

Steps
1. Select three to five images you've used in past learning materials. (ideally from the program you have been using for all activities throughout this book)
2. Apply the Rule of Thirds grid to each image (you can use a photo editing tool or simply imagine the grid).
3. Evaluate how well each image aligns with the Rule of Thirds and, if needed, brainstorm ways to improve the composition.
4. Write down your ideas for future reference.

Go Deeper
If you'd like some additional resources to help with this topic, try these:
- Digital Photography School's Rule of Thirds guide (digital-photography-school.com/rule-of-thirds)
- Photzy's free "Understanding the Rule of Thirds" guide (photzy.com/the-rule-of-thirds-explained-and-when-to-use-it-free-quick-guide)
- Shotkit's "Rule of Thirds in Photography" article (shotkit.com/rule-of-thirds)

Activity 6-2. Visual Hierarchy Analysis

Objective
Develop your ability to apply visual design principles to learning materials by critically analyzing real-world examples and understanding their influence on viewer attention.

Steps
1. Choose a piece of marketing material (an advertisement, website homepage, or product packaging) and analyze its visual hierarchy.
2. Identify how the design uses movement, focus, contrast, brightness, size, and proximity to guide the viewer's attention.
3. Write a brief summary of your observations and how these principles could be applied to your next learning design project.

Go Deeper
To spark new ideas as you work through this activity, try these resources:
- Interaction Design Foundation's article on visual hierarchy (interaction-design.org/literature/topics/visual-hierarchy)
- Canva's tutorials on design elements and principles (canva.com/learn/visual-hierarchy)
- NN/g's article on visual hierarchy in UX (nngroup.com/articles/visual-hierarchy-ux-definition)

Activity 6-3. Content Makeover

Objective
Transform text-based content into visually compelling and informative learning resources by applying a variety of design principles to strengthen comprehension.

Steps
1. Select a text-heavy slide or document from a previous training program (ideally the one you have been using for all activities throughout this book).
2. Redesign it using the principles discussed in this chapter, such as incorporating relevant imagery and multimedia principles and applying visual hierarchy.
3. Write a brief explanation of your design choices and how they improve the learning experience.

Go Deeper
For inspiration, explore these additional resources on this topic:
- Duarte's video on slide design makeovers (duarte.com/resources/webinars-videos/what-would-duarte-do-slide-design-makeovers-thank-you)
- Visual design hacks for the nondesigner from NN/g (nngroup.com/videos/visual-design-hacks)

Chapter 7
Execute a Successful Learning Campaign

> Content is king, but distribution is queen, and she wears the pants.
> —Jonathan Perelman, media strategist

Seven million dollars. That was the average cost of running a 30-second Super Bowl television ad in 2024. That's up from $2.2 million in 2002. Large corporations use Super Bowl Sunday to raise awareness about their products and services because tens of millions of people around the globe watch the event and its memorable halftime shows. Comprehensive marketing efforts often start on social media weeks before the game, teasing innovative, funny, or surprising ads designed to attract maximum attention (Majidi 2024). Marketers couldn't ask for a more captive audience.

Remember the Snickers ad with the tagline, "You're Not You When You're Hungry"? It showed a team of rugby players, and in its midst was petite TV icon Betty White. One player says to another player, "Mike, you're playing like Betty White out there." Mike's girlfriend comes over and hands Betty White a Snickers, which immediately turns Betty into the big, tough rugby player Mike.

The ad was part of a multi-channel marketing campaign, including television commercials, social media, and experiential marketing. Snickers maintained a consistent core message across all channels, which further helped reinforce brand recognition and build trust with consumers.

Memorable Super Bowl TV commercials speak to our emotions, making us laugh or cry and often making us think. An individual 30-second commercial is usually part of a larger marketing campaign, just like the Snickers ad, a strategically planned series of actions that promote a product, service, or cause and improve brand awareness and sales to a target audience. Marketing campaigns often involve a variety of channels and always have a specific goal. The first is to get people's attention, while the ultimate goal is to entice them to buy a product or service. Marketing campaigns are most successful when the audience believes the company understands what they need and want.

What can we, as L&D professionals, learn by studying effective marketing campaigns? First, we can learn how to get people's attention (we covered a few techniques for capturing learners' attention in chapter 1). After we've generated this initial buy-in and excitement, we can then focus on marketing campaigns to learn how to encourage learners to take action and acquire new knowledge, skills, and behaviors.

Marketers can teach us how to use a variety of techniques, including identifying recurring programs that we can automate. Recurring programs on topics such as onboarding, compliance, and health and safety include a lot of mundane administrative tasks, so if we can save time and money by automating those, we can focus our attention on designing outstanding content and creating learning opportunities that engage and inspire more learners over time. We talk more about this in chapter 8.

We'd all like to create experiences with such attention-grabbing hooks and captivating content that learners wait eagerly for the next installment, just like people anticipate the next great Super Bowl ad. In this chapter, we'll examine the keys to creating best-in-class learning campaigns, including planning strategically, aligning to overall company goals, segmenting your target audience, personalizing assets, orchestrating the delivery of content, and measuring impact and success.

Campaigns Versus Journeys

You might be wondering if marketing campaigns are similar to the customer journeys discussed in chapter 3—and if learning campaigns are similar to learner journeys. In a nutshell, they're related but not the same. Customer journeys (and learner journeys) focus on specific audiences and are "always on." Journeys are highly personalized because different customers or learners enter and exit at their own pace and in their own time. A journey is a strategic way of looking at how an *individual* interacts with a brand or learning content.

Campaigns, on the other hand, are associated with a *broader target audience*, usually a specific segment within a customer base. Campaigns often center on one-time or recurring tasks and have clear start and end dates. With that distinction in mind, let's review how we can leverage the power of campaigns in L&D and dive deeper into how they work.

The way L&D professionals usually discuss campaigns is not the way marketers talk about them. Often, marketers talk about a combination of marketing campaigns and the orchestration of marketing journeys. To make the links between the two disciplines a little easier to understand, we've slightly altered that traditional understanding of a marketing campaign, with apologies to our marketing friends.

In this book, we define the *learner's journey* as a big-picture, high-level strategic plan that helps us understand each step a learner takes as part of a learning experience. Going back to our LuxeKitchens example, the learner journey includes all the steps sales consultants have to complete, from lead management to follow-ups, as they try to increase sales numbers.

A *learning campaign*, on the other hand, is the tactical execution of specific elements of the overall learner journey. Thus, the *learner journey* is the sum of all the related *learning campaigns*. For LuxeKitchens, one learning campaign might focus on lead management while another focuses on kitchen selection or negotiation and closing a sale; these campaigns are part of one learner journey that leads a sales consultant from the initial lead management all the way to the follow-up once a kitchen has been sold.

With these definitions in mind, let's explore how to leverage the power of journeys and campaigns and design unforgettable learning experiences.

Elements of a Marketing Campaign

Campaign marketing is an aspect of direct marketing that's usually called *customer-relationship marketing*. It is about "gathering, analyzing, and using information about individual customers and prospects" (Housden and Thomas

2002). Once a marketer has collected customer and prospective customer information, they can communicate with the target audience by sharing valuable, relevant content. In the marketing world, campaigns are always brand-centric, meaning that they focus on increasing our attention and reaction to a specific brand (Hannouz 2021). Remember the Snickers Super Bowl commercial? It used consistent brand messaging across all channels: Snickers is the solution if you're hangry! It positioned itself as more than a chocolate bar: Snickers can help you if you don't feel like yourself. The humor used in the ad is still used today to identify the Snickers brand. The company even created an app that told users who they would be when hungry.

When marketers plan campaigns, they think about specific goals, such as increasing awareness of a brand and introducing or improving sales of a new product or service. The target audience isn't the driving factor. Campaigns are sent to predefined audience segments, often with little thought about how individuals within them will react. Marketing campaigns are usually linear, discreet, and time-based. They include several essential elements and corresponding tasks (Table 7-1).

Table 7-1. Marketing Campaign Tasks

Marketing Campaign Element	Task
Goal	Identify what you want to achieve with your campaign.
Message or purpose	Answer the question, "Why are you running a campaign?"
Audience	Select the people who will be part of your campaign.
Deliverables	Work through what you want to send, when, and where.
Execution plan	Build out a communication, adoption, and rollout plan.
Measures of success	Identify key performance indicators.

Campaigns allow marketers to automate processes and improve scalability. Instead of focusing on one-off pieces of content, they think strategically about multiple pieces of content, how to create it, repurpose it as needed, and push it out through marketing automation tools. Campaigns are never written in stone, and their flexibility allows marketers to react in the moment to adjust the output, making the experience more meaningful for customers. Because they use automation and repurpose content, campaigns also allow marketers to decrease costs over time, improving the return on investment in the long run.

Now, let's move on to discussing how marketers compose a customer journey through a process known as *journey orchestration*. This aspect of the marketer's playbook is most similar to what L&D professionals do in learning campaigns.

Customer Journey Orchestration

When orchestrating a customer journey, marketers pay attention to individual customers and their unique experiences. Customers enter and exit the journey at different points in time, often re-enter after exiting, and might even repeat some steps. Each customer triggers the touchpoints of a journey at different times, and interacts with the brand differently (Hannouz 2021).

Marketers try to focus as much as possible on personalized experiences while also aligning the customer journey with overall company goals. They use data to adjust customer journeys as needed. In the L&D environment, the most successful learner journeys are also tailored and personalized for individual learners and aligned with overall organization goals.

> ★ **Terms You Should Know**
>
> **Marketing Campaign and Journey Orchestration**
> A *marketing campaign* is a series of activities to promote a product or service using a variety of media, including (but not limited to) email, social media, and print advertising. They are brand-centric, segment-driven, linear, and designed to share a message with a wide audience to achieve a specific goal, such as increasing sales. Campaigns are usually executed for a well-defined period. In L&D, we can use learning campaigns to push content to a specific audience to help move them to action.
>
> *Journey orchestration* is the process of coordinating and managing a customer experience in real time across various channels and touchpoints. The goal is to create personalized experiences that encourage customers to continue interacting with a brand. In journey orchestration, marketers focus on individual customers, not large groups, and tailor experiences to each customer as much as possible, which is an ongoing and adaptive process. In L&D, a learner journey is part of an overall strategic plan and includes the tasks and touchpoints necessary for an individual learner to achieve a specific larger organizational goal.

How to Market a Blockbuster

We'll try to make some of the abstract concepts we've discussed more concrete by illustrating them with a simplified example of how marketers might plan for an upcoming blockbuster movie release. Let's consider two strategies—one using a marketing campaign and the other a customer journey.

Create a Marketing Campaign

To create a marketing campaign, the studio that produced the blockbuster movie could rent a billboard before the premiere to promote it. The billboard would show a static message that targets a broad audience (the geographic region in which the billboard is located and drivers who commute on the highway) and stay up only during a specific timeframe (one month). A commuter would see the billboard and decide to watch the film on opening weekend. After the screening, they don't interact further with the movie studio.

Orchestrate a Customer Journey

To orchestrate a customer journey, the movie studio could use the large email subscriber lists it has gathered from previous blockbuster events to tailor a digital experience for each customer based on their preferences, including film genre, VIP status, location, and other factors. The studio would send personalized email invitations to happy hours before weeknight showtimes, special weekend matinee deals for families, and discounted tickets to other films if the recipient purchases two or more tickets for the blockbuster. After the movie leaves theaters, the studio would continue to personalize the moviegoer experience with additional promotions related to its streaming platform and future films.

Deciphering Learning Campaigns

As we explained, in L&D we use a rough mix of journey orchestration and marketing campaigns to create a learning campaign. In this section, we'd like to suggest a more precise and nuanced way of thinking about learning campaigns to offer our participants the best learning experiences.

Recall that the learner journeys discussed in chapter 3 included many touchpoints. After each touchpoint is completed, participants either have learned something new or can do something differently. Each touchpoint is linked to a particular learner goal. The sum of all learner goals is the overall journey goal.

When we envision an overarching learning campaign, we see each touchpoint as a smaller campaign. This means that we can view our learner journey as a series of learning campaigns, each with a goal derived from the learner goals we've identified on our learner journey map. Figure 7-1 should help you see the connections clearly.

Figure 7-1. The Learner Journey's Relationship With the Learning Campaign

Phase	Pretraining Day 1	Training Week 1
Learner Goals	Buy in to the new sales curriculum	Use CRM effectively to capture leads from various lead sources (e.g., email, phone, walk-ins)
Touchpoints	**Create excitement:** Get buy-in and manage expectations	**Manage leads:** Phone skills, email etiquette, and CRM workflow
Channels and Interactions	Join learning community on MS Teams	• 30 min vILT in Zoom on lead sources • 5–10 min simulation in Storyline on the CRM workflow
Says or Asks	"How will this training help me?"	"Interesting, I guess there's a better way to deal with leads."
Feels or Thinks	Overwhelmed and confused	Unsure
Does	Join all learning activities while working in familiar ways	Try to include new ways of capturing leads
Feedback And Data	MS Teams, email, and video analytics; manager observations	Zoom, email, and LMS analytics; manager observations; number of qualified leads

(Left axis: Learner Emotional State; Right axis: Learning Campaign; Bottom axis: Learner Journey)

As we noted, marketing campaigns traditionally focus on an audience segment, rather than specific personas. But in a learning campaign, we believe it's important to focus on personas for each campaign and answer the question "Why?" This focus supports our key goal of personalizing all learning experiences as much as possible, which goes hand-in-hand with an essential principle we discussed in chapter 4: *Share the right content at the right place at the right time.* Learning campaigns need to rely heavily on a content strategy. Our understanding of learning campaigns also includes defined starting and ending dates and the need to measure success.

Best Practices for Creating Your Learning Campaigns

When creating learning campaigns, start with your goals and purpose before thinking about your target audience, deliverables, execution plan, and how you will measure results and success. Go back to your learner journey map, examine the first touchpoint, and use that as the starting point for your first campaign.

What if someone in your organization suddenly submits a new training request? In that case, you would vet the ask and confirm that there is a legitimate learning need associated with a business need. Always try to avoid saying yes if someone asks for training for no clear reason! After confirming the need is legitimate, identify where the specific request sits in the learner journey and begin your work. Let's review a step-by-step list of five best practices for creating a learning campaign (Figure 7-2).

1. Set Your Goals, Purpose, and Message

The first question to ask yourself is, "What am I trying to achieve with this learning campaign?" Given that you have already identified where in the learner journey the campaign sits, you know the goal because it's the same as the learner goal identified for a particular touchpoint. Now you need to identify any key performance indicators that go above and beyond the outcomes you want to see at the learner level.

Returning to our LuxeKitchens example, imagine a stakeholder has requested training to improve consultants' phone skills as part of the lead management process. The goal: "Sales consultants need to learn to take clear and precise notes while on the phone and enter them into the customer relationship management (CRM) system to improve lead quality." This will result in increased customer satisfaction and higher sales, which are the overall business needs.

Figure 7-2. Five Key Steps for Creating Learning Campaigns

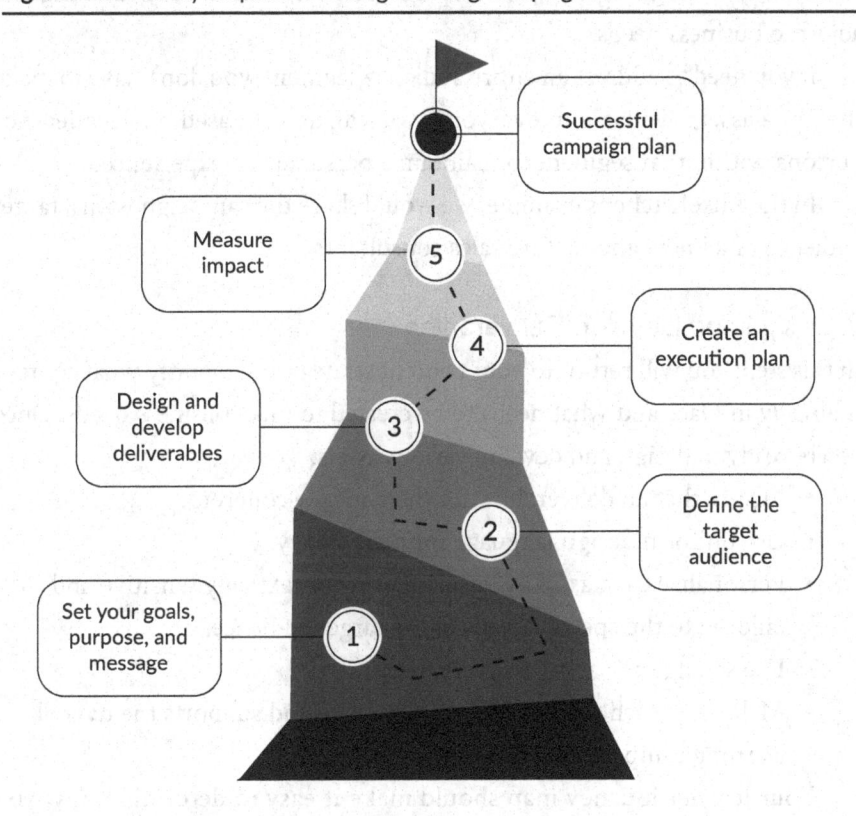

- 5 — Measure impact → Successful campaign plan
- 4 — Create an execution plan
- 3 — Design and develop deliverables
- 2 — Define the target audience
- 1 — Set your goals, purpose, and message

Based on this information, we could summarize the message and purpose: "Improve your day-to-day phone skills for error-free CRM entries that will lead to higher sales." In this phase, you would also think about your CTA for each asset.

2. Define the Target Audience

The next task is to identify your target audience. Unlike a marketer, learning designers look at multiple segments by going back to the learner personas. You created the learner journeys with the personas in mind. When a new business request comes through, always double-check to see if those personas align with the request. Most of the time, you'll be good to go. However, if the business request is quite specific, you might have to augment your target audience, add other personas, or remove some personas. In the end, you may need to add an entire audience segment to your campaign, so be flexible in your thinking and adjust to business needs.

If you need to address an entire audience segment, you don't have to make the same assets available to everyone; you can adjust based on each learner persona within that segment to maintain a personalized experience.

In the LuxeKitchens example, we would share the campaign with a target audience of all new and mature sales consultants.

3. Design and Develop Deliverables

In this step, you will return to your content strategy and identify what content is already in place and what needs to be created to meet business needs. Once you're ready to design and develop various assets:

- Ensure that all deliverables are thematically coherent.
- Use uniform design language for consistency.
- Personalize each asset by ensuring it is contextually sensitive and tailored to the specific needs of the target audience.
- Use strong messaging in every asset.
- Make sure each deliverable has a purpose and supports the overall learning campaign and business need.

Your learner journey map should make it easy to determine how you want to deliver, publish, and share because you have already identified the best delivery channels.

At LuxeKitchens, content exists in several places—in the CRM Help Site, in standard operating procedures, and in soft skills courses. All three contain content we could use to create training for improved phone skills. We would also want to talk to store managers to get real-world examples to use in the learning campaign.

In the learner journey map for LuxeKitchens, we identified some applicable interactions, including AI-based role-play tools, e-learning with group activities, interactive videos, simulations, and a community of practice. In this stage of creating a campaign we would need to be more specific as we focus on improving phone skills.

An abbreviated version of a learning campaign for improving phone skills might look like the graphic in Figure 7-3.

Figure 7-3. Sample Learning Campaign for Improving Phone Skills

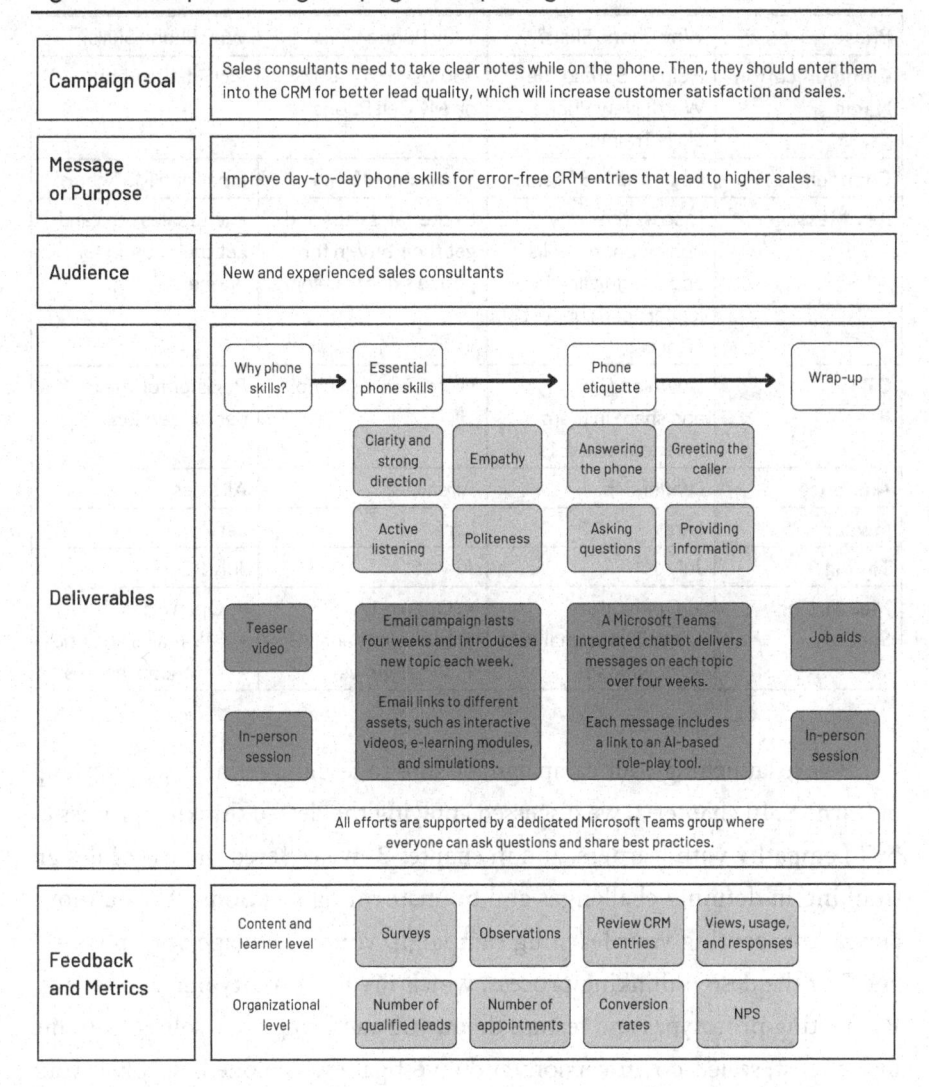

Campaign Goal	Sales consultants need to take clear notes while on the phone. Then, they should enter them into the CRM for better lead quality, which will increase customer satisfaction and sales.
Message or Purpose	Improve day-to-day phone skills for error-free CRM entries that lead to higher sales.
Audience	New and experienced sales consultants
Deliverables	Flow: Why phone skills? → Essential phone skills → Phone etiquette → Wrap-up. Essential phone skills includes: Clarity and strong direction, Empathy, Active listening, Politeness. Phone etiquette includes: Answering the phone, Greeting the caller, Asking questions, Providing information. Teaser video. Email campaign lasts four weeks and introduces a new topic each week. Email links to different assets, such as interactive videos, e-learning modules, and simulations. A Microsoft Teams integrated chatbot delivers messages on each topic over four weeks. Each message includes a link to an AI-based role-play tool. Job aids. In-person session. In-person session. All efforts are supported by a dedicated Microsoft Teams group where everyone can ask questions and share best practices.
Feedback and Metrics	Content and learner level: Surveys, Observations, Review CRM entries, Views, usage, and responses. Organizational level: Number of qualified leads, Number of appointments, Conversion rates, NPS.

4. Create an Execution Plan

The next step is to work on your execution plan. As described in chapter 4, you'll need to create a communication, adoption, and rollout plan that includes messaging to promote the campaign and keep engagement high. Given that it is a small subset of an overall learner journey, there is no need to create an in-depth adoption and rollout plan. Your plan might look something like Table 7-2, which is an excerpt of a larger communication plan.

Table 7-2. Sample Communication Plan Excerpt

Phase	Why Phone Skills?	Why Phone Skills?	Why Phone Skills?
Communication Name	Help Us Spread the Word! New Phone Skills Training	You Used to Call Me on My Cell Phone	Pick up the Phone
Channels	Email and MS Teams	Email and MS Teams	Email and MS Teams
Key Message	Discuss the "why" behind phone skills and training and how leaders can support efforts.	Excite sales reps and get their buy-in for phone skills training.	Excite sales reps and get their buy-in for phone training.
CTA	Download info and share in team meetings and 1:1s.	Watch teaser video.	Register for the in-person session.
Audience	Leadership	All sales	All sales
Owner	Lara	Lara	Lara
Timing	July 1	July 15	July 22
Measure of Success	• Open rates • MS Teams analytics • Downloads	• Open rates • MS Teams analytics • Video views	• Open rates • MS Teams analytics • Attendance rates

Before launching your campaign, be sure to test and refine it with a group of learners. In chapter 2, we discussed applying the design thinking process to build empathy with learners, and in chapter 3, we covered the use of design thinking in defining challenges and brainstorming solutions. As you move closer to executing your learning campaign, you can engage with phases 4 and 5 of the design thinking process, which involve prototyping and testing. By creating prototypes and testing them, you can bring your solutions to life in low-cost, scaled-down versions and investigate which one best solves your design challenge. Ideally, you'll share the prototype with a wide audience and test its impact. AI tools provide a low-cost solution to support prototyping and testing.

In our LuxeKitchens example, we would create low-fidelity e-learning modules and conduct live role plays before programming them into an AI tool. We would release the assets to learners and get feedback in the moment and later, after they take part in the entire campaign. We would then repeat and improve the solution until it hits the mark.

Sometimes, we might have to reverse course, taking another look at our learner personas or problem statements if a solution doesn't have the desired effect. We could also do A/B testing to try out several types of deliverables, messaging, and timing.

5. Measure Impact

Before you release a campaign, be sure to plan how you will measure its impact. You already have learner goals and KPIs in place but you'll still need to establish a reporting baseline and cadence. You also need to identify which tools to use, such as your LMS or LXP, Google Analytics, or Tableau. We'll discuss some of those options in chapter 9.

As you collect data points about the content and the overall campaign, turn that data into insights. Where in the campaign do most participants return for a second look? When do they drop off? Consider whether the content is too difficult, too easy, or repetitive. Do you know who is dropping off? Take the time to interpret the data you've collected and use it to tell a visually appealing story.

In the LuxeKitchens story, we would measure learner outcomes in this training by distributing surveys and observing employees on the phone. We'd also review CRM entries to ensure accuracy. Views, usage, responses, and engagement with assets provide insights about the training content. From an organizational perspective, we'd look at the number of qualified leads correctly entered into the system, the number of appointments generated by phone conversations, and the resulting conversion rate. The Net Promoter Score, which we'll discuss in chapter 9, would show us if customers are satisfied.

From Marketing to L&D: Four Campaign Approaches

Now that we've covered the basics of campaign creation, we can dive into specific types of marketing campaigns that translate well to the L&D world. Instead of a comprehensive list, we'll focus on four highly effective approaches: email and text; experiential; social media and influencer; and cause related.

Email and Text Marketing Campaigns

Email is often the first thing that comes to mind when we think of marketing campaigns. However, while email is a powerful tool and the most common type of marketing campaign—it is just one of many tools in the marketer's toolbox. Email marketers try to move customers to action in a few simple steps:

1. They send and track a series of emails.
2. They collect metrics around email opens and clicks to an accompanying landing page.
3. They use automation tools to track customers' digital footprints and collect more information.
4. They use the information collected to personalize the purchasing experience.

Here are a few statistics about the prevalence of email (Kirsch 2023):

- In 2022, more than 340 billion emails were sent and received.
- More than 4.6 billion people use email daily.
- In 2023, 38 percent of brands were increasing their email budgets, while only 10 percent were cutting them.

Email marketing is closely connected to mobile marketing. According to What'stheBigData (2024):

- 60.67 percent of website traffic comes from mobile devices.
- 92.3 percent of internet users consider accessing the internet through their smartphones compared with other devices.
- There are more than 5.3 billion mobile internet users globally.

In addition, according to Mailchimp (2023), 41 percent of consumers prefer text messages over email.

You'll find more details about the value of email in chapter 8, which focuses on how to effectively use technology to improve your email game. It's important to know that users spend roughly 10 seconds reading an email. So, it's no surprise that the elements that make an email successful include the length of the message, its visual attractiveness, its structure, calls to action, effective copy, the subject line, and graphics (Malkani 2022). If you follow our guidelines from chapters 6 and 7 on visuals and writing good copy, your learners will be much more likely to open those emails! Aside from great visuals and good copy, how can we take advantage of emails in L&D and ensure success? We've gathered some key ideas in Table 7-3.

Table 7-3. Using Email for Marketing Success

Marketing Tactic	Description	L&D Use
Subscriber segmentation	Only reach out to customers who are truly interested in your brand (i.e., people who have opted in to your emails).	Design a process in which employees can sign up for emails, which will increase the actions learners take.
Message personalization using dynamic content	Dynamic content refers to digital content that automatically changes based on customer data saved in a marketing automation tool. Content might include text, images, audio, or video. It personalizes the experience and enhances user engagement. For example, an email features a personalized message and product recommendations.	Create an email course that shares different content based on the learner's job role and is sent out at the learner's preferred time of day.
Email automated campaigns	Emails are either action- or time-triggered. For example, a customer downloads an e-book and receives an email (action). Or a newsletter email is sent out every Monday morning (time).	Send an email when a learner completes the first level of a training course, reminding them of the upcoming assessment and additional resources. Or send an email on the first day of the new hire onboarding program to manage expectations.

In L&D, emails can be used in a variety of ways. Simple, stand-alone email campaigns allow you to break existing content into chunks over time. Emails can also be useful as part of an overall learning campaign consisting of many modalities. Either way, learn from the marketers and use segmentation and personalization to speak directly to learners and automate the process as much as you can.

A Real-World Lesson for L&D

One of Bianca's favorite email-supported campaigns was part of an onboarding program. She was asked to transform a one-hour training program about a company's competitors that wasn't in-depth enough for the sales team or inspiring excitement among the administrative team. In response, she developed a learning campaign that started with a short in-person kick-off to set the tone and then moved online.

Over four weeks, Bianca created and shared multiple emails through a marketing automation platform. The emails included information about the company's biggest competitors and were personalized to the recipient's job role using dynamic content. A sales team member received much more in-depth emails with multiple resource links, while those in administration got shorter emails with fewer links.

Alongside the emails, Bianca and her team put a chatbot in Slack and used it to push out timed content to support the content in the emails. In other words, the chatbot ran on a separate campaign schedule aligned with the email campaign. The timing of the messages depended on the recipient's time zone and job role. The data showed that people on the sales team often spent time learning after working hours instead of during working hours.

At the end of the four weeks, Bianca gathered everyone in person for a debriefing session. Learners reported being much more engaged because of the highly personalized content and spaced repetition. These factors also enhanced knowledge transfer. New hires felt better informed and prepared to do their jobs. Salespeople were able to talk on the phone with more confidence more quickly when asked about competitors, and they closed deals sooner.

Experiential Marketing Campaigns

The term *experiential marketing* was first coined in 1999 by Bernd Schmitt, a professor of marketing at Columbia University. The term describes "live interaction which uses consumers' insights and emotions to connect them with a brand" (Doherty 2022). The goal of experiential marketing is to create a memorable experience, which then creates a competitive advantage. Historically, experiential marketing has referred to a physical experience, but today, marketers try to replicate physical experiences in the digital world. There are five things that should be part of experiential marketing or an experiential learning campaign. Customers or learners should:

1. Use their senses (sight, sound, touch, taste, and smell).
2. Experience emotions.
3. Be engaged intellectually and creatively.
4. Take action, usually in a physical way.
5. Relate to the experience socially or in a way that appeals to their desire for self-improvement (Doherty 2022).

Real-World Lessons: M&M's and Barbie

Let's now analyze two examples of experiential marketing campaigns you might be familiar with. The first is for M&M's candies, and the second is for the movie, *Barbie*.

A few years ago, Mars created an immersive pop-up shop for M&M's candies in New York City. The company was launching a new flavor and wanted input from customers, so they created what they called "flavor rooms," each with décor and a fragrance unique to a specific flavor. They also offered visitors snacks and drinks, including an M&M's-themed cocktail—many of these appeared on customers' social media pages. This is an example of a physical experience that expanded into the digital sphere through customers' actions.

In 2023, Warner Bros. Entertainment promoted its film *Barbie* to audiences of all genders, ages, and backgrounds using unique trailers. One popular element was an AI tool that allowed moviegoers to generate a selfie with Barbie or feature themselves as the character in a variety of professions, color stories, and personalities, all aligned with director Greta Gerwig's vision of Barbie's meaning. The result? A feel-good story for moviegoers and a powerful promotion tool for the film. This is a creative example of using digital technologies in the experiential marketing space.

Lessons for L&D

As learning designers, we have many options for including engaging physical and digital experiences in our training programs. For example, Bianca worked on an immersive experience for which the original ask was a two-hour, in-person live event discussing a product's advantages and use cases for employees at company headquarters. She knew the task, as described to her, would be boring and wouldn't drive the results the organization was looking for, so she asked to make some changes in the brief.

She proposed a free-flowing, in-person event with six booths. At one booth, for example, learners would be immersed in the history of the product using QR codes placed on a large backsplash depicting images of the product evolving over time. At another booth, learners would sit back and relax with popcorn to watch a short video about the lifestyle of a customer using the product. At yet another booth, the physical product would be on display for learners to touch and interact with. Throughout the event space and hidden in deliverables, learners would collect clues as part of a scavenger hunt.

This creative theme would carry through the full learning experience, from invitation emails to giveaways to thank-you emails, creating a cohesive, lively atmosphere. An event-focused app would tie everything together, allowing Bianca's team to gamify the experience. At the end, the most engaged learners would win prizes.

The organization agreed to her proposal and the event was a huge success. Learners even asked for more events like it in the future. Bianca and her team were asked to take the experience on the road so employees beyond headquarters could immerse themselves in the new product and help the company sell more.

Social Media and Influencer Campaigns
Involving third-party platforms, especially social media, and using the power of influencers in marketing campaigns is an effective way to expand reach and create awareness.

Social Media and Social Learning
Social media marketing refers to the use of platforms such as Instagram, TikTok, YouTube, LinkedIn, and Facebook to share content and connect with customers and colleagues. Because most consumers use social media to watch videos, view photos and stories, network, share content, access news, and shop for products and services, social media marketing is a logical way to find them.

Social media allows marketers to engage with customers in unique ways and on their own terms. This type of marketing is ultimately about *relationship building*—using market research, paid advertising, and online communities to respond to customers and prospects (Mishra and Baldus 2022). Organizations of all kinds can monetize their presence on social media by promoting their products, and, as you can imagine, social media offers many data points that can help organizations learn more about their customers.

Note, however, that this might be challenging to introduce into your learning designs because many organizations have strict social media policies. Fortunately, many education and training technology solutions have built-in social capabilities that you can consciously build into your campaigns.

Another way to translate social media campaigns to L&D is to include *social learning*—what we do when we're talking about work, sharing insights, and observing work processes, decisions, techniques, and tools (Britz 2020). Once you have identified how to integrate social learning into your campaign, you can look at tools to help you along the way.

One of our favorite ways to bring social learning into a campaign is using a direct messaging tool. Most organizations have something in place like Microsoft Teams or Slack. In the email learning example we shared earlier, Bianca set up a chatbot within Slack environment and also created a channel just for conversations about competitors. This evergreen channel was used by new hires and salespeople who had been with the organization for years. It became the hub for everything about competitors, where each representative shared insights on what they heard from customers and new assets and products competitors brought to markets.

A Real World Lesson for L&D

One outstanding example of a successful social media campaign is Apple's #ShotOniPhone campaign, which started in 2015. The company began a contest for customers to share photos taken on an iPhone, which were then posted on 10,000 billboards around the world. In 2017, Apple opened its Instagram account to crowdsource more content. The campaign is still going strong and has more than 16 million entries on Instagram alone!

Influencer Campaigns

Influencer marketing is a type of social media marketing that uses social networking sites and individuals who have established a network of friends, acquaintances, and strangers. The power and impact of influencers lie with their followers and on their authenticity, reliability, and credibility (Freberg et al. 2022). When we hear the word *influencer*, we often think about celebrities, but most are average people who are considered experts in a specific field, such as gardening, travel, or beauty products. They derive status because of their expertise and use that influence when they communicate with followers on social media (Ziewiecki and Ross 2021). Influencers may receive free or discounted products or money in return for their endorsements.

Influencers as Champions for L&D

Where do influencers fit into learning campaigns? In chapter 4, we talked about champions and ambassadors who can help us spread the word about a learning experience. They are the equivalent of Instagram influencers in a marketing campaign.

Bianca recalls an event she worked on in which champions brought a system rollout to life for a sales force of more than 1,000 people. The organization was introducing a new CRM, and everyone needed to be on board. The biggest pain points in the old system were that it took too long to enter information, the interface wasn't easy to navigate, and the overall data entry process was cumbersome. When the sales force heard about the new CRM, everyone shut down immediately, uninterested in learning a new system they assumed would be as frustrating as the previous one.

The champions were early adopters of the new system, used it every day for several weeks, and saw firsthand the time savings gained. Bianca and her team integrated the champions into a learning campaign around the new CRM. These early adopters shared best practices, tips, and tricks and became the go-to resources if other employees had questions. Champions even hosted webinars and open office hours as everyone got up-to-speed on the new system. Their influence within the company made the learning campaign a success. Word-of-mouth is always the best kind of marketing!

Cause-Related Campaigns

Cause-related marketing is a collaboration between companies and nonprofit organizations in which companies donate money, goods, or services for a social cause they believe in when customers buy a product. These campaigns are often considered an important part of a company's corporate responsibility program (CRP). Campaigns vary based on the donation type, product type, duration, and geographical scope (Galan-Ladero et al. 2021). Marketers find that cause-related marketing creates a valuable positive view of a brand and loyal customers.

Danone yogurt company's 1 Danone = 1 Life Seed campaign is a good example of successful cause-related marketing. When consumers purchase a Danone yogurt, seeds are donated to farmers in developing countries. This initiative is part of Danone's "One Planet. One Health" initiative and focuses on sustainability, health, and community well-being.

Learner Communities Volunteer for a Cause

To translate cause-related marketing to an L&D environment, organizations might volunteer staff time to certain charities as part of a learner experience. Volunteer days are also a great way to improve participants' social and interpersonal skills.

If we consider the situation of the sales reps at LuxeKitchens, for example, we might decide that a day away from the store serving the community could improve both their morale and customer-handling skills. As part of the ongoing campaign around lead management, the L&D team could send out an email halfway through the existing campaign to promote upcoming volunteer days. Sales reps could then sign up for the days that fit their schedules. After everyone volunteers, a debrief in the form of a team huddle could ask the sales reps to reflect on their experience and talk about how it could be translated into their day-to-day interactions.

Things to Consider When Creating Your Learning Campaign

Now that we've introduced the different campaign types, we'll turn to a few final considerations to keep in mind when designing and deploying learning campaigns.

A learning campaign should be integrated into everything else you do. If you're running a learning campaign for the first time, but learners don't know that they are part of it, they won't expect multiple assets over time and may not make the connection between an email you sent and an AI-based role-play tool. Integrate the campaign into your organization's other learning experiences to ensure everyone makes those connections. And include your team and any other members of the organization you recruited to contribute to the campaign. Designing and running campaigns isn't a one-person job (Decker 2024).

A good learning campaign requires a consistent mission, vision, and visual identity. You already know why you want to run your campaign (purpose), and you have set out goals to measure its success. For a learning campaign to really make a difference, it should have an aspirational aspect—a mission and vision. Where do you want to take your learning content or program in the future, and what do you have to do to get there?

As you run the learning campaign, maintain consistency with your brand while also instilling a unique identity, mission, and vision for the campaign. Link the mission, content, vision, look, tone, and voice of your brand with the campaign, and let all elements shine at every single touchpoint. An effective learning campaign has a clear message, is memorable, is easy to scale, translates across mediums, and brings value to the audience (French 2023).

Something else to consider: A good learning campaign never overlooks permission, so always include preference options in your emails. Just because people work in your organization doesn't mean they want or should receive a bunch of emails or text messages. If a recipient wants to opt out completely, make sure the campaign as a whole still works without a glitch. Also, try using system emails sent from an LMS or LXP, which can be edited to stand out more. These are considered transactional emails and don't have to adhere to common laws and regulations.

Finally, a successful learning campaign always starts small and is flexible, adapting to learners' needs along the way and tying back to learner journey goals and content strategy. This will help create a consistent and valuable learner experience.

Create Effective, Holistic Learning Campaigns

Learning campaigns and learning paths are easily mistaken for one another, even though they are distinctly different concepts. What makes learning campaigns special is that they go hand-in-hand with strong, continuous communication plans and change management, especially in organizations new to learning campaigns.

It's best to approach your learning campaigns holistically as if crafting a story rather than just assembling components randomly. Every element should contribute to a unified and effective learning experience. Each asset must have a clear purpose and a goal beyond performance objectives. Each campaign as a whole must support business goals and strategic objectives, a positive learning culture, and continuous learning. In other words, great learning campaigns are not just a collection of deliverables—they are built around learners. Learning campaigns should spark curiosity and draw in participants with seamless integration of content, context, and visuals.

Learning campaigns always require strategic planning. While this stage may require more initial effort from L&D than traditional methods of design, the long-term benefits are significant. Once established, campaign content can be repurposed, shared strategically, and updated to deliver far greater results than any conventional training program.

Campaigns also require stakeholder support to succeed. When their support is secured early in the process, convincing them of the value of learning campaigns becomes much easier. Start small by piloting a section of a larger program to demonstrate how learning campaigns can effectively improve learner engagement, increase content relevance, and cultivate a thriving L&D culture.

A Final Thought

We urge you to consciously choose to run your learning campaign using the strategies and best practices discussed in this chapter. Without proper planning and buy-in from your organization, any learning campaign will fall flat. Draw inspiration from some of the marketing campaigns that surround you every day; with that inspiration, create the best possible learning experiences for your audience.

Activity 7-1. A Successful Learning Campaign

Review the program you have been working on throughout this book. You should already have a learner persona, a high-level learner journey, and a content strategy. Pick one step out of the learner journey and design an unforgettable learning campaign using several campaign types.

Objective
Design a learner-centric campaign with strong, measurable goals and a series of four to five cohesive deliverables.

Steps
1. Define your goal, purpose, and message.
2. Define your target audience.
3. Design the deliverables.
4. Create an execution plan.
5. Identify measures of success.

Chapter 8
Level Up Learning With Marketing Technology

> Marketing technology is the key to delivering the right message to the right person at the right time through the right channel.
> —David Edelman, renowned marketing executive

Sarah, an L&D manager, was drowning. Her company was on the rise, adding new teams and products at a dizzying pace. Each new hire meant a new training program to build. Once brimming with creative energy, Sarah was now buried in administrative tasks—scheduling classes, sending reminders, and fielding a constant barrage of registration questions. Strategic planning and innovative course design? Those were luxuries she could barely dream about.

One bleary-eyed evening, while battling a particularly stubborn registration system, Sarah stumbled on an article about marketing automation. Could these tools, designed to streamline marketing campaigns, hold the keys to untangling her L&D workflow? Intrigued, she began studying the world of marketing technology, or *martech*, as it is commonly known. She quickly discovered tools that could automate registration confirmations and personalize communications, and they seemed like the lifeline she needed.

Sarah developed a plan for boosting efficiency and enhancing learner engagement with the help of martech tools. When she got the green light from her leadership team, she quickly implemented new automation solutions and experimented with a number of these tools.

The results were nothing short of transformative. As the time spent on repetitive tasks shrank, Sarah's capacity for strategic planning expanded exponentially. This, in turn, rippled through the organization, affecting:

- **Learner engagement.** Employees received timely, relevant course recommendations, leading to a significant boost in participation rates and completion scores.
- **Data-driven insights.** Analytics from email campaigns offered valuable insights into learner preferences, allowing the L&D team to tailor course content with laser-like precision.
- **Operational efficiency.** Automation of routine tasks freed up the L&D team to focus on high-value activities, such as curriculum development and personalized coaching.
- **Return on investment (ROI) improvement.** The enhanced learning experience translated into measurable improvements in employee performance and retention.

We've found this to be the typical experience when L&D professionals first adopt marketing technology tools. They discover that these tools don't just simplify workflows and free up a little time; they open space for more strategic thinking and content development and ultimately help create more effective learning. In this chapter, we'll share how you can apply martech tools across L&D, specifically focusing on marketing automation and email marketing.

The future of L&D is automated—jump on board!

★ Terms You Should Know

Martech
Martech, or *marketing technology*, is a big toolbox full of software that can help plan, run, and measure a marketing campaign. By using these tools, marketers can automate repetitive tasks, gain insights about their customers, and work smarter, not harder.

Automation for L&D

Automation has revolutionized how marketers work, and it can do the same for L&D. You can use automation tools to say goodbye to repetitive tasks and hello to engaging, personalized learning experiences. You can also leverage data-driven insights to streamline processes and save valuable time for strategic planning, content creation, and effective program analysis. The best way to illustrate the possibilities is with a short case study from Zapier, a software company specializing in automation tools.

An L&D Success Story

In 2022, Zapier's L&D team created a suite of automated workflows to manage administrative tasks, allowing them to focus more on areas in which the personal touch is essential, such as coaching and facilitating. The shift to automation saved more than 1,000 hours of work annually and provided a more consistent, high-quality learning experience.

The L&D team's journey began by identifying a large group of repetitive tasks that could be automated. They compiled a wish list for what they wanted their so-called "L&D robot" to do, which included:
- Create, coordinate, and track live internal workshops.
- Deploy intelligent promotion strategies.
- Enhance the learning experience with prework, recaps, and surveys.

The backbone of their L&D robot was a workflow automation platform that connected various other tools and platforms to create a seamless workflow. For example, the automation software retrieved workshop details from a database, created calendar events, assigned tasks, scheduled reminders, and delivered personalized messages to facilitators and learners. By using automation, Zapier's L&D team was able to:
- Schedule workshops automatically.
- Promote workshops intelligently.
- Enhance learner messaging.

The results couldn't have been better. The new martech tools minimized human error, increased workshop attendance twenty-fold, and ensured timely communication with participants.

The Zapier example demonstrates how automation can revolutionize the way L&D teams approach their work. By automating repetitive tasks and leveraging data-driven insights, we can create more engaging, personalized, and effective learning experiences while saving time and resources. Now, let's examine another real-world story.

Blended Learning Streamlined

A few years ago, Mike led a year-long blended learning project that involved 42 workshops in 40 different cities. There was an enormous amount of data to manage, ranging from registrations to communicating workshop details and directions. Each participant registered via an online form, providing their name, email address, and the date and location of the workshop they wanted to attend. Based on this information, participants were enrolled in online learning courses, as well as an email drip campaign corresponding to their selected workshop's date and location. Mike and his team used several tools—including Survey Gizmo, Zapier, GoTo Meeting, Rise (the LMS), and Google Sheets—to organize the data into a performance dashboard for the workshops.

> ★ **Terms You Should Know**
>
> **Drip Campaign**
> An email *drip campaign* is a series of scheduled messages sent to an email inbox, like a slow drip from a faucet. Each email in the sequence informs, engages, or persuades the recipient about a topic or product. It's a way to stay in touch with people in an automated but somewhat personalized way.

Without the help of automation, Mike's team would have had to spend many hours downloading data, sorting out the relevant fields into three separate spreadsheets, and then manually importing them into the other software. This repetitive process would have involved transferring learner registration data from the registration form to the LMS, email marketing platform, event management system, and reporting dashboard every week. Processing this data would have been a tedious, time-consuming task, especially because they'd have to do it 42 times! It would have consumed hours of valuable time, diverting their attention from more strategic initiatives.

However, with automation, this data transfer happens seamlessly in the background, freeing up the team to focus on creating and delivering exceptional learning experiences.

Fortunately, Mike was able to use Zapier to automate this tedious work (but you could also use other tools, including Make, Automate.io, and Microsoft's Power Automate). Figure 8-1 shows a simple representation of how the system worked.

Figure 8-1. Automation Process for Mike's Multi-City Workshops

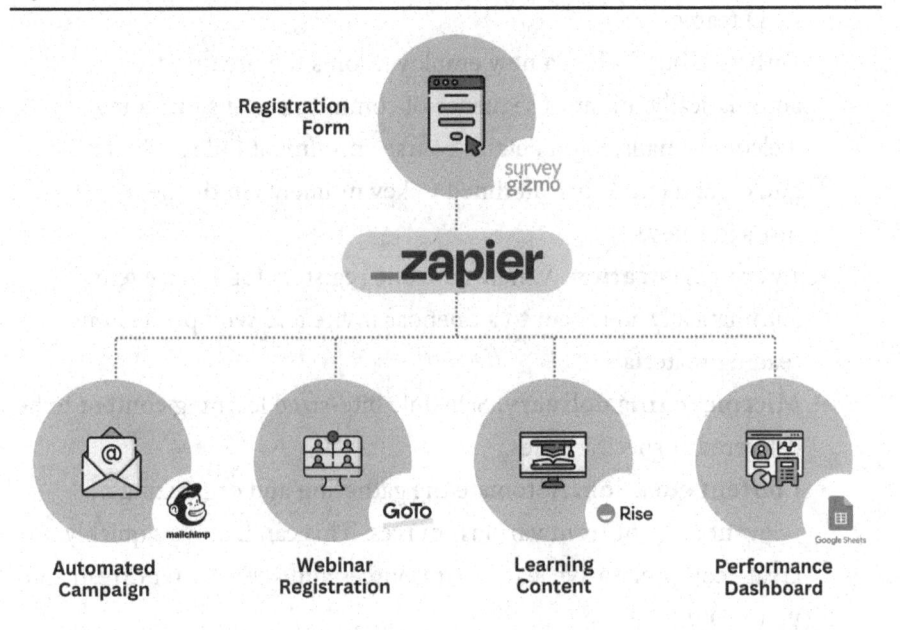

We want to emphasize that Mike was not and is not an automation expert. The automation he created for this project is an example of how you can create personalized solutions, even with limited experience. It's doable for everyone!

Automation can significantly streamline your L&D processes, saving time and resources while providing a more consistent, high-quality learning experience. It is never about replacing the human connection in L&D; it's about allowing you to focus on what truly matters—creating engaging learning experiences and igniting a passion for growth.

In the next section, we'll examine specific ways to apply marketing tools and automation to your own learning initiatives.

Automation to Level Up L&D Initiatives

Here are just a few examples of tasks for which automation can help improve your programs:

- **Triggered enrollments.** Automatically enroll learners in a webinar platform when they register for a specific event. This ensures a seamless experience for learners and reduces manual work for L&D teams.
- **Onboarding.** When a new employee joins the organization, automatically initiate a sequence of communications including welcome emails, login details, course enrollment links, orientation guides, and check-ins, all timed to key moments in the new hire's journey.
- **Event registration.** When someone registers for a live event, automatically add them to a calendar invite and send presession reading materials.
- **Microlearning delivery.** Schedule bite-sized learning content to be delivered at specific times.
- **Content curation.** Automate the gathering and organizing of relevant content from various sources. This can help you quickly create comprehensive learning resources and keep content fresh and up to date.
- **Completion certificates.** Automatically email personalized certificates upon course completion. This small touch can go a long way in recognizing learners' achievements and encouraging further engagement.
- **Content refresh reminders.** Set reminders to review specific learning content based on predefined intervals.

The possibilities for automation in L&D are vast, limited only by your imagination. It allows L&D professionals to save time and focus on important projects, leading to better results for their organizations.

Get Started

Getting started can seem daunting if you're new to marketing automation in L&D. However, five simple steps can help you begin your automation journey with confidence (Figure 8-2).

Figure 8-2. Five Steps to Jumpstart Your L&D Automation

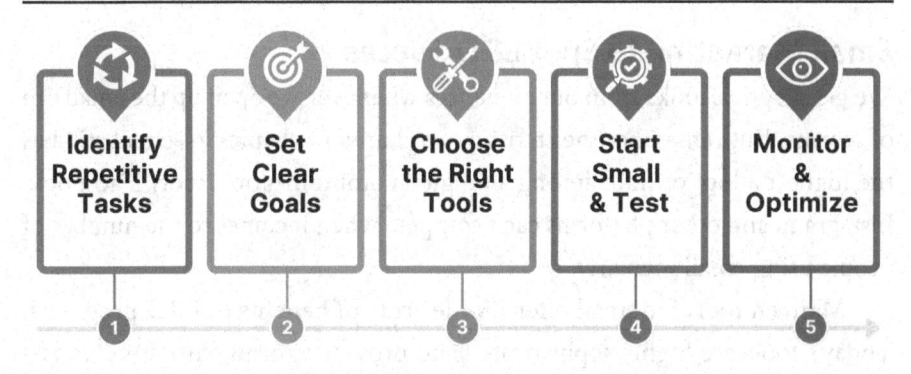

| 1. Identify Repetitive Tasks | 2. Set Clear Goals | 3. Choose the Right Tools | 4. Start Small & Test | 5. Monitor & Optimize |

By following these steps, you'll be well on your way to successfully implementing marketing automation in L&D initiatives:

1. **Identify repetitive tasks.** List all the repetitive, time-consuming tasks in your L&D workflow, such as sending enrollment reminders, distributing feedback surveys, or generating completion certificates. These are prime candidates for automation.
2. **Set clear goals.** Define what you want to achieve with automation. Do you want to increase learner engagement, improve completion rates, or save time on administrative tasks? Having specific goals will guide your automation strategy and help you measure success.
3. **Choose the right tools.** Research and select marketing automation tools that align with your goals, budget, and existing tech stack. Look for platforms that offer a wide range of features, integrations, and user-friendly interfaces.
4. **Start small and test.** Begin by automating one or two simple tasks and testing the results. This will help you gain familiarity with the tools and processes without overwhelming your team. As

you see success, gradually expand your automation efforts to more complex workflows.
5. **Monitor and optimize.** Continuously monitor the performance of your automated workflows and gather feedback from learners and stakeholders. Use these insights to optimize and refine your automation strategy over time.

Email Marketing to Spur L&D Success

We get skeptical looks from our audiences whenever we open up the email can of worms. But remember the statistics we shared in chapter 7—email still has the highest adoption rate among all digital communication tools. Facebook, Instagram, and other platforms can't compete when it comes to the number of people using email regularly.

Martech tools for email offer a wide array of benefits to L&D programs. Today's tools are highly sophisticated and provide valuable insights into engagement, open rates, and click-through rates. This is data that can be used to evaluate the effectiveness of your content and inform data-driven decisions for continuous program improvement.

What Makes Email Marketing Valuable?

Let's consider why we should use email for L&D. First and foremost, email is familiar; most people use it daily. Almost everyone has an email address and knows how to use it, unlike many other communication tools. This means you don't have to worry about special training or a learning curve—and neither will the people you're training. Don't underestimate the importance of the comfort most people feel with using email. In addition, email is accessible on most devices, making it convenient for reviewing learning materials on the go. This flexibility allows for more self-paced learning and empowers learners to control their development.

Email has a secret superpower that other digital tools can't match; it can make your messages seem like they're written just for the reader. Imagine being able to greet each person by name or show different content to different groups—that's what email can do! This is *personalization*, and it's like having a magic wand that turns a mass message into a one-on-one conversation. With simple tricks like merge tags (think of them as fill-in-the-blanks for names or other details) and dynamic content (which changes based on who's reading it), you can make each email feel special. This personal touch makes people more likely to read and engage with your messages. It's like the difference between getting a generic flyer and a letter addressed just to you (Figure 8-3). Which one would you pay more attention to?

Figure 8-3. A Sample Personalized Marketing Email

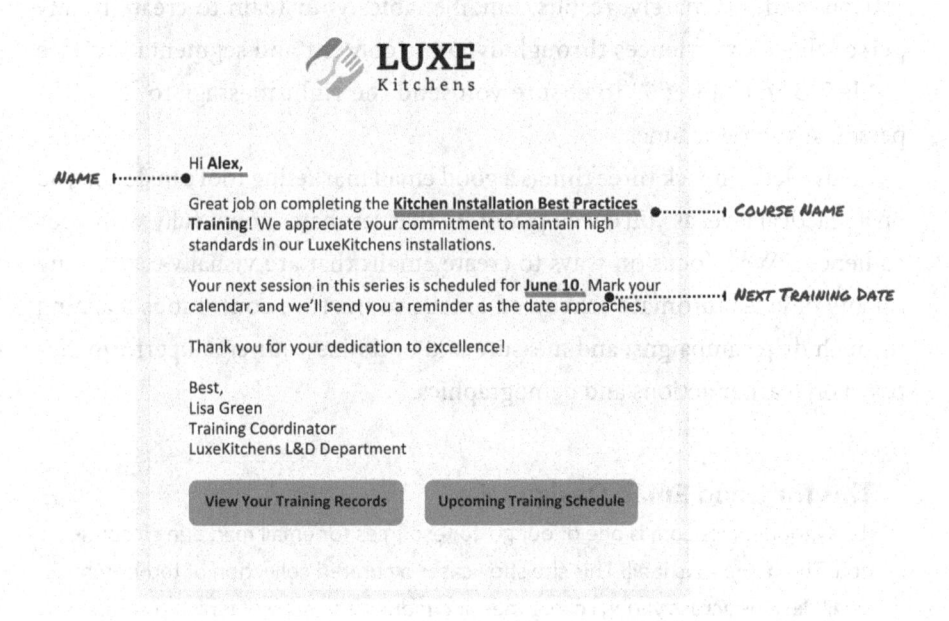

LUXE Kitchens

NAME ··········• Hi **Alex**,

Great job on completing the **Kitchen Installation Best Practices** •··········· COURSE NAME
Training! We appreciate your commitment to maintain high standards in our LuxeKitchens installations.

Your next session in this series is scheduled for **June 10**. Mark your •··········· NEXT TRAINING DATE
calendar, and we'll send you a reminder as the date approaches.

Thank you for your dedication to excellence!

Best,
Lisa Green
Training Coordinator
LuxeKitchens L&D Department

[View Your Training Records] [Upcoming Training Schedule]

Email technology provides L&D professionals a valuable way to gauge learner engagement and make data-driven decisions about content effectiveness. You can embed links to relevant resources or quizzes directly within each email and then monitor who has accessed the content, along with specific details about who clicked each link. You can also determine who in your program hasn't interacted with the content at all. This data provides a clear picture of how (or if) people engage with your learning materials.

Another advantage of using email for learning is its versatility. It can serve a variety of purposes, including delivering training materials, providing updates or reminders, and even conducting surveys and gathering feedback. Email is a valuable tool for both formal training programs and informal learning initiatives.

Reaching larger audiences with minimal effort and cost is another benefit of using email. Unlike hosting traditional classroom training, which requires physical space and resources, you can send an email to multiple recipients at once without any additional expenses.

In short, email marketing tools, which are often undervalued in the L&D world, can become a secret weapon for boosting program visibility, participation, and, ultimately, results. Email enables your team to create highly personalized experiences through dynamic content and segmentation (see Table 7-3 in chapter 7) to ensure you send the right message to the right person at the right time.

Now, let's unpack three things a good email marketing tool can do for you on a practical level as you develop content that resonates powerfully with your audiences. We'll focus on ways to create emails that are visually captivating on any device, automate scheduled emails to nurture continuous learning through drip campaigns, and measure and optimize your email performance based on learner actions and demographics.

Tips for Good Email Design

Reallygoodemails.com is one of our go-to resources for email marketing inspiration. The name says it all! This site showcases a curated collection of top-notch email designs across various categories and industries, many of which you can easily adapt to your specific L&D needs. It also offers easy search and filter options, highlights best practices, and provides educational content. It's an invaluable tool for L&D pros who want to enhance their email campaigns.

Another tool we've found useful is Email Love (emaillove.com), which curates a collection of beautiful and effective email designs from various industries. It's a great resource for understanding how successful companies use layout, color, imagery, and typography to create engaging email experiences.

How to Create Visually Captivating Emails

As you learned in chapter 5, the first impression of your content matters a lot. A captivating email design can be the difference between a click and a delete in a crowded inbox. If you've ever tried to cobble together a visually appealing email within Outlook or Gmail, you'll appreciate the design capabilities of email marketing tools, which offer a wide range of design templates and customization options. These tools make it easy for even nondesigners to craft beautiful and professional-looking emails with drag-and-drop tools, custom colors, fonts, and built-in image editing.

Compare the two emails in Figure 8-4. Both are asking for feedback on a recent training event. Which one is likely to get more responses?

Figure 8-4. Two Versions of the Same Email Request

In addition to aesthetic appeal, effective email design includes mobile responsiveness as well as the hallmarks of good writing we've already discussed—clear and concise messaging and a strong CTA. These factors can significantly affect the success of an email campaign by increasing open rates, click-through rates, and, ultimately, organizational performance. Ensuring mobile responsiveness is especially crucial because more than 60 percent of email recipients access their emails on mobile devices.

How to Automate and Personalize Emails

With a little automation, you can unlock the potential of scheduling personalized emails based on enrollment, completion, and important learning milestones to ensure learners stay on the right path. There are three important ways to use email marketing tools for your L&D programs—scheduled campaigns, drip campaigns, and adaptive campaigns—and we'll discuss the value of each now.

Scheduled Campaigns

Scheduled campaigns operate on a set timetable, like setting an alarm for your educational content. You decide when learners receive new material, whether it's for upcoming training sessions, webinars, or course enrollment deadlines. This approach is perfect for ensuring that learning opportunities are timely and align with broader educational goals or organizational milestones. It's an effective way to keep learners informed and engaged with regular updates.

Notice that the scheduled email reminder in Figure 8-5 is visually appealing with a clean, professional design featuring a high-quality image of a luxury kitchen. As with all good emails, it is personalized and addresses the recipient by name ("Hey Alex"), which helps to capture attention and create a more engaging experience. Additionally, the message includes a clear CTA with a prominent "register now" button, allowing readers to take immediate action directly from the email. This combination of visual appeal, personalization, and an easy-to-use CTA button makes the email both attractive and effective in driving engagement.

Drip and Adaptive Campaigns

Email drip campaigns gradually send or "drip" content to learners over time, similar to watering plants in measured amounts. Content is released incrementally based on predefined schedules or specific triggers, which might include a learner completing a module, expressing interest in a topic, or reaching a particular milestone. Drip campaigns support continuous learning by providing relevant information when the learner is most likely to need it, which helps to progressively reinforce knowledge and skills.

Figure 8-5. A Scheduled Email Reminder for an Upcoming Training Event at LuxeKitchens

![Email reminder showing Subject: Join Our Exclusive Viking 7 Series Webinar, with a LuxeKitchens branded image of a luxury kitchen stove]

Hey Alex,

Be part of a luxury kitchen revolution with the new **Viking 7 Series Range**. This exclusive webinar will turn you into a sales pro.

- **Key Features:** Learn about its self-cleaning system and precision cooking modes.
- **Expert sales tips:** Connect with clients' culinary dreams.
- **Exclusive strategies:** Stand out in the high-end market.
- **Live Q&A with specialists:** Get insights and answers.

Don't miss out! **Monday, March 18 at 9am Eastern**

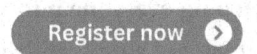

Register now ▶

P.S. Explore the Viking 7 Series range on our website.

Alex Kendricks,
VP of Sales Development

Unsubscribe

For example, imagine that LuxeKitchens is about to add a new oven to their product catalog. To ensure a smooth rollout and prepare their sales team, they could create a targeted drip campaign leading up to and following the launch date. The campaign might look like the one in Figure 8-6.

Figure 8-6. LuxeKitchens' New Product Email Drip Campaign

Drip Campaign
Triggered relative to new product launch date

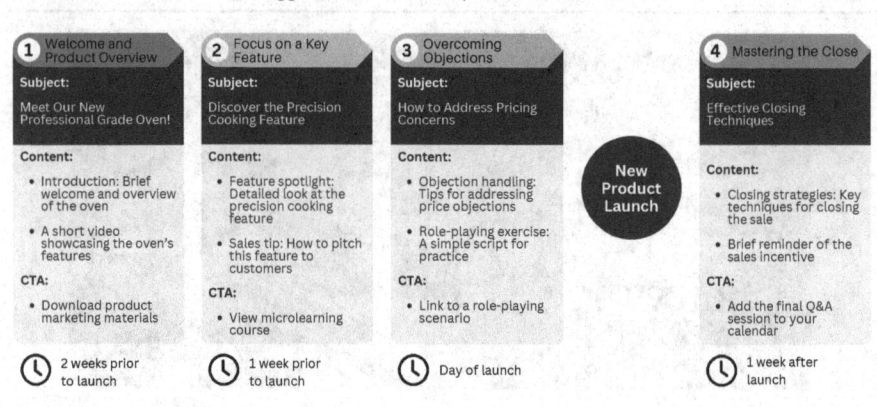

1. Welcome and Product Overview
Subject: Meet Our New Professional Grade Oven!
Content:
- Introduction: Brief welcome and overview of the oven
- A short video showcasing the oven's features

CTA:
- Download product marketing materials

⏱ 2 weeks prior to launch

2. Focus on a Key Feature
Subject: Discover the Precision Cooking Feature
Content:
- Feature spotlight: Detailed look at the precision cooking feature
- Sales tip: How to pitch this feature to customers

CTA:
- View microlearning course

⏱ 1 week prior to launch

3. Overcoming Objections
Subject: How to Address Pricing Concerns
Content:
- Objection handling: Tips for addressing price objections
- Role-playing exercise: A simple script for practice

CTA:
- Link to a role-playing scenario

⏱ Day of launch

New Product Launch

4. Mastering the Close
Subject: Effective Closing Techniques
Content:
- Closing strategies: Key techniques for closing the sale
- Brief reminder of the sales incentive

CTA:
- Add the final Q&A session to your calendar

⏱ 1 week after launch

This automated email series would be delivered to the LuxeKitchens sales team at pre-determined intervals. Each email would contain crucial information and resources related to the new oven, ensuring the team is fully equipped for successful sales efforts from day one.

The beauty of this approach is its versatility. The same email cadence can be adapted easily for future product launches. LuxeKitchens can create separate drip campaigns with tailored content to target different audience segments, like the installation team, keeping everyone informed and prepared.

Adaptive campaigns, which are a type of drip campaign, offer personalized learning experiences tailored to an individual's actions, preferences, and performance. These campaigns use data analytics (and may also use AI) to adjust the learning content, pace, and complexity in real time based on the learner's interactions and progress. This strategy ensures that each learner receives a customized learning path that addresses their unique needs and goals, maximizing engagement and effectiveness by catering directly to their learning journey.

Now, imagine that the LuxeKitchens training team wants to use email automation to deliver targeted content based on each installer's level of engagement. In Figure 8-7, you'll see a simple example of what that might look like, with each email containing content based on the recipient's previous interactions.

Figure 8-7. An Adaptive Email Campaign at LuxeKitchens

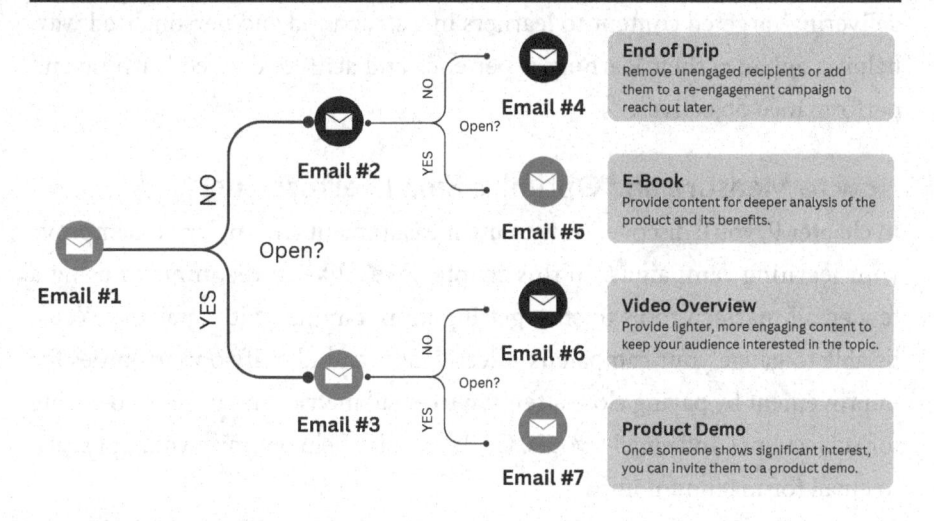

```
Email #1 ──YES──> Email #2 (Open?)
         │              ├──YES──> Email #4 ──NO──> End of Drip
         NO             │                           Remove unengaged recipients or add
         │              │                           them to a re-engagement campaign to
         │              │                           reach out later.
         │              └──YES──> Email #5 ──> E-Book
         │                                      Provide content for deeper analysis of the
         │                                      product and its benefits.
         └──YES──> Email #3 (Open?)
                        ├──NO──> Email #6 ──> Video Overview
                        │                      Provide lighter, more engaging content to
                        │                      keep your audience interested in the topic.
                        └──YES──> Email #7 ──> Product Demo
                                                Once someone shows significant interest,
                                                you can invite them to a product demo.
```

Initially, all installers would receive an email introducing the oven, highlighting upcoming training sessions, and showcasing features with a video. The email platform would then track whether installers open the email. At the end of the campaign, segments of installers would receive content based on their interactions with each email they received. For example, highly engaged installers who opened all three emails in the sequence would be invited to an in-depth product demo. Less engaged installers who didn't open any of the emails could be removed from future mailings or, better yet, moved into a re-engagement campaign with a new hook, emphasizing the importance of training and a registration incentive. This dynamic approach would ensure that all installers get the information they need. Highly engaged installers would get access to more in-depth resources, while those who needed a nudge would receive a reminder with an additional incentive.

Whether you choose the structured timing of scheduled campaigns, the gradual engagement of drip campaigns, or the personalized touch of adaptive campaigns, each strategy offers unique benefits for a learning program. Your selection should match your goals, learner requirements, and the context of your learning programs. Note: Email campaigns often serve as elements within larger learning initiatives, which themselves are part of an organization's overall L&D strategy.

In L&D, we have found that drip campaigns are especially valuable for delivering targeted content to learners in a structured and personalized way, helping enhance their learning experience and achieve desired learning and performance objectives.

How to Measure and Optimize Email Performance

In chapter 9, you'll discover how to use measurement and analytics to improve your learning campaigns. In this chapter, we'd like to recommend using a few email martech tools to start getting more familiar with analytics. You'll be able to gauge your campaigns' effectiveness and identify opportunities for improvement by paying close attention to email metrics and using A/B testing for subject lines and email layouts. CTAs can also help optimize your approach to email for maximum impact.

Email Metrics

Tracking key email metrics such as open rates, click-through rates, and unsubscribe rates is vital for assessing the effectiveness of your L&D campaigns. Specifically, you'll need to track these metrics:

- **Open rates** show the percentage of recipients who opened your email. High open rates indicate your subject lines are compelling and relevant to your audience. If your emails have low open rates, you should make your subject lines more engaging or review the timing of your emails.
- **The click-through rate (CTR)** measures the percentage of email recipients who clicked on one or more links within an email. This metric is crucial for understanding how engaging your email content is and whether it motivates recipients to take action, such as enrolling in a course or accessing learning materials. If the CTR is low, consider improving the content's relevance, CTA clarity, or the overall design of your emails to make them more appealing.
- **Unsubscribe rates** tell you how many people opt out of your mailing list after receiving an email. Monitor unsubscribe rates to identify opportunities to improve your emails. A low unsubscribe rate indicates you're delivering relevant and valuable content.

As we noted in chapter 7, it's important to respect those in your organization and never flood their inboxes.

Overall, email metrics can help you unlock better campaign performance, engagement, audience preferences, and send times, fueling smarter strategies in the long run. By closely monitoring these metrics, you can gain valuable insights into how well your email campaigns resonate with your audience. Use this feedback loop to continuously improve your email strategies, ensuring that your learning initiatives are effective, engaging, and valuable to your recipients. Adjusting your campaigns based on these insights can lead to higher engagement, better learning outcomes, and more successful L&D initiatives.

A/B Testing

We touched on the value of A/B tests for content such as headlines in chapter 5. Now we'll look at how to make those tests a little easier using marketing tools. Remember that in an A/B test you create two versions of something (such as an email, a website layout, or a social media post) and show them to different groups of people. Then, you monitor which version performs better based on your goals (more clicks or more sign-ups, for example). Figure 8-8 shows an A/B test for a LuxeKitchens training email.

Figure 8-8. A/B Testing an Email for LuxeKitchens Training

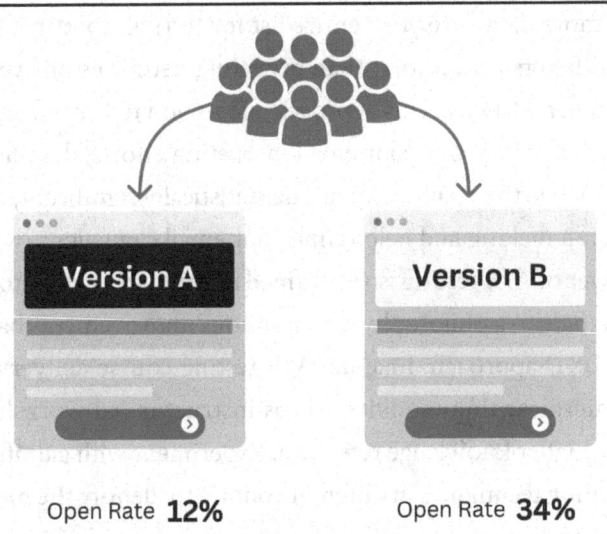

Version A — Open Rate **12%**

Version B — Open Rate **34%**

Email marketing platforms help you run A/B tests by splitting your subscriber list into segments. The steps would look something like this:
1. **Pick your test.** Decide what element you want to test—subject lines, CTA buttons, or email content, for instance.
2. **Segment your list.** The platform randomly divides your list into groups (A and B).
3. **Variation delivery.** Each group receives an email with a different version of the element you're testing.
4. **Track and analyze.** The platform monitors which version gets more opens, clicks, or conversions.
5. **Winner declared.** The platform identifies the most effective version based on results.

By testing variations of your content with A/B testing, you can gather data to make smarter choices and improve learner engagement, course registrations, or materials such as videos and online courses.

One note about doing A/B testing: This kind of testing typically requires larger email lists to achieve statistically significant results, with many experts recommending at least 1,000 contacts per variant. However, you can still benefit if you've got a smaller list. Even with fewer than 1,000 subscribers, A/B testing can still provide valuable insights to guide your email strategy. To make the most of a limited audience, consider running tests over longer periods to accumulate more data. Use your entire list for testing, splitting it evenly between A and B versions. Rather than expecting definitive answers, focus on identifying general trends. This approach allows you to learn from your audience and gradually improve your email marketing efforts, despite the smaller sample size. While the results may not be statistically significant, they can still inform decision making and help refine your email campaigns over time.

The power of A/B testing isn't confined to email marketing tools. Instead, view it as a *mindset*—a philosophy of continuous improvement that permeates your entire L&D approach. Imagine A/B testing course delivery methods—like using microlearning modules versus instructor-led workshops—to see which drives higher knowledge retention. Experiment with gamified elements or social learning techniques in different cohorts to identify the most engaging format. You can even A/B test different assessment methods to ensure they accurately gauge competency development.

By embracing this data-driven approach, you move beyond assumptions and be empowered to make informed decisions, constantly iterating and refining your L&D programs to deliver the most effective learning experiences possible. Remember, A/B testing isn't just about email clicks; it's about unlocking the true potential of learning through the power of experimentation and data-driven insights.

The key to successful A/B testing is setting clear goals for each experiment (such as higher open rates, increased course registrations, or more views of a video). Segmenting your audience whenever possible allows you to tailor messages to specific needs and preferences. Analyzing results is valuable for gleaning insights and using them to refine your future campaigns iteratively. Start small, experiment, and apply what you learn to your L&D efforts.

More Martech Worth Considering

While automation and email marketing tools are powerful upgrades for L&D professionals, the martech landscape offers a wide range of other tools that can help create engaging, personalized learning experiences. There are thousands of martech tools out there, but we like leveraging these six in an L&D context.

Incorporating these additional martech tools into your L&D strategy can help create more engaging, personalized, and data-driven learning experiences. By exploring the full range of martech possibilities, you can stay at the forefront of L&D innovation and drive better outcomes for your learners and organization.

Interactive, Personalized Video

Interactive video platforms allow you to create dynamic, personalized content that adapts to learner input and behavior. By incorporating interactive elements like quizzes, branching scenarios, and clickable hotspots, you can create immersive learning experiences that drive engagement and retention. Tools like Mindstamp, Vimeo, and Stornaway.io enable L&D professionals to transform passive videos into active learning opportunities.

Landing Pages

Landing pages are single web pages designed to convert visitors into leads or customers. In an L&D context, they can be used to promote specific courses, workshops, or learning resources. Creating targeted, visually appealing landing pages can capture learner interest, drive registrations, and gather valuable data on learner preferences and behaviors. Although most email marketing automation tools have landing page functionality built in, tools like Lu.ma, Unbounce, and Leadpages offer more sophisticated options and simplify the process of creating and optimizing these pages for maximum impact.

Marketing Webinar Platforms

Webinar platforms designed for marketing purposes offer a range of features that can enhance L&D webinars, such as customization of the webinar interface, integrated registration forms, detailed analytics on attendee behavior, and automated webinar sequences, including prerecorded webinars that simulate live experiences. Leveraging tools like Demio, LiveStorm, or BigMarker can create engaging, interactive learning experiences that foster collaboration and knowledge sharing among remote learners.

Sales Enablement Platforms

Sales enablement platforms help sales teams access, share, and use content that supports the selling process. In an L&D context, these platforms can be used to curate and distribute learning content, reinforce training, and provide performance support; some even have dedicated training functionality. Tools like Seismic, Highspot, Trumpet, and Journey.io enable L&D teams to create centralized content hubs, track content usage and effectiveness, and deliver just-in-time learning.

Data and Analytics

Data and analytics tools help organizations collect, analyze, and visualize data to gain insights and make data-driven decisions. In L&D, these tools can help you evaluate training effectiveness and improve the quality of your content. By leveraging tools like Google Analytics, Tableau, or Looker, L&D teams can better understand learner behavior, optimize learning programs, and demonstrate the ROI of L&D initiatives to stakeholders. We'll discuss Google Analytics and Tableau in more detail in chapter 9.

Generative AI Technology and L&D

AI is rapidly transforming many industries, and L&D is no exception. This powerful technology offers exciting opportunities to create more engaging learning experiences. Let's explore how AI can empower L&D professionals:

- **Beat creative blocks.** AI tools like ChatGPT can suggest topics, prompts, and examples to help you overcome writer's block. Imagine generating a list of potential e-learning course topics based on keywords. This helps identify gaps and spark innovation.
- **Repurpose content with ease.** AI can analyze existing content and adapt it for different formats or audiences. Think about automatically creating summaries, key takeaways, and quizzes from long-form articles.
- **Create learning strategies.** AI tools can customize learning strategies by adapting content to your learners and their environment. They can simplify complex topics and automate feedback, making learning more effective and engaging.
- **Craft compelling learning materials.** AI writing assistants like Jasper.ai and Grammarly can help create more engaging course descriptions and content. These tools offer suggestions and optimize for clarity and impact, ensuring your content aligns with learning objectives.
- **Visualize learning with AI.** AI-generated images and graphics, like those from DALL-E or Midjourney, can enhance learning content. Simply describe the image you need, and AI can create a custom graphic or infographics. As you've seen, we've used these tools to create some of the images in this book.

Remember, AI is a partner, not a replacement. As Irina Nica from HubSpot says, "AI lets us offload repetitive tasks, freeing us for more strategic work." The collaboration between AI and human expertise paves the way for a future of personalized, efficient, and effective learning.

Ready to engage with AI tools? Here's your action plan:
1. **Identify repetitive tasks** that AI tools can automate.
2. **Experiment with AI content creation tools** to generate ideas and draft content.
3. **Explore AI-generated visuals** to enhance your learning materials.
4. **Analyze data** to tailor learning strategies for individual and organizational goals.
5. **Stay informed** by following industry experts and attending relevant events on AI in L&D.

This approach allows you to leverage AI's power while maintaining the human touch that is essential for effective learning. Check out the recommended resources in this book for more information about AI-powered learning and education, as well as a list of experts we recommend following.

Get Started With Email Marketing in L&D

Now that you understand the power of email marketing for L&D, it's time to get started. Here's a step-by-step guide to help you begin your email marketing journey. You'll notice many of these steps are familiar because they align with the steps for developing an effective learner journey and learning campaign.

1. Define Your Goals

Clearly outline what you want to achieve with your email marketing efforts. Do you want to increase course registrations, improve learner engagement, or boost completion rates? Specific, measurable goals will guide your strategy and help you track progress.

2. Choose an Email Marketing Platform

Select a tool that aligns with your needs and budget. Consider factors like ease of use, automation capabilities, design options, and integration with your existing L&D tech stack. For those just getting started, we like MailerLite for their robust, full-featured free plan for up to 1,000 subscribers and ConvertKit, which has a generous free plan for up to 10,000 subscribers.

3. Build Your Email List

Start collecting email addresses from your learners. You can gather this information through course registration forms, surveys, or by offering valuable content in exchange for their contact details. Remember to obtain explicit permission and provide an easy way for learners to unsubscribe.

4. Segment Your Audience

Divide your email list into smaller groups based on common characteristics, such as job role, department, learning preferences, or past course completions. This will allow you to create targeted, relevant content for each segment.

5. Plan Your Email Campaigns

Develop a content calendar outlining the types of emails you'll send, their frequency, and the key messages you want to convey. Consider a mix of promotional emails (course announcements), educational content (tips and resources), and engagement emails (surveys or quizzes).

6. Design Your Emails

Use your chosen email marketing platform to create visually appealing, mobile-responsive templates that align with your brand guidelines. Keep the layout clean, concise, and easy to navigate. Use images, videos, and interactive elements to make your emails more engaging.

7. Test and Refine

Before sending an email to your entire list, conduct thorough testing to ensure the message displays correctly across different devices and email clients. Send test emails to yourself and your colleagues to proofread the content and check for broken links or formatting issues.

8. Monitor and Analyze Performance

Once your email campaigns are up and running, regularly track key metrics like open rates, click-through rates, and unsubscribe rates. Use this data to identify areas for improvement and optimize your future campaigns.

9. Continuously Improve

Embrace a culture of experimentation and continuous improvement. Regularly conduct A/B tests to refine your email content, subject lines, and CTAs. Stay updated on the latest email marketing trends and best practices, and don't be afraid to try new approaches to keep your learners engaged.

☆ ☆ ☆

By working through these steps, you'll be well on your way to leveraging the power of email marketing to enhance L&D initiatives and drive better learning outcomes.

> **Email Marketing for L&D: A Checklist**
> - ✓ Assess your current email communication with learners. Are you leveraging the full potential of email to engage, inform, and motivate your audience?
> - ✓ Identify one area where email marketing could enhance your L&D initiatives. It could be onboarding, course promotions, or post-training reinforcement.
> - ✓ Select an email marketing platform and start building your email list. Begin with a small pilot campaign to test the waters and gain valuable insights.
> - ✓ Experiment, analyze, and refine your approach based on data-driven insights. Continuously seek ways to improve your email marketing efforts to deliver the most effective learning experiences possible.

Remember, the key to success with email marketing in L&D is to focus on providing value to your learners. The learner personas we discussed in chapter 2 can guide you in understanding what your audience truly cares about. By consistently delivering relevant, engaging content that addresses their needs and preferences, you'll foster a culture of continuous learning and drive meaningful results for your organization.

Data Protection and Privacy in Internal Email Marketing Campaigns

Even for internal email marketing campaigns, organizations should prioritize data protection and privacy. While regulations like GDPR and CAN-SPAM may apply less strictly to internal communications, it's crucial to maintain ethical practices. This includes having a lawful basis for data processing, minimizing data collection, ensuring transparency, providing opt-out options, and securing employee information. By treating internal campaigns with the same level of care as external ones, companies can maintain trust, comply with regulations, and create a culture of respect for privacy—all while effectively delivering learning content to employees.

Going Forward With L&D Tech

We've explored the amazing potential of marketing technologies for L&D; now, it's time to put these ideas into practice. Here are three simple, practical tips to get you started:

- **Collaborate with marketing.** If you have a marketing team, they are a goldmine of knowledge and tools for creating engaging content. Connect with them and tap into their expertise and resources to level up your training programs.
- **Start small and scale up.** The world of martech is vast and complex, but don't let that overwhelm you. Begin with tools that offer free trials or low-cost plans. You can test what works best for your organization's L&D needs before investing more time and money later.
- **Keep learning and innovating.** The digital landscape is constantly changing, with new tools and technologies popping up every day. Set aside some time to read about and explore new options. By staying ahead of the curve, your training programs will remain relevant and effective.

We also suggest consulting two resources as you begin:

- **StackRadar** is your friendly neighborhood martech guide. It breaks down marketing tools in simple terms—showing you what's out

there and how they stack up—it's perfect for when you're figuring out which tools you need.
- **Chief Marketing Technologist (Chiefmartec).** This blog, written by Scott Brinker, is Martech 101. It's known for its yearly map of marketing tools (Spoiler: There are a lot!) and for explaining trends and strategies in a way that won't make your head spin.

You don't need to be a tech expert or completely change your approach to workflows to start using martech in your L&D programs. It's all about making smart, informed decisions to create engaging learning experiences.

A Final Thought

The world of marketing technology offers a wealth of opportunities for L&D professionals to enhance their training programs. By embracing tools like the ones discussed in this chapter, L&D teams can create more engaging, personalized, and effective learning experiences. As the digital landscape continues to evolve, L&D professionals who harness the power of marketing technology will be well-positioned to deliver dynamic, effective learning experiences that drive organizational success. Remember, as tech entrepreneur Matt Blumberg once said, "Reaching the inbox isn't your goal—engaging people is."

Activity 8-1. Start Your Automation Journey Here

Objective
Now that you understand the power of automation in L&D, it's time to take action. To begin your automation adventures, start with these three tasks.

Steps
1. **Conduct an automation audit.** Review your current L&D workflows and identify areas where automation can be applied. Make a list of repetitive tasks that could be streamlined with automation tools. Some of the most common tasks that work well if automated include course enrollment and registration processes, certificate generation, and email notifications for learning-related activities (such as registration, due dates, and event reminders). These tasks are repetitive, data-driven, and often involve multiple steps, making them ideal for automation.
2. **Explore automation tools.** Research marketing automation platforms and tools that align with your needs and budget. Take advantage of free trials or demos to get a hands-on feel for how these tools can support your L&D initiatives. One of the best ways to begin this research is to create a comprehensive list of your current tools and systems, and then search for compatible automation platforms. Understanding your existing tech stack is crucial for finding automation tools that integrate well. Zapier, for instance, supports thousands of apps, so knowing your current tools helps narrow down the most suitable options.
3. **Engage stakeholders.** Start conversations with key stakeholders—including teams in IT, HR, and department heads—about the potential of incorporating automation in L&D. Share the insights you've gained from this chapter and discuss how automation can support overall business goals and drive learning outcomes. In your conversations, be sure to note the potential time and cost savings of automation, and make sure to back them up with concrete examples and metrics. Stakeholders are often most interested in the bottom line. Providing clear, quantifiable benefits helps make a strong case for automation.

Activity 8-2. Automation Audit Worksheet

Objective
Use this worksheet to get started on your automation journey.

Steps
1. **Identify repetitive tasks.** List three to five repetitive, time-consuming tasks in your L&D workflow.
2. **Set clear goals.** What do you want to achieve with automation? List two to three specific goals.
3. **Choose the right tools.** Research and list three potential marketing automation tools that align with your goals and budget.

Tool	Key Features	Price Range

4. **Start small and test.** Choose one to two simple tasks from step 1 to automate first.
5. **Monitor and optimize.** Define how you'll measure success for each automated task.

Automated Task	Success Metric	Review Frequency

Action Plan
Identify your next three steps for implementing marketing automation in your L&D initiatives.

Activity 8-3. Improve Your L&D Email Subject Lines

Objective
Improve the effectiveness of your L&D email communications by analyzing and optimizing recent subject lines, ideally from your onboarding program (or the program you have been using for all activities throughout this book).

Steps
1. **Look through your sent L&D emails from the past month.** Choose three important emails with different purposes (for example, a course announcement, a reminder, or resource sharing). Write down the subject lines used for these emails.
2. **Analyze subject lines.** Input each subject line into a subject line analyzer tool and record the scores and key feedback for each. We like using these programs:
   - Coschedule
   - SendCheckIt
   - SubjectLine
3. **Brainstorm new versions.** For each original subject line, brainstorm five new versions. Try to incorporate variety (such as personalization, questions, urgency, and benefits). Aim to address any weaknesses identified by the analyzer tool.
4. **Test and optimize.** Input your new subject lines into the analyzer tool and record scores for each new version. Identify the highest-scoring version for each original subject line.
5. **Reflect and plan for action.** Compare your highest-scoring new subject lines with the originals. Note any patterns or insights you've gained about what makes an effective subject line. Write down two to three specific strategies you'll apply to future L&D email subject lines.

Optional Extension
If time allows, create a simple A/B test using an email marketing tool for your next L&D email. Use your original subject line and your new, highest-scoring version and watch the results unfold.

Activity 8-4. Do Your Own A/B Testing

Objective
Conduct A/B tests using an email marketing platform to optimize L&D email communications and make data-driven improvements.

Steps
Choose from these items to run an A/B test. (Pick one or try them all!)

1. **CTA optimization.** Don't settle for a bland "Enroll Now." Test a more descriptive CTA highlighting the value proposition, like, "Explore the Course and Boost Your Skills." See which one compels learners to click to gain valuable clues about what motivates them to take the next step.
2. **Content format exploration.** Cater to diverse preferences. Experiment with a plain text email that delivers concise information versus a visually rich email packed with images and infographics. Track which format grabs attention better and use that information to shape future content creation choices.
3. **Personalization power.** A/B test an email personalized with the learner's name and department against a generic one. Gauge how personalization influences open rates and engagement. Based on the data, determine if it's worth the extra effort for your audience.
4. **Timing tune-up.** Send emails at different times of the day or week to see when learners are most receptive. Discover the optimal sending window to maximize open rates and engagement, aligning your communication with their natural rhythms.

Chapter 9
Measure the Impact of Your Efforts

> Without data, you're just another person with an opinion.
> —W. Edwards Deming, engineer, statistician, and writer

Think of the last time you ate at a restaurant. Was it one of those places with just five carefully curated items on the menu? If so, it was probably easy to decide what to go for. Or was it an establishment with 50 items on the menu plus six daily specials? In that case, you probably found it challenging to figure out what tickled your fancy. Either way, if you loved what you ate, you probably told some friends about the place and maybe even posted a review online.

Now, consider this question, inspired by a discussion by James Clear in *Atomic Habits*: Would you be inclined to leave a more positive review for the restaurant with more dishes or the one with fewer items on the menu? Or would your review depend entirely on the quality of the dishes you ate? We think it's much more likely that your review would be based on the quality of the food and how satisfied you felt afterward, don't you?

When measuring learning impact, many organizations focus on the number of learners who completed a certain amount of training instead of their engagement, satisfaction, and behavior change. This is as nonsensical as evaluating a restaurant based only on the number of dishes. In L&D,

we need to shift our focus to measures that will help us understand and demonstrate how effective our training is and how our efforts affect learners and organizations.

This is yet another case in which we can learn by thinking more like marketers because they understand and use measurement to their advantage. In marketing, measurement examines how effective specific efforts are over time and explores their results. In short, when measuring effectiveness, marketers ask basic questions, including "What's working and what isn't?" and "Where should we spend more (or less) money?"

The first steps in measuring anything are:
1. Setting clear goals
2. Segmenting the audience
3. Collaboratively laying out the customer journey
4. Breaking the customer journey into smaller campaigns

If these steps sound familiar, it's because they summarize everything we've walked you through in this book so far. Along the way, marketers also identify which data to track and measure and when to make necessary adjustments. In this chapter, we'll explore the data marketers use to measure the effectiveness of their content and, in turn, the results for the organization. We will borrow some of those approaches and talk about how we can augment data and analytics in L&D.

How Marketers Think About Measurement

Measurement helps marketers plan future strategies and optimize what they do to improve results. Most marketers know that data matters. A reported 58 percent want to work on their data analysis skills, 57 percent want to learn about new technology solutions and platforms, 54 percent want to become better at visualizing data, and half want to be more proficient in building the dashboards they use to understand their data better (Funnel 2023).

Traditional marketing models focus on offline marketing efforts, but today online and offline strategies coexist, which creates new challenges. Marketers must now look at data from multiple sources and then aggregate it into a meaningful measurement plan. Not long ago, marketers coined the term *unified marketing measures* (*UMM*) to describe the task of combining online and offline measures into a single plan.

Despite knowing the importance of measurement, many marketers still struggle with data and metrics. A 2023 Funnel survey found that 50 percent worried about the quality of their data, 35 percent were concerned about adequately compiling data, and 34 percent relied on nonmarketing data gatherers or analysts (employees with data knowledge and skills who work outside the marketing department). The survey also found that marketers weren't taking advantage of automation. Some 64 percent said they didn't automate populating data reports or dashboards, 59 percent saw an opportunity to improve how they visualized data, 54 percent didn't automate the cleaning of their data, and 44 percent struggled to collect data from multiple sources. And a surprising 34 percent of marketers didn't know how to share data with their teams.

Does all this seem familiar? We bet it does. As L&D professionals, we face some of the same challenges and uncertainty.

L&D's Approach to Measurement

In spite of all the challenges, most marketers are excited about using data to improve their work; unfortunately, many L&D teams aren't quite there yet. A survey found that only about one in four organizations have L&D departments that know how to effectively use data from their training programs. L&D teams have access to a lot of data but struggle to analyze it and use it to make their training better or prove its value (Baska et al. 2019; Chaston 2015). It's like having a powerful luxury car but not knowing how to drive it.

L&D professionals lag behind marketers when it comes to measuring and using data. We often rely on an LMS as our only source of data, even though our modern learning experiences venture beyond the e-learning and instructor-led sessions administered through an LMS. Our dependence on LMS-based data hampers our ability to measure the impact of multi-layered learning campaigns consisting of deliverables that sit outside the LMS. As a result, we don't have a true picture of the effectiveness of our programs and cannot tie the impact back to organizational goals.

The good news is that we don't need new, expensive marketing platforms that feed many attribution models into one overarching platform for the best outcomes (although we wouldn't say no to those!). Rather, we suggest leveraging the marketers' idea of *unified measurement* in our learning designs as much as possible and broadening our thinking about how and what we measure.

A Few Essential Terms

Data, metrics, and KPIs are all terms commonly used in both marketing and L&D. Although often used interchangeably, each term has a distinct meaning. *Data* refers to the raw numbers marketers collect from a variety of sources, including websites, social media platforms, and email campaigns. We can find a lot of important data, for example, on our LMS or LXP, and through social media. However, all this data is meaningless without context and interpretation.

Metrics, on the other hand, are quantitative measurements, derived from the data, that help marketers make sense of it. Metrics help marketers understand how well their marketing campaigns are performing. The same holds for metrics in L&D. We start with data from our LMS or LXP, or other data sources, and then start asking if the data tells us that the training has met our goals.

Key performance indicators are specific metrics marketers use to track the progress of particular parameters over time. KPIs may include one or more metrics. They are strategic, reflecting the overall success of a campaign and its influence on the business. Examples of KPIs include revenue growth, profit margins, and customer satisfaction. They help marketers make informed decisions. For L&D professionals, KPIs might include how much each sales consultant has increased their sales numbers or improved their customer service skills in the three months following a training course. Both metrics have a direct influence on the overall business. In short, all KPIs are metrics, but not all metrics are KPIs. This means that metrics are like the building blocks of KPIs. KPIs are essential for measuring the overall success of any marketing campaign and are usually summarized in reports that visualize their success (Rennell 2021).

> ### ⭐ Terms You Should Know
>
> **Data, Metrics, and KPIs**
> *Data* is a collection of facts and figures from various sources, including organization websites, LMSs, LXPs, and social media. Data always needs context to become meaningful. *Metrics* are groups of data points that help track the performance of a process or activity in the context of the organization's goals. In the L&D environment, we would consider employee satisfaction with training or a higher rate of successful interactions with customers to be positive metrics. *KPIs* are a set of metrics that help us monitor progress in achieving business goals. A monthly rate of growth in sales can be a KPI for both marketers and L&D pros.

Benefits of Measuring L&D's Impact

The marketer's motto could be, in the words of British mathematician Lord Kelvin, "If you cannot measure it, you cannot improve it." Learning designers certainly could benefit from this way of thinking.

By measuring their effectiveness, marketers gain efficiency and cost savings, and more easily convert leads into sales. If L&D professionals focus on becoming more data literate and measure the impact of their work, they will reap similar rewards. Let's consider the most valuable benefits of establishing good measurement practices.

Goal Achievement

Metrics and KPIs help marketers determine whether their efforts have met the goals set at the beginning of a campaign. Those campaign goals are tied to organizational goals that affect the organization's bottom line. The same is true for learning campaigns.

Clarity and Focus

Clear goals and metrics allow marketers to work together toward achieving a goal by focusing on one outcome, which tends to improve team morale as well. With focus comes better alignment with stakeholders and business goals. Of course, L&D professionals also benefit from working together with greater clarity and focus and aligning with stakeholders and business goals.

Accountability

With strong metrics and KPIs in place, marketers can hold themselves accountable for reaching the goals they set out to achieve. Everyone has a role to play. Unfortunately, in L&D, we often see colleagues running from one request to the next without being held accountable for things that matter, such as good content that resonates with learners, improving behavior, and helping make changes to the bottom line.

Data-Driven Insights

Tracking and monitoring data and regularly adjusting their efforts to achieve their goals allows marketers and L&D professionals to make informed decisions based on facts, not emotions or hunches.

Real-Time Optimization

With data-driven insights, marketers can make decisions in the moment. They don't have to wait until a campaign runs its course or goes off the rails to react. This rapid response mode isn't a concept familiar to most L&D professionals, but we can get closer if we integrate good measurement habits into our routines.

Resource Allocation

When marketers identify what's working well, they can use that information to allocate more resources to successful campaigns and move away from less successful initiatives. The same should be true in L&D, but we often don't think in terms of reallocating resources in this way.

Improved ROI

Measuring outcomes and results over time helps marketers understand which parts of a campaign are working well and which areas need more attention. This helps direct investment toward the channels that best achieve organizational goals. Our colleagues in L&D often discuss improving ROI, but we rarely see examples of how to measure ROI well.

What Is Progressive Profiling?

Marketers collect data in many clever ways that, as customers, we're not always aware of. *Progressive profiling* is a common approach to capturing customer information over time and sharing content in return for that information. Here's how it works:

> If you go to the LuxeKitchens website, you might enter your name and email address to download a short e-book on the basics of good kitchen design. The company has now captured your name and email and has linked that data to your IP address. The next time you visit their website, you might decide to download a video that walks you through the process of choosing the right cabinets. The site recognizes you and populates the request form with your name and email address but then asks for even more information—your city, zip code, and occupation. And the next time, when you register for a webinar with a sales consultant and kitchen planner, everything is prepopulated on the form except your budget for a kitchen renovation. Each transaction becomes easier for you, and with each transaction, the organization learns more about you as a customer.

How would progressive profiling translate to the world of L&D? We might decide to use metrics about our learners' existing knowledge to prepopulate an email newsletter sharing specific learning campaigns they would be interested in and that align with their goals and aspirations. That newsletter could then link to a survey in which we ask them about their preferred time to learn, which we could then leverage for future training initiatives. Or, we could use text messages to achieve the same goal. Digital data allows us to be innovative, stepping outside the LMS box to deliver what's relevant to our learners in their moment of need, and learn more about our learners in the process.

A Closer Look at Data and Metrics

As we already know, data refers to raw information and metrics are data points that provide context to this information, all of which helps marketers make informed decisions. Marketers use a variety of data and metrics that can also be used by L&D professionals.

Types of Data

In previous chapters, we've talked about several types of data L&D professionals can capture. Here is a brief recap.

Demographic Data

Marketers use this information, gathered from marketing automation tools, when creating buyer personas. Demographic data includes information about the characteristics and preferences of customers—age, gender, location, education, and so on. As a learning designer, you use the same information when you create learner personas. Data from an HR department is often the starting point.

Attitudinal Data

Marketers can collect information about attitudes in two ways: through customer interviews and via product or service ratings and reviews. If you conduct learner persona interviews, you have the opportunity to learn a great deal about your learners' attitudes, feelings, and emotions.

Behavioral Data

When customers follow a customer journey, their actions and interactions provide a wealth of information for marketers, including clicks, views, downloads, and shares. As you become more proficient using learner journeys and learning campaigns, you can also collect behavioral data along the way. Your LMS or LXP will gather some of this information.

Outcome Data

Information about the results of a marketing campaign, such as customer retention, is part of outcome data. You can collect the same kinds of information when your learners complete a learner journey or campaign.

☆ ☆ ☆

Now that we've discussed the many types of helpful data, we need to make it actionable by putting it in context and using metrics to tell a story.

Types of Metrics

Metrics are sets of data points marketers and business leaders use to contextualize data. First, we'll discuss vanity and actionable metrics. We'll then consider leading and lagging indicators, which are equally valuable.

Vanity and Actionable Metrics

Numbers are seductive, and some can be misleading. *Vanity metrics* are data points that look impressive on paper but don't help you make decisions and often lack a clear ROI. Social media metrics usually fall into this category. For example, the number of followers doesn't necessarily tell your company how well a specific piece of content resonated with customers. The same holds true for the number of learners who attended your training sessions. That number only tells you how many learners attended, not if they learned anything! Vanity metrics can be helpful, but they need to be contextualized further.

Actionable metrics, on the other hand, are the heroes of data-driven decision making. They are tangible and provide true insights to guide strategic action. Engagement with a social media post, such as a comment or a share, usually counts as an actionable metric because it can tell an organization how well content resonated with the audience. People generally don't share posts they don't find interesting or useful (McLachlan 2023). For your L&D content, you could examine engagement during a virtual live session by looking at how many learners clicked into activities or worksheets or how many posted questions or comments, which would tell you much more than pure attendance numbers.

The distinction between vanity and actionable metrics isn't always cut and dry. Context matters. What's actionable for one organization might be vanity for another. The key is to understand how metrics connect to your unique goals and inform strategies that drive results in your organization. In Table 9-1, we categorize some L&D metrics as vanity and some as actionable, adding a key question you can ask to tease out the importance of each. You may disagree based on the preferences of your L&D team and your organization, so explore what works best in your specific case.

Table 9-1. Vanity Versus Actionable Metrics

Vanity Metrics		Actionable Metrics	
Types of Data	Relevant Questions	Types of Data	Relevant Questions
Enrollment numbers	How many learners are enrolled in a course or program?	Learner engagement	How often and how long did learners interact with the course content and activities?
Course completions	How many learners completed the course?	Learner satisfaction (free-form feedback)	How satisfied were learners with the course content, delivery, and outcomes?
Average course ratings	What average rating did learners give a course?	Learner retention	How well did learners remember and apply what they learned after completing the course?
Number of course views or downloads	How many courses were viewed or downloaded?	Learner performance	How did learners perform on assessments, assignments, or projects related to the course objectives?
Seat time	How much time did learners spend on a course or a program?	Business impact	How did the learning program contribute to organizational goals such as productivity, quality, customer satisfaction, or revenue?

Leading and Lagging Indicators

Leading and *lagging indicators* are common terms in data measurement. You can think of them as drivers or catalysts of an end result. They are inputs or actions you take today and that will hopefully positively influence your KPIs tomorrow. You can use those indicators as benchmarks—when they're achieved, it signals the likelihood of meeting your overall KPIs and goals. They measure progress and are an early indicator of success. For marketers, leading indicators include website traffic, time-on-site, social media engagement, and the number of leads in the pipeline. As an L&D professional, you can look at engagement during training sessions, results from knowledge checks, and observations.

Lagging indicators measure your current production, outputs, and performance. They measure output that's already occurred to gain insight into future success. These indicators are triggered by a certain event. For example, let's say you ran an event; a lagging indicator is the number of people who attended. In marketing, lagging indicators include revenue, churn rates, ROI, and profit. In L&D, they'll differ depending on the type of training involved but might include increased sales numbers after the training program, such as those we saw in our LuxeKitchens example.

Leading indicators are much harder to measure, whereas a lagging indicator is easier to measure, but much more difficult to change. By combining leading and lagging indicators, you can create a fuller, richer picture of the trends, challenges, and successes in any learning experience and align your goals with overall organizational goals.

Let's first consider an example from the marketing world. If visits to a website are high, but visitors don't convert to paying customers, the company might not meet its revenue forecast. Marketers would have to compare several leading and lagging indicators to help them identify the disconnect—perhaps it's a subpar website user experience—and fix the issue.

For an example from L&D, let's return to our learner journey map, where we identified feedback points and metrics across the journey. Some of these points are vanity metrics, others are actionable metrics, and all of them are leading indicators. The lagging indicator is our overall journey goal. This means that as learners go through this journey, or individual campaigns within the journey, we can identify whether we will meet our journey goal, which is tied to our overall business objectives. The moment we realize learners aren't meeting the predetermined learner goals, it's time to adjust before it's too late! The true magic of learner journeys and campaigns happens in the moments when we measure what matters and make decisions based on that data.

In our LuxeKitchens case study, we looked at usage, engagement, and the number of qualified leads, to name just a few metrics, all of which are leading indicators. If CRM use is high and learners are engaged with additional training content, they will learn how to use the CRM more efficiently, resulting in a higher number of qualified leads. That number of qualified leads is one indicator that the company will meet its overall goals of boosting kitchen sales across different brands by 3 percent year-over-year.

What to Measure, When, and Where

Marketers look at different metrics based on the customer journey. They capture metrics that drive traffic at the top of the marketing funnel and engagement metrics at the bottom. Marketing automation tools capture the vast majority of these metrics, whether a customer is browsing on their home computer or frolicking around the neighborhood on a mobile device. With the inclusion of more and more smart technologies in our lives—from thermostats to watches to cars—the amount of data that's collected daily is increasing exponentially. Everything can be tracked everywhere, at any time.

In the following sections, we'll discuss some of the most common measures marketers use and draw parallels to L&D. All marketers are focused on how engaging their content is, and they don't make decisions based on just a few metrics. They look at the overall impact of a marketing campaign and its components and aggregate all the information to make informed decisions. That's certainly a process L&D could learn from.

Cost per Acquisition

The *cost per acquisition* (*CPA*) refers to the total cost of acquiring one new paying customer. The goal for any organization is to keep the CPA as low as possible. It's calculated by dividing advertising spending by the number of new customers acquired. If marketers have a high CPA, it means that they spend a lot of money on ads and on achieving a high rank in Google's search results. The higher a company ranks, the more likely customers will see their products.

Marketers use the *Quality Score* formula to help ads move up higher in the rankings. The formula depends on a variety of factors related to the quality of a company's website content, including keyword relevance, user experience, and click-through rate. If a company has engaging content, it will pay less to move up in ad rankings and, therefore, lower its CPA. Good marketers use their CRM systems and market research to understand which customer leads to focus on in their advertising and how to drive those "hot leads" to become paying customers (Chi 2023).

There is no direct equivalent to CPA for L&D, but you can consider how a Quality Score might show whether your content resonates with learners, just as it tells marketers about the quality of their website content. In the content strategy chapter, we discussed how content includes the written word, images, and multimedia, *not* the channels (an LMS, for example) through which you deliver the content. You care most about how engaged your learners are with a piece of content and if it drives them to take action, so in the case of L&D, CPA means *cost per action*. In other words, what investment in content will result in the desired actions or behavior change by your learners?

Customer Lifetime Value

The *customer lifetime value (CLTV)* metric looks at a company's entire business relationship with a customer and estimates the total value (often measured in revenue) the organization can expect from a single customer account. Ideally, an organization receives more revenue from a customer than it spends on acquiring them, retaining them, and cross-selling to them. CLTV reveals how important certain customers are, which helps make decisions. For example, the organization might decide to adjust marketing efforts to attract more of those high-value customers by offering improved customer service and engagement and developing different customer touchpoints—or enhancing management of unprofitable customers. Aside from the monetary value, companies also look at the strategic value a customer can bring through referrals or positive word of mouth (Mandal 2023). CLTV is a forward-looking concept that gives marketers a predicted or expected value, not a precise number (Fader 2020). Marketing automation tools and CRMs capture all the data points marketers need to calculate the CLTV.

Of course, you don't measure the results of your L&D work in "learner revenue." Even thinking about distinguishing between valuable and not-so-valuable learners seems outrageous. But there is a parallel here. First, you can explore a metric called employee lifetime value (ELTV). Instead of looking at revenue, ELTV looks at the anticipated contribution an employee will bring to an organization over their tenure. The formula is:

$$\frac{\text{Average yearly revenue}}{\text{Total number of employees}} \times \text{Average length of an employee's tenure in years} = \text{ELTV}$$

As you can see, the ELTV is calculated as an average. A high ELTV positively influences business outcomes. It helps you understand the optimal path for new hires to contribute, shows the importance of L&D, and provides data sets to better understand the employee life cycle. Onboarding and ongoing L&D initiatives usually have a significant influence on ELTV (Van Vulpen n.d.).

The ultimate question is: Can you measure the results of your L&D offerings on ELTV? We admit that this is a little bit far-fetched and probably not the most valuable metric, but stick with us while we add one more piece to the puzzle.

One scholar took this question to the next level and looked at the student engagement value (SEV) derived from the CLTV (Balasooriya et al. 2018). In an academic environment, CLTV can be derived by looking at the profitability of enrollments. First, identify high-performing students versus weak performers who might drop out of a program, and then define the student life cycle as all interactions a student has with the learning offerings. This seems a lot like our learner journey, doesn't it? We can now look at factors—borrowed from marketing and revised for L&D—that tell us whether learners are engaged and how they engaged with the content to tell us more about the SEV:

- **Recency.** Has the interaction between the learner and the learning offerings occurred recently?
- **Frequency.** How often does the learner interact with the learning offerings?
- **Investment.** How much time does the learner invest in our learning offerings? (Don't just look at seat time but at social learning activities as well.)
- **Maintenance.** How much time and effort does the L&D team spend maintaining a learning offering that a learner can engage with?
- **Retention and churn.** How many learners leave the organization? Or, more granular, how many learners drop out of a learning offering?
- **Referrals.** How many learners does each learner interact with?

- **Risk costs.** Does the learner have the prerequisite knowledge to take part in the learning offering?
- **Performance.** How well does a learner perform during and after the learning offering?

The last criterion doesn't exist in the CLTV calculation, and we omitted "discounts" for this book. All these metrics can be captured through your LMS, LXP, or third-party platforms, as well as HR data. In summary, the ELTV is probably not a good measurement of L&D success; however, we do like using those additional planes from Balasooriya's CLTV to think about learner engagement.

Now, we have come full circle. If you can identify that a learner isn't bringing the desired value to your organization—that is, they aren't as engaged as you would like—you could create a learning campaign that brings these learners along for the ride. This would allow you to use resources differently and make a difference in their lives.

Goal Completion Rate

The *goal completion rate* (GCR) is the percentage of users who have completed a specific goal or action that marketers have established for a campaign. For instance, one goal might be downloading an e-book or subscribing to a newsletter. Marketers track GCR using Google Analytics to determine the relevance and value of their content to users. The formula for calculating GCR is:

$$\frac{\text{The number of users who have completed the goal}}{\text{The total number of visitors to the website}} \times 100 = GCR$$

Marketers use this metric to optimize their campaigns, websites, and content. A higher GCR indicates that users are more engaged with the content. If a GCR is low, marketers will analyze existing data and sometimes reach out to users directly for feedback.

In the training and talent development context, goals and actions might include watching a video or attending a live session. In this case, completion rates and attendance rates are essentially GCRs. Remember, however, that these are vanity metrics unless you contextualize them. For example, if attendance rates are low, you could reach out to learners to find out why they aren't attending. Maybe the content isn't relevant. In that case, you would try to react and adjust the offering to increase attendance rates. When content is more relevant, learners are more engaged.

If the problem is that the session's timing just doesn't work, you can adjust it. Never just take the GCR at face value. Always take the time to dig a bit deeper, ask learners questions about the content, and see your GCR go up!

Engaged Time

Marketers use sophisticated methods to track the total amount of time a user is interacting with websites. They monitor how often the user is moving their cursor, clicking, playing audio or video clips, and scrolling in an active tab in their browser window. By analyzing user behavior, marketers can dig deeper into the digital footprints and interactions of their customers to optimize their user experience.

Tools like Mouseflow track users' navigation patterns, which organizations can then use to improve the design of their web pages, putting key information where users spend the most time. Heatmaps, which visually represent various data points, can also guide marketers in making those decisions (Kotler et al. 2020).

In L&D, facilitators can glance around a room and determine the level of learner engagement during a live learning session. But we usually don't know how actively engaged learners are with a piece of digital content. Most LMSs track video views but don't provide data about video drop rates—the percentage of viewers who stop watching before reaching the end. Yet, this data is essential if you want to know when learners lose interest or find content irrelevant or when the video needs improvements to boost clarity and engagement.

Experience API (xAPI) can help shed some light on engagement, but many learners are adept at knowing how and when to engage with a piece of content while multitasking on the side! Even so, however, measuring the time learners are engaged with our content is a valuable indicator of its impact and effectiveness.

Social Media Engagement and Sentiment Analysis

As the name suggests, this metric measures how much an audience engages with content on social media, including likes, comments, and shares. It's a great indicator of how relevant content is to a user. Many marketing automation tools capture this information. Facebook, for example, has a specific Facebook Insights dashboard with various data points from page views to story reach and post engagement. This tool can even distinguish between organic traffic and paid engagement (Lipschultz 2022). This holds true for most other social media platforms too. Other platforms, such as Hootsuite, allow marketers to dive deeper into their social media metrics across a variety of platforms.

When it comes to social media, brands are trying to build trust with their customers and engage them in authentic conversations. Marketers use a technique called *social media listening*, in which they monitor conversations and interact and engage with audiences. A process called a *sentiment analysis* helps marketers make sense of conversations and surveys online, categorize opinions, and identify trends (Lipschultz 2022). This is a way to go beyond quantitative feedback.

As a learning designer, you can consider comments and shares to find out whether the content resonates with learners. Again, "likes" are often just vanity metrics, but if you augment them with comments, you can draw a more complete picture. Many modern LMSs and LXPs can report on social activity on the platform, while Viva Engage and similar social learning communities are valuable for collecting data. You can also use a variety of AI tools to analyze that data.

Sentiment analysis is powerful because it allows you to dig deeper into learners' feelings and emotions, truly understanding what works and what doesn't work for them. You can then respond by adjusting training in the moment to improve their experience.

Net Promoter Score

The *net promoter score* (*NPS*) consists of a single statement, "I will recommend this product or service to others." Customers rate their response to this prompt on a scale of zero to 10. Someone who selects zero to six is considered a detractor; seven to eight is a passive consumer, and nine to 10 is a promoter. The NPS is calculated by subtracting the detractors from the percentage of promoters (Phillips and Phillips 2023). Marketers often use this prompt to determine customer loyalty and potential business growth after someone purchases and uses a product. A frequent follow-up question is, "Why did you give this rating?"

The NPS works beautifully in L&D environments. It is quick and easy to implement and provides actionable insights. When you talk to your business stakeholders about your training's NPS, the idea will resonate with them because it's a familiar metric.

Sources of Data and Metrics in L&D

We can find data about our learners in many places, both within and outside our organizations. Internal sources might include our LMS or LXP, survey and test tools, and Microsoft or Google Suite. Microsoft and Google can capture data from emails and calendars, allowing organizations to glimpse how teams collaborate and what individuals spend more or less time on. External sources of data might include social media platforms, web analytics, and market research. The growth of AI-supported technologies will create even more usage and engagement data.

Data Use in LuxeKitchens Training

Let's revisit the LuxeKitchens example to see how different data sources can be combined into actionable takeaways. LuxeKitchens has access to a vast amount of training data from many sources. They use an LMS that tracks registration, the use of digital assets, and attendance for each session, along with Level 2 results. For Level 1 feedback, the company uses a survey tool. Their email marketing tool sends engaging emails to their target audience and holds information about all emails sent, their open rates, and click-through rates.

The company uses an AI-based role-play tool that captures data on usage and engagement. Managers enter observations manually into a spreadsheet. Customer satisfaction survey results are stored in a separate system, which includes questions about every step in the customer journey, and the customer journey is aligned with the learner journey. During sales conversations, sales consultants use a performance tool built on WordPress to look up product information.

A tool called Mixpanel captures information from the WordPress site, including user data, page views, role, region, store, and data about content on the site, such as video and PDF views. This is combined with information from Amazon Web Services (AWS) and a data warehouse called Redshift.

This is a lot of data to keep track of! Somehow, the LuxeKitchens L&D team needs to aggregate the data into one view and tie it back to business outcomes—and that's when dashboards come into the picture.

To aggregate the data, the L&D team needs a common denominator that ties everything back to an individual learner. This would usually be an email address or employee ID. Next, the team would build a Power Business Intelligence (BI) Dashboard, which is a single page that aggregates data from many sources and tells a clear story through data visualization.

The LuxeKitchens BI Dashboard would include:

- Level 1 feedback
- Level 2 metrics
- Usage and engagement details for all training offerings categorized by delivery channel and region
- Data showing how many sales consultants opened the email promoting an upcoming in-person event, how many registered for the event, and how many showed up
- Level 3 data captured from managers' observations using a Likert-type scale
- Customer survey results correlated to each step of the learner journey
- Visualization of how training initiatives for each step of the learner journey affected customer survey results

Data can be fed into the BI dashboard either through FTP containers or email reports, which the dashboard could pull automatically. The real magic of the dashboard happens in the visualization of the effect of training initiatives. The L&D team can track training effectiveness by correlating training activities with sales performance at the store level. They can also analyze the cost per training session to optimize resource allocation and budgeting and evaluate geographic patterns in training uptake to identify areas that need additional focus. The possibilities are endless, and therefore, setting up a BI Dashboard isn't for the faint of heart. It requires a strong technical background and an understanding of how data and databases work.

The LuxeKitchens developmental teams could also use a *learning record store*. An LRS, such as Watershed or Learning Pool, does the same things as a typical BI dashboard, but focuses on learning data and analytics by default, bringing together data from an entire learning ecosystem—including xAPI data—and collecting, storing, and distributing it.

If all this discussion of databases and dashboards seems overwhelming, don't let that deter you. The best approach is to start small with the data points and metrics you have access to and build your plan step-by-step to meet your needs.

> **Opt In to Build Trust**
>
> Understanding where and how employees spend their time helps us provide training offerings accordingly, but not all employees feel comfortable with the methods organizations use to collect data. To ease any discomfort, we can provide opt-in choices for data collection across our organizations. This might be done through consent forms that describe the data collection process.
>
> Building trust between employees and organizations is more important than ever today. If we give the option to opt-in, we also need to ensure employees can update their data collection preferences at any time. We also need to clearly communicate what data is being collected, how it will be used, and who will have access to it. Organizations should only collect the data that's absolutely necessary to measure the goals they set out to achieve (Deloitte 2024).

Your Measurement Strategy

You now understand the components that make up a marketer's toolkit for measuring the results of a marketing campaign, as well as the enormous variety of data and data analysis approaches you can consider when measuring the results of your learning experiences. Now, it's time to formalize your measurement strategy.

A measurement strategy has two parts:
1. What data, metrics, and KPIs do you want to measure?
2. How are you measuring? How will you implement your process?

When you have a clear strategy in place, you can align your efforts with the goals of your organization, measure progress against key objectives, analyze what's working and what isn't, prioritize initiatives, and provide helpful documentation for stakeholders.

Design Your Strategy

To start designing your strategy with an end goal in mind, follow these steps.

Hold a Collaborative Meeting With Your Stakeholder

Stakeholders might want to jump straight into a solution, but the initial meeting isn't the time for that. In this meeting, remind stakeholders why they need the help of L&D specialists and discuss how they want to measure success. At LuxeKitchens, the impetus for new and better training was simple: a decrease in sales. During the meeting, consider what you know about the learner journey. Each step includes a learner goal, and the sum of those learner goals is the overall business goal, including KPIs that were put in place from the beginning. The overall business goal for the LuxeKitchens training was to increase sales by 3 percent year-over-year (a lagging indicator).

Add Your Learner and Business Goals

Choose the right metrics and indicators to track your progress. The metrics for your learning goals are leading indicators, which tell you if you can meet your overall business goal. Imagine the metrics as a trail of breadcrumbs. If you follow all the crumbs, you will make it to your overall goal! In the learner journey map, we identified those metrics for each step in the Feedback and Metrics row. Take another look to determine if anything needs to be adjusted, especially now with your stakeholders in the room.

Add Your Metrics

When you're satisfied with the metrics, add them to your measurement strategy. Use the Measurement Map (developed by Bonnie Beresford) to visualize leading and lagging indicators and summarize stakeholder meetings (Figure 9-1).

Figure 9-1. Bonnie Beresford's Measurement Map

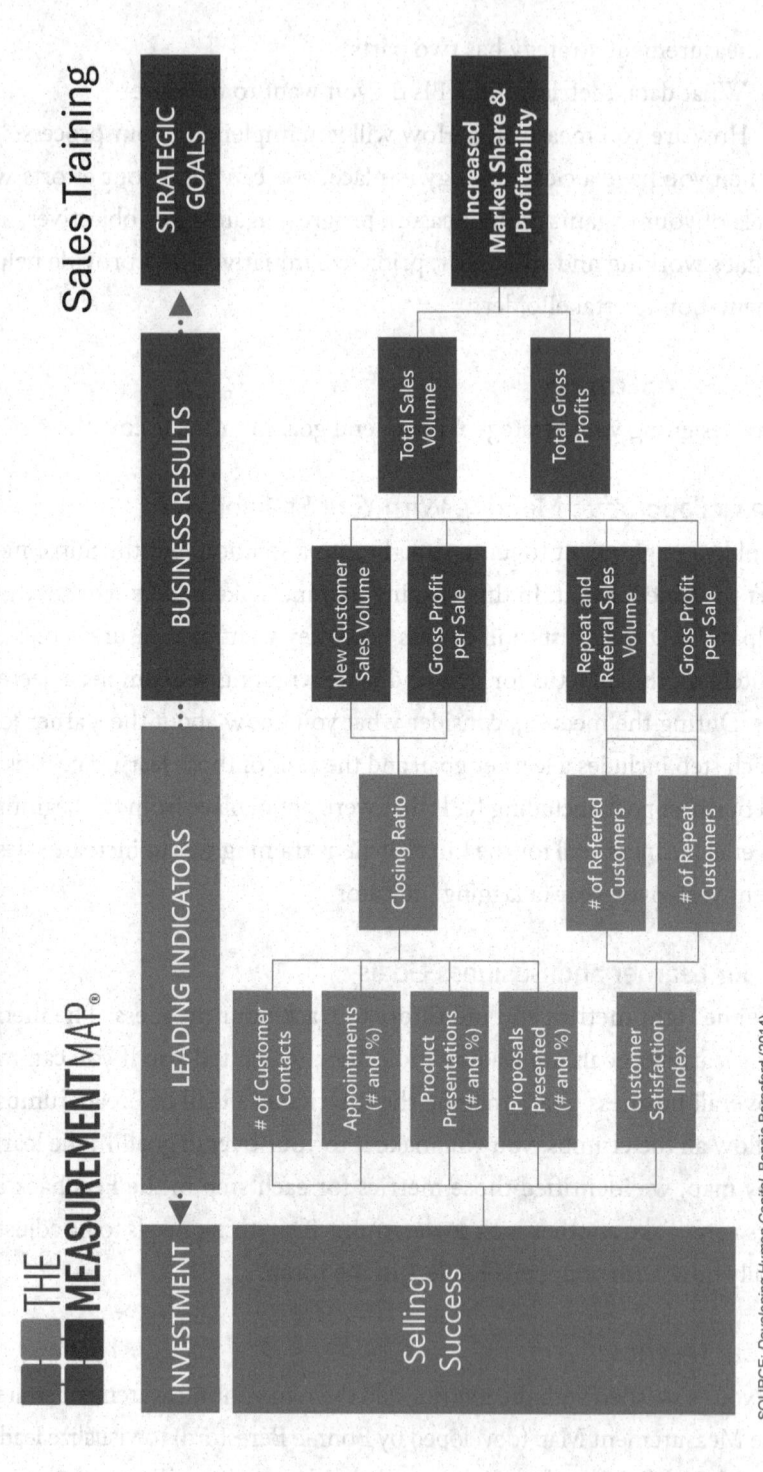

Sales Training

INVESTMENT	LEADING INDICATORS	BUSINESS RESULTS	STRATEGIC GOALS
Selling Success	# of Customer Contacts Appointments (# and %) Product Presentations (# and %) Proposals Presented (# and %) Closing Ratio Customer Satisfaction Index # of Referred Customers # of Repeat Customers	New Customer Sales Volume Gross Profit per Sale Repeat and Referral Sales Volume Gross Profit per Sale Total Sales Volume Total Gross Profits	Increased Market Share & Profitability

THE MEASUREMENTMAP®

SOURCE: *Developing Human Capital*, Bonnie Beresford (2014)
"The Measurement Map® and the Measurement Map logo are registered trademarks of Bonnie Beresford & Associates, LLC

Add Your Tools and Data Collection Methods

Mine your implementation planning to determine the tools and methods you want to use to collect data from various sources. Add these to your measurement strategy. This includes reporting processes, such as when you want to pull data, where you'll get it from, who your study population is, and who is responsible for it. Have additional collaborative meetings with your team and stakeholders to identify the different parts of the reporting process. You might also be able to leverage cross-departmental resources.

Thinking through a measurement strategy from the business perspective often feels counterintuitive to L&D professionals. We're used to measuring Level 1 (reaction) to Level 5 (ROI) data. Borrowing from marketing, we're suggesting that you flip the usual script and start with your stakeholders and the business goal and work your way backward from there. The metrics you collect for each step of the learner journey fall primarily into traditional L&D Levels 1 through 3, while business results and strategic goals fall under Levels 4 and 5.

Implement the Strategy

It's finally time to implement your measurement strategy. Your goal will be to use the insights you've gained to improve learning content, design, delivery, and maybe even the evaluation process.

You have tracked and collected information, analyzed and interpreted findings, and identified patterns, trends, gaps, and opportunities. Summarize these in a clear report and, whenever possible, visualize the results for your stakeholders so they can follow along easily and understand your recommendations. If necessary, rethink your goals, KPIs, and any other aspects of your measurement strategy that don't seem adequate.

Use Qualitative Data to Enhance Your Story

Quantitative data alone never tells the whole story when measuring the impact of a learning experience. You should always add qualitative information to capture the full picture. This requires blending several methodologies, including surveys, interviews, focus groups, observations, and pre- and post-learning experience tests, to gather feedback from learners and stakeholders. Couple that with other internal and external information, including likes, comments, shares, and usage and engagement data from an LMS, LXP, Microsoft or Google Suite, Google Analytics, or LRS to measure the entire learning experience.

We suggest using a baseline—developed through pre-assessments and observations—and perhaps a control group to compare the performance of learners before and after the learning experience. Control groups offer an ideal way to test several different modalities and identify what resonates most with a target audience. For example, do they connect more with a live webinar or a video? However, stakeholders may argue that a control group isn't representative because external factors might have influenced the group.

In our LuxeKitchens example, a possible external factor could be a shortage of kitchen appliances. As a result of customer dissatisfaction about the shortages, sales consultants wouldn't be able to sell as many kitchens as usual, meaning sales (business goal) would go down. Compare that to a group that received new training. They would be faced with the same shortage of appliances. If their sales were up after the training, it is safe to assume that this is due to the training program because they were able to sell kitchens despite the shortages.

It is never enough to track qualitative information; you always need to use it to tell a story. Ideally, tie it back to your learner journey, highlighting successes across the journey and showing how each lagging indicator adds up to achieve your overall business goal. Use dashboards, charts, and graphs to visualize the story, presenting your data and insights in an engaging way.

AI's Emerging Role in Measurement

With the expansion of AI-powered tools, we will see some aspects of the measurement process become simplified, especially for tasks related to automating data collection and computational or repetitive tasks. Today, 63 percent of marketers' time is spent on data cleaning and management (Funnel 2023). This is an instance in which AI can help us save time by doing these tedious tasks in minutes instead of hours. Yet humans remain crucial to the success of any measurement project. We will continue to integrate tech stacks, identify the right metrics, and verify data quality up front. It's projected that 37 percent of marketers will begin using AI for data cleaning and management. Finding opportunities to use AI and upskill employees on its use will be crucial as we move forward.

Organizations will need people who are data literate and enjoy working with numbers! In the next section, we share some resources to help put your measurement strategy into action.

> **Why Data and Analytics Matter**
> Despite the value of becoming more data-driven, 28.9 percent of organizations don't measure learning outcomes. Here are a few relevant statistics:
> - 47.7 percent of organizations use oral feedback from users and executives.
> - 38.2 percent use statistics and analytics from a learning platform.
> - 36.8 percent use evaluations with metrics.
>
> For those organizations that do measure outcomes:
> - 63.2 percent are interested in empowering individual performance.
> - 63.2 percent want to increase employee engagement.
> - 48.7 percent want to upskill employees to respond to market conditions.
> - 47.4 percent are focused on revenue growth (Learningbank 2023).

Tools to Improve Measurement

Data analysis might not be among the core skills and capabilities of most L&D professionals, but it needs to be. You can improve your skills by working collaboratively with your marketing team and learning how they approach data-driven decisions. Consider when you might use a cross-functional approach to leverage the resources and expertise of your marketing colleagues.

With the rise of digital marketing, options to measure results and success have expanded exponentially. It's easy to get lost in *how* we measure something versus *what* we want to measure. Decisions about the latter take more planning and finessing and set the tone, determining whether your measurement strategy can be successful in the long run.

A comprehensive discussion of measurement tools could fill an entire book, so we've simply selected two that L&D can leverage: Google Analytics and Tableau. (Power BI and Mixpanel are also great tools to use, but we won't review those here because we previously discussed them.)

Google Analytics

Google Analytics is a platform that gathers data from websites and apps to provide insight into your business. It collects the number of users, new users, sessions, sessions per page, page views, pages per sessions, average session duration, and bounce rate (Lipschultz 2022). After creating a Google Analytics account, you'll need to add a small piece of JavaScript code to each page of your site or e-learning module, which will then collect data. For example, the code might collect information about where a visitor to the site came from and package that information before sending it to Google Analytics, which would then use this information to create reports. Work with your IT or marketing department to identify the learning-related pages to which you would like to add the JavaScript, such as landing pages or pages within your LMS or LXP. The best part? It's all free!

Return to the metrics that you identified as part of your measurement strategy and add Google Analytics as a source to capture that information. Let's review some simple metrics you might include.

Visitors and Traffic Sources

How many unique learners visited the video you recently uploaded? The more visitors you have, the higher the interest. And, if you know where those visitors are coming from (for example, a link in email or directly), you can focus your efforts on those channels to promote learning in the future.

Keywords

What keywords did your learners search for in the LMS, the LXP, or your intranet? If a specific keyword shows up over and over, try to identify the reason. Is it an emerging skill that your employees need? Understand what content learners are looking for.

Time on Site

How long did a learner spend on the site where you posted that video? Did they just navigate there without even engaging with the video? Did they spend hours on the same page even though the video was only two minutes long? Both scenarios can tell you how engaged a learner is. If they navigate away quickly, they aren't engaging with the content. If they spend hours on the same page, they may have forgotten to close the tab.

Device
Are learners using their mobile devices or a desktop or laptop to access your training? The answer to this question allows you to design solutions that best fit your audience's habits. For example, if the content isn't responsive and most of your learners access it through a mobile device, they will end up being frustrated and won't engage or learn.

Tableau
Tableau is similar to Google Analytics. It allows you to connect different cloud databases and apps, such as Salesforce, Google Ads, SAP, and ServiceNow. Some of Tableau's features are free, while others are paid.

Similar to Google Analytics, Tableau aggregates information from various sources into one easy-to-use platform and visualizes your data—a feature that sets it apart from Google Analytics. The company suggests that no coding experience is needed to use Tableau, but it is still helpful to have some knowledge of coding to ensure you're pulling the right datasets and asking the right questions. Tableau uses a drag-and-drop interface and writes optimized SQL queries to bring data together.

Let's say you have a large Excel file with registration and attendance data, as well as feedback for your training session. Tableau allows you to visualize this information and identify trends and patterns. You can add more data sources to your reports and dashboards for a fuller picture. The key is to make sure you're tying metrics back to goals discussed with your stakeholders at the beginning of the project.

The Ongoing Impact of Measurement
Only by measuring what we do can we show our impact on learners and organizations. Measurement isn't a one-time thing; it's an ongoing, intentional effort. It isn't just about the smile sheets you hand out after a session or share after an online experience; it's about understanding your learning data and making sense of the results for your organization. It's about collecting data at

the content level, not just at the learner experience or business level (a fact often overlooked). Measurement is your North Star and a powerful connection to your organization.

A data-driven mindset helps us make decisions and fosters curiosity and innovation because we ask the right questions at the right time. In addition, we are more open to adjusting our training offerings in the moment instead of waiting. This continuous and iterative approach to testing means we learn and optimize our offerings regularly. Using data wisely also allows us to be more learner-centric and empathetic. We understand our learners better and meet them where they are, creating more relevant and valuable content that resonates with the target audience.

Measurement always needs to be intentional. As L&D pros, we can't wake up one morning and decide we want to measure all our efforts. Measurement is part of any good design and needs to happen before we even think about the content and delivery channels we want to use.

In this chapter, we've focused on measuring specific learner journeys and learning campaigns, but there's something to be said about planning for measurement regularly each year. Think about how you can improve your overall measurement processes and plan for the resources you will need, including the tools and people to ensure you have enough budget available.

A good measurement practice not only allows you to align with stakeholders but also aligns instructional designers with one another, ensuring they are asking the right questions and designing training that brings value to the learner and the organization. Remember, just because you can measure something doesn't mean you should. Always consider your why, and answer the question: "What is the impact?"

A Final Thought

You won't become data-driven in your L&D function overnight. You'll first need to get people excited about the prospect. It's crucial to get your organization to buy in because a lot of the data you need may be outside L&D's control, and you'll need supporters to help you get access. Focusing more on making decisions based on data is a cultural shift and will require patience and a talent for advocacy.

Activity 9-1. Tell a Story With Data

Visualize a data set you have access to (ideally from your onboarding program or the program you have been using for all activities throughout this book) using the free version of Tableau.

Objective
Visualize data and identify trends and patterns in a large dataset.

Steps
1. Sign up for the free version of Tableau.
2. Pull an extensive report from your LMS or LXP.
3. Drag and drop the data into Tableau to create a visual dashboard.

Conclusion
Small Steps, Big Impact

Well, friend, you've done something remarkable by reaching the end of this book. You've unlocked secrets that top marketers have been using for decades to connect with customers and drive revenue.

Now what? Now, you can use those insights to transform how people learn. This isn't theory. This isn't wishful thinking. These are field-tested tactics that can revolutionize your learning programs.

Your Next 24 Hours

Pick one technique to implement tomorrow. Maybe something you read resonated with you immediately. Start with that. If you have trouble choosing a starting point, try one of these:

- Transform your most-ignored course title into a headline that demands attention.
- Craft an email that makes mandatory training seem like a VIP invitation.
- Run your first A/B test (even a small one).

Why start small? Because momentum beats meditation. Every successful marketer starts with a single campaign, a single test, and a single win.

Your New Marketing-Inspired Mindset

You now have multiple effective marketing strategies to engage your audiences, and you can implement them to transform learning for your organization or your clients.

Your toolkit includes:
- Audience insights that make learners feel seen and understood
- Strategic designs that blend emotion with hard science
- Tech tools that turn manual tasks into automated magic
- Analytics that prove your impact (and justify your next budget)

Let's Not Stop Here

Most L&D pros will read this book, nod their heads, and go right back to doing what they've always done. But you want to go further—you've proven that by making it this far.
- Join the conversation online using the #TrainLikeAMarketer.
- Stay in the loop at TrainLikeAMarketer.com.
- Join fellow marketing-minded L&D pros in our Train Like a Marketer LinkedIn group at linkedin.com/groups/14552471.

Whether you're crafting learning content for corporate audiences, freelance clients, or internal teams, you now hold the marketer's power to transform content into experiences that captivate, convince, and convert. Think of this as your creative brief for revolutionary learning campaigns that help people grow, develop, and achieve more.

A strategy is set. The tools are ready. The audience awaits. Time to show them what learning can be.

The revolution starts with you. Let's make this happen.

Remember, the best time to transform your learning programs was yesterday. The next best time? Right now.

Recommended Resources for Deeper Learning

Curious to learn even more? We've got the goods! These resources are like the cheat codes for thinking like a marketer. For the latest and greatest (and to avoid dead links), you can also head over to TrainLikeAMarketer.com for a constantly updated list.

Chapter 1
We highly recommend these two great resources for learning more about the intuitive and deliberative thinking and cognitive biases:
- ***The Persuasion Code: Decoding the Brain's Secrets to Win People Over* by Christophe Morin and Patrick Renvoise.** This book explores the science behind persuasion, using a mix of brain science and marketing strategies. The authors explain how effective persuasion appeals to the brain's primal decision-making regions and introduce a model for influencing people's behavior. The key takeaways are that emotions and simple messages are crucial for persuasion.
- **Decision Lab's list of cognitive biases** (thedecisionlab.com/biases). This is a comprehensive resource for understanding various cognitive biases and heuristics that influence human decision making and behavior.
- ***Thinking, Fast and Slow* by Daniel Kahneman.** This book explains how our two thinking systems, the intuitive and the deliberate,

influence our decisions and behaviors. By understanding these cognitive systems, we can optimize decision making in both personal and professional contexts, as well as enhance the effectiveness of learning designs.

Chapter 2

Here are some great examples, tips, and templates for creating personas:

- **Vennage user persona examples** (venngage.com/blog/user-persona-examples). This article provides a comprehensive overview of user personas, showcasing how these semifictional representations enhance product design and marketing strategies. It emphasizes the importance of understanding users' demographics, motivations, and pain points to create effective personas that resonate with the target audience. It also links to practical templates.
- **Marketsplash persona examples** (marketsplash.com/persona-examples). This article presents user persona examples to illustrate how to effectively understand and engage your target audiences. It highlights the importance of creating detailed personas by showcasing real-world examples, which help teams tailor their marketing strategies and product developments to meet user needs and preferences.
- **Hubspot: Make My Persona** (hubspot.com/make-my-persona). This is a free, interactive persona generator. It guides you through a series of questions to gather essential demographic and psychographic information, enabling you to tailor your marketing strategies effectively. The tool also offers professionally designed templates, making it easy to visualize and share personas with team members.
- **QoQo** (qoqo.ai). QoQo is an AI-powered companion designed to enhance the UX design process by streamlining user research and ideation. It helps you generate user personas, identify challenges, and organize ideas.

Chapter 3

By employing design thinking, you can tailor learning experiences to what learners truly need, rather than depending on past training data or making uncertain choices based on intuition versus concrete feedback. Here are some great resources if you want to learn more about the design thinking process:

- **IDEO's design thinking page** (ideou.com/pages/design-thinking). This page explores the concept of design thinking, emphasizing its role in transforming how organizations develop products and services. It outlines the methodology, which combines human-centered design with technological feasibility and economic viability, and provides tools and steps for mastering this approach.
- **Interaction Design Foundation** (interaction-design.org/literature/topics/design-thinking). This resource provides an in-depth exploration of design thinking to better understand users and create innovative solutions. It emphasizes the importance of challenging assumptions and redefining problems to foster creativity and collaboration. The resource also includes various tools and methodologies that can help you effectively implement design thinking in your projects.
- **IBM's design thinking courses** (ibm.com/design/thinking). IBM outlines its unique approach to design thinking, emphasizing a user-centered methodology tailored for large enterprises. The framework is built on three core principles: a focus on user outcomes, restless reinvention, and diverse empowered teams.

And here are some valuable virtual examples and templates for creating learner journeys. These templates are versatile tools designed to help you visualize and analyze the entire customer experience, providing a structured framework for mapping out each stage of a customer's interaction with a product or service. The templates allow you to identify key touchpoints, pain points, and opportunities for improvement throughout the customer journey. They can easily be adjusted to L&D.

- **MIRO's customer journey map template** (miro.com/templates/customer-journey-map)

- **MURAL's customer journey map template** (mural.co/templates/customer-journey-map)
- **LUCID's customer journey map template** (lucidchart.com/pages/templates/customer-journey-map)

Chapter 4

These examples, tips, and templates will help you learn more about curation:

- **The CURATED Model for Content Creation in L&D** (mike-taylor.org/2023/09/07/the-c-u-r-a-t-e-d-model-can-help-anyone-master-content-curation). This model offers a comprehensive framework for effective content curation by breaking down the process into seven key steps: collect, understand, refine, arrange, transform, elevate, and disseminate. It also provides a structured approach to content curation, helping you systematically process and share valuable information with your audience.
- **The Complete Guide to Content Curation** (blog.hootsuite.com/beginners-guide-to-content-curation). This is a comprehensive overview of the content curation process, emphasizing its importance in social media strategy. The guide outlines essential steps for effective curation, including determining a content mix, scheduling posts, and regularly reviewing and adjusting strategies to align with audience preferences.
- **The Ultimate Guide to Curation for L&D** (learn.filtered.com/thoughts/the-ultimate-guide-to-curation-for-ld). This guide covers the key elements of curation, curating learning pathways, distribution of curated content, and the benefits of effective curation. It's specifically written for L&D professionals, making it a valuable resource.

Chapter 5

Mastering the art of simple, clear writing isn't easy. These resources can help:

- **Center for Plain Language** (plainlanguage.gov/guidelines). This is a valuable destination for anyone who wants to learn how to write in plain language. The organization's website provides a

variety of resources for writers and editors to improve the clarity of their writing.
- **Apple's Writing Style Guide: A Masterclass in Simple, Clear Writing** (support.apple.com/guide/applestyleguide/welcome/web). Apple's guide is a valuable resource for anyone who wants to learn how to write clear and concise prose. By following the guidelines in the style guide, writers can improve the readability and clarity of their writing.
- **Writing for Busy Readers** (writingforbusyreaders.com). Spearheaded by Harvard University's Todd Rogers, this is a one-stop hub that includes a book, workshops, and a tech-savvy newsletter to transform everyday communicators into effective writers for busy audiences everywhere.

Chapter 6

Understanding multimedia learning principles and how to design visuals for learning can be made easier if you review a few basic resources:

- ***E-Learning and the Science of Instruction* by Ruth Colvin Clark and Richard E. Mayer.** This book is a must-have for multimedia learning designers. Clark and Mayer go beyond guesswork, offering research-based recommendations for using multimedia effectively. The book even explores the ideal situations for each approach. Packed with practical advice, this book condenses extensive research to help you craft superior experiences that boost learning outcomes.
- **The Ultimate Guide to Visual Hierarchy** (canva.com/learn/visual-hierarchy). Designing layouts where important elements grab attention first is a core principle called visual hierarchy. This resource from Canva offers a primer on the concept.
- **The Interaction Design Foundation's Guide to the Rule of Thirds** (interaction-design.org/literature/article/rule-of-thirds-examples). This definitive guide provides examples that explain the Rule of Thirds. The visual examples show how the principle is applied in different scenarios, helping you understand how to align key elements within a composition for maximum impact.

- **A Practical Guide to Designing With Faces** (designshack.net/articles/graphics/a-practical-guide-to-designing-with-faces). Designing with faces can be a powerful way to connect with your audience and add a human touch to your work. This resource provides a practical guide to the strategic use of faces, which can lead to more captivating, relatable, and memorable designs.
- *Visual Design Solutions: Principles and Creative Inspiration for Learning Professionals* by **Connie Malamed.** This book is for anyone who wants to improve their instructional materials with strong visual design. It is an excellent resource offering practical tips and examples for creating clear and engaging visuals that enhance learning and retention.
- *Graphics for Learning: Proven Guidelines for Planning, Designing, and Evaluating Visuals in Training Materials* by **Ruth C. Clark and Chopeta Lyons.** This bestselling book summarizes the guidelines for the best use of graphics for instructional materials, including multimedia, texts, working aids, and slides. The guidelines are based on the most current empirical scientific research and are illustrated with a wealth of examples from diverse training materials.

Do you want to explore the world of data visualization? Here are a few terrific tools we have used and recommend:

- **Flourish** (flourish.studio). Flourish Studio is an interactive data visualization tool that enables you to create stunning charts, maps, and animated stories from any dataset. It offers a user-friendly platform where you can easily transform complex data into engaging visual content, making it suitable for many applications, including L&D.
- **Tableau** (tableau.com). This is a powerful data visualization and business intelligence platform that has a range of products for data analysis and insights. It offers several products and capabilities to connect data sources and create interactive visualizations, dashboards, and stories with drag-and-drop functionality.
- **Canva Graph Maker** (canva.com/graphs). This is a user-friendly platform for creating a wide variety of charts and graphs, allowing

you to visually represent data effectively. It has more than 20 types of customizable graphs (including bar charts, line graphs, and pie charts) enabling you to import data from CSV files or spreadsheets and easily embed your content in presentations or reports.

Chapter 7

If you would like to become a campaign pro, try some of these resources for additional tips, examples, inspiration, and templates:

- **HubSpot—The Ultimate Guide to Marketing Campaigns** (blog.hubspot.com/marketing/marketing-campaigns). This in-depth guide for creating and executing effective marketing strategies outlines different types of marketing campaigns, including email, content, social media, acquisition, and paid advertising campaigns, while detailing their unique goals and approaches.
- **20+ Best Direct Marketing Examples for You to Learn** (avada.io/resources/direct-marketing-examples.html). Access more than 20 creative and effective campaigns that illustrate the power of direct marketing strategies, such as Nestlé's KitKat Chunky mail campaign. Each example emphasizes the importance of clear CTAs and targeted messaging to effectively drive engagement and conversions.
- **Seven Marketing Campaign Examples That Do Brand Storytelling Well** (columnfivemedia.com/marketing-campaigns-examples-tips). Explore seven successful marketing campaign examples, and gain insights and tips for creating effective strategies. The article highlights notable campaigns from brands like Coca-Cola and Nike, showcasing innovative approaches that engage audiences and drive results. It emphasizes the importance of clear objectives, creative storytelling, and understanding target demographics to enhance campaign effectiveness and achieve desired outcomes.
- **Campaigns of the World** (campaignsoftheworld.com). This comprehensive platform showcases innovative advertising campaigns from around the globe. It features a diverse collection of creative works, allowing you to explore marketing strategies and trends across different industries. The site highlights notable campaigns,

such as Schwarzkopf's "Icons of You" (which celebrates diversity) and Surfshark's bold initiatives.

Chapter 8

These are two useful tools to automate your tech stack and improve the efficiency of your L&D work:

- **Zapier** (zapier.com). This tool cuts your busy work by connecting your favorite apps and automating repetitive tasks. You can use prebuilt templates or create your own to set off a chain reaction within different apps, like sending emails, enrolling learners, and managing data—all triggered by a single action. It's like having a personal assistant for your digital world.
- **Power Automate** (microsoft.com/en-us/power-platform/products/power-automate). Part of the Microsoft Power Platform suite alongside Power Apps and Power BI, Power Automate is a platform for automating tasks and workflows, similar to Zapier. If your organization uses Microsoft products, you might already have a license for this software.

For those interested in AI-powered learning and education, we recommend following these two experts who are leading the charge in this space:

- **Ethan Mollick** is a professor at the Wharton School of the University of Pennsylvania. He specializes in exploring the implications of the AI-driven era for work and education. Connect with him on Substack or LinkedIn.
- **Philippa Hardman** is a leader in applying AI tools and techniques within an L&D context. Connect with her on Substack or LinkedIn.

Chapter 9

There are many resources out there that take a more detailed look at data-driven design than we ever could in this book. Here are a few we recommend:

- *Data-Driven Learning Design* by **Lori Niles-Hofmann** (loriniles.com/ebook). This e-book provides guidance on leveraging data to enhance instructional design decisions. It emphasizes the importance of understanding learners' digital body language to

make informed choices that lead to effective learning experiences. This resource also aims to empower L&D teams to transition from traditional roles to becoming strategic business drivers through data-informed methodologies.
- **The L&D Detective Kit** (kevinmyates.com/l%26d-detective-kit). Kevin Yates's resource is designed to help L&D professionals measure the impact of training and learning initiatives. It provides tools and techniques for investigating and demonstrating how learning programs influence workplace performance and business goals. It offers practical strategies for using fact-based evidence to measure what matters most in learning initiatives.
- *Data and Analytics for Instructional Designers* **by Megan Torrance.** This book helps you leverage data and analytics to enhance learning experiences. It covers key concepts in data analytics, learning metrics, and statistical analysis while providing practical frameworks for collecting, analyzing, and using data in instructional design. It aims to empower L&D professionals to make data-driven decisions and demonstrate the impact of learning initiatives on organizational performance.

References

Agius, A. 2024. "Customer Journey Maps: How to Create Really Good Ones." HubSpot Blog, April 17. blog.hubspot.com/service/customer-journey-map.

Andrews, D.H., T.D. Hull, and J.A. Donahue. 2009. "Storytelling as an Instructional Method: Definitions and Research Questions." *Interdisciplinary Journal of Problem-Based Learning* 3(2): 6–23.

Baker, K. 2024. "Customer Segmentation: How to Segment Users and Clients Effectively." HubSpot Blog, April 18. blog.hubspot.com/service/customer-segmentation.

Balasooriya, I., J. Conesa, E. Mor, and M.E. Rodríguez. 2018. "Student Engagement Value (SEV): Adapting Customer Lifetime Value (CLV) for a Learning Environment." In *Advances on P2P, Parallel, Grid, Cloud and Internet Computing: Proceedings of the 12th International Conference on P2P, Parallel, Grid, Cloud and Internet Computing (3PGCIC-2017)*, 601–610.

Bandura, A. 1977. *Social Learning Theory*. Englewood Cliffs, NJ: Prentice Hall.

Beresford, B. n.d. "The Measurement Map." themeasurementmap.com.

Borkin, M.A., Z. Bylinskii, N.W. Kim, et al. 2016. "Beyond Memorability: Visualization Recognition and Recall." *IEEE Transactions on Visualization and Computer Graphics* 22:519–528.

Breeze, J. 2018. "Here's Looking at You!" LinkedIn Pulse, August 13. linkedin.com/pulse/20140813103409-1146575-here-s-looking-at-you.

Britz, M. 2020. "Social Learning @ Work—Quick Start Guide." markbritz.com/social-learning-work-a-quick-start-guide.

Bulgren, J. A., D.D. Deshler, and B.K. Lenz. 2007. "The Use of Analogies and Metaphors in the Teaching of Science Concepts." *Journal of Research in Science Teaching* 29(10): 1065–1079.

Chi, C. 2023. "Cost per Acquisition (CPA): A Beginner's Guide." HubSpot Blog, June 21. blog.hubspot.com/marketing/cost-per-acquisition.

Clark, R.C. 2012. *Scenario-Based E-Learning: Evidence-Based Guidelines for Online Workforce Learning.* San Francisco: Pfeiffer.

Clear, J. 2022. *Atomic Habits: An Easy and Proven Way to Build Good Habits and Break Bad Ones.* New York: Penguin Random House.

Decker, A. 2024. "The Ultimate Guide to Marketing Campaigns." HubSpot Blog, July 7. blog.hubspot.com/marketing/marketing-campaigns.

Deloitte. 2019. "Global Human Capital Trends Report." deloitte.com/us/en/insights/focus/human-capital-trends/2019.html.

Deloitte. 2024. "2024 Global Human Capital Trends." deloitte.com/us/en/insights/focus/human-capital-trends.html.

Dietz, D. 2012. "Transforming Healthcare for Children and Their Families: Doug Dietz at TEDx San Jose, CA 2012." TEDx Talks video. youtube.com/watch?v=jajduxPD6H4.

Doherty, Á. 2022. "Experiential Marketing in a Digital Era." In *The SAGE Handbook of Digital Marketing*, edited by Annmarie Hanlon and Tracy Tuten. Thousand Oaks, CA: SAGE.

Fader, P. 2020. *Customer Centricity: Focus on the Right Customers for Strategic Advantage.* Philadelphia: Wharton School Press.

Finelli, R. 2023. "Employee-Led Training Helps the Learner, the Teacher, and the Company." Kaplan, March 15. kaplan.com/about/trends-insights/employee-led-trainings.

Flesch, R.F. 1979. *How to Write Plain English: A Book for Lawyers and Consumers.* New York: Harper and Row.

Freberg, K., B.G. Smith, and L. Silva. 2022. "How Influencers Influence: Conceptualizing the Influencer Map for Marketing." In *The SAGE Handbook of Social Media Marketing*, edited by Annmarie Hanlon and Tracy Tuten. Thousand Oaks, CA: SAGE.

French, K. n.d. "How to Run Effective Marketing Campaigns (Guide + Template)." Column Five Media. columnfivemedia.com/how-to-run-content-marketing-campaigns.

Fuentes-Claramonte, P., C. Ávila, A. Rodríguez-Pujadas, et al. 2015. "Reward Sensitivity Modulates Brain Activity in the Prefrontal Cortex, ACC and Striatum During Task Switching." *PLoS ONE* 10(4). journals.plos.org/plosone/article?id=10.1371/journal.pone.0123073.

Funnel. 2024. "Marketing Data State of Play 2024: Transformation: How AI (+ Your Data Skills) Will Change Everything." funnel.io/marketing-data-state-2024.

Gadziola, M., and D. Wesson. 2016. "The Neural Representation of Goal-Directed Actions and Outcomes in the Ventral Striatum's Olfactory Tubercle." *Journal of Neuroscience* 36(2): 548–560. jneurosci.org/content/36/2/548.

Galan-Ladero, M.M., C. Calera-Casquet, and H.M. Alves. 2021. *Cause-Related Marketing: Case Studies From a Global Perspective*. Switzerland: Springer International Publishing.

Game Storming. 2011. "How-Now-Wow-Matrix." Game Storming, January 5. gamestorming.com/how-now-wow-matrix.

Gentner, D., J. Loewenstein, and L. Thompson. 2003. "Learning and Transfer: A General Role for Analogical Encoding." *Journal of Educational Psychology* 95(2): 393–408.

Getto, G., J.T. Labriola, and S. Ruszkiewicz. 2023. *Content Strategy: A How-to Guide*. New York: Routledge.

Gilovich, T., D. Griffin, and D. Kahneman. 2002. *Heuristics and Biases: The Psychology of Intuitive Judgment*. Cambridge: Cambridge University Press.

Google. n.d. "How Google Analytics Works." Google Analytics Help. support.google.com/analytics/answer/12159447.

Google. 2022. "What Creators Should Know About Google's August Helpful Content Update." Google Search Central Blog, August 18. developers.google.com/search/blog/2022/08/helpful-content-update.

Hannouz, M. 2021. "Campaign Management Versus Customer Journey Orchestration." Repackaged Blog, September 21. repackaged.tech/en/blog/campaign-management-vs-customer-journey-orchestration.

Hartley, J., and M. Trueman. 1983. "The Effects of Headings in Text on Recall, Search, and Retrieval." *British Journal of Educational Psychology* 53(2): 205–214.

Haven, K. 2007. *Story Proof: The Science Behind the Startling Power of Story.* Westport, CT: Libraries Unlimited.

Heath, C., and D. Heath. 2007. *Made to Stick: Why Some Ideas Survive and Others Die.* New York: Random House.

Henley, C. 2021. "Motivation and Reward." Chapter 37 in *Foundations of Neuroscience* by C. Henley. Published by the author. openbooks.lib.msu.edu/neuroscience/chapter/motivation-and-reward.

Housden, M., and B. Thomas. 2002. *Direct Marketing in Practice.* London: Routledge.

Immordino-Yang, M.H., and A. Damasio. 2007. "We Feel, Therefore We Learn: The Relevance of Affective and Social Neuroscience to Education." *Mind, Brain, and Education* 1(1): 3–10.

Johnson, D.D., and M. Kress. 1972. "Readability and Learning Outcomes." *Journal of Educational Research* 65(8): 337–342.

Jordan, L. 2020. *Techniques of Visual Persuasion: Create Powerful Images That Motivate (Voices That Matter).* Indianapolis: New Riders.

Kahneman, D. 2011. *Thinking, Fast and Slow.* New York: Farrar, Straus, and Giroux.

Kalyanaraman, S., and S.S. Sundar. 2006. "The Psychological Appeal of Personalized Content in Web Portals: Does Customization Affect Attitudes and Behavior?" *Journal of Communication* 56(1): 110–132.

Kandinsky, W. (1911) 1977. *Concerning the Spiritual in Art.* Translated by M.T.H. Sadler. New York: Dover Publications.

Kannengiesser, U., and J.S. Gero. 2019. "Design Thinking, Fast and Slow: A Framework for Kahneman's Dual-System Theory in Design." *Design Science* 5. doi.org/10.1017/dsj.2019.9.

Kanwisher, N., J. McDermott, and M.M. Chun. 1997. "The Fusiform Face Area: A Module in Human Extrastriate Cortex Specialized for Face Perception." *Journal of Neuroscience* 17:4302–4311.

Kapp, K.M., and R.A. Defelice. 2019. *Microlearning: Short and Sweet.* Alexandria, VA: ATD Press.

Kirch, K. 2024. "The Ultimate List of Email Marketing Stats for 2023." HubSpot Blog, July 29. blog.hubspot.com/marketing/email-marketing-stats.

Kolb, D.A. 1984. *Experiential Learning: Experience as the Source of Learning and Development*. Saddle River, NJ: Prentice-Hall.

Koliska, M., and K. Oh. 2023. "Guided by the Grid: Raising Attention With the Rule of Thirds." *Journalism Practice* 17(2): 354–373. doi.org/10.1080/17512786.2021.1916402.

Kotler, M., T. Cao, S. Wang, and C. Qiao. 2020. *Marketing Strategy in the Digital Age: Applying Kotler's Strategies to Digital Marketing*. Singapore: World Scientific Publishing.

Kuehnl, C., D. Jozic, and C. Homburg. 2019. "Effective Customer Journey Design: Consumers' Conception, Measurement, and Consequences." *Journal of the Academy of Marketing Science* 47(3): 551–568.

Learningbank. 2023. *2023 The Nordic Learning Trends Report*. learningbank.io/nordic-learning-trends-report-2023.

Lindgaard, G., G. Fernandes, C. Dudek, and J. Brown. 2006. "Attention Web Designers: You Have 50 Milliseconds to Make a Good First Impression!" *Behaviour & Information Technology* 25(2): 115–126.

Lipschultz, J.H. 2022. "How Organizations Measure, Manage and Monitor Digital Marketing." In *The SAGE Handbook of Digital Marketing*, edited by Annmarie Hanlon and Tracy Tuten. Thousand Oaks, CA: SAGE.

Mailchimp. n.d. "Text Message Marketing Guide." mailchimp.com/resources/text-message-marketing.

Majidi, M. 2024. "Average Cost of a 30-second Super Bowl TV Commercial in the United States from 2002 to 2024." Statista, February 7. statista.com/statistics/217134/total-advertisement-revenue-of-super-bowls.

Malamed, C. 2015. *Visual Language for Designers: Principles for Creating Graphics that People Understand*. Gloucester, MA: Rockport Publishers.

Malkani, A. 2022. "Reinventing Email Marketing Through a Personalisation Strategy." In *The SAGE Handbook of Digital Marketing*, edited by Annmarie Hanlon and Tracy Tuten. Thousand Oaks, CA: SAGE.

Mandal, P.C. 2023. "Management of Customer Lifetime Value in Organizations: Strategies and Initiatives." *Journal of Business Ecosystems* 4(1): 1–15. Durham: IGI Global.

Marketing Evolution. 2022. "What Is Unified Marketing Measurement?" marketingevolution.com/marketing-essentials/unified-marketing-measurement.

Mayer, R.E. 2020. *Multimedia Learning*, 3rd ed. Cambridge: Cambridge University Press.

Mayer, R.E., W. Bove, A. Bryman, R. Mars, and L. Tapangco. 1996. "When Less Is More: Meaningful Learning From Visual and Verbal Summaries of Science Textbook Lessons." *Journal of Educational Psychology* 88(1): 64–73.

Mayer, R.E., and R. Brünken. 2006. "The Influence of Personal Relevance on Learning and Memory." *Learning and Individual Differences* 16(2): 182–193.

Mayer, R.E., and L. Fiorella, eds. 2021. *The Cambridge Handbook of Multimedia Learning*, 3rd ed. Cambridge: Cambridge University Press.

McEwen, L.F. 2016. "Do Drip Campaigns Really Work?" Pinpointe, July 15. pinpointe.com/blog/do-drip-campaigns-really-work.

McLachlan, S. 2023. "Vanity Metrics: Definition and Examples for Marketing." Hootsuite Blog, September 21. blog.hootsuite.com/vanity-metrics.

Medina, J. 2014. *Brain Rules: 12 Principles for Surviving and Thriving at Work, Home, and School*. Updated and Expanded. Seattle: Pear Press.

Mind Tools for Business. 2023. *Learning and Development in Organizations: Reflecting on 20 Years of Research*. mindtools.com/wp-content/uploads/2023/10/MTB0004-20th-Anniversary-Annual-Report_2023-FV_compressed-1.pdf.

Mishra, K.E. and B.J. Baldus. 2022. "Strategic Directions in B2C Social Media Marketing." In *The SAGE Handbook of Social Media Marketing*, edited by Annmarie Hanlon and Tracy Tuten. Thousand Oaks, CA: SAGE.

Morin, C., and P. Renvoise. 2018. *The Persuasion Code*. Hoboken, NJ: Wiley.

National Center for Education Statistics. 2013. *Adult Literacy in America.* Washington, DC: US Department of Education.

Needle, F. 2021. "20 Creative Ways to Repurpose Content." HubSpot Blog, February 5. blog.hubspot.com/blog/tabid/6307/bid/27256/5-creative-ways-to-recycle-content.aspx.

Neslin, S.A. 2022. "The Omnichannel Continuum: Integrating Online and Offline Channels Along the Customer Journey." *Journal of Retailing* 98:111–132.

Nielsen, J. 1997. "How Users Read on the Web." Nielsen Norman Group, September 30. nngroup.com/articles/how-users-read-on-the-web.

Nielsen Norman Group. 2008. *Writing for the Web: Scannable, Concise, Objective,* 2nd ed. Nielsen Norman Group.

Paivio, A., and K. Csapo. 1973. "Picture Superiority in Free Recall: Imagery or Dual Coding?" *Cognitive Psychology* 5:176–206. doi.org/10.1016/0010-0285(73)90032-7.

Palazón, M., M. Lopez, M. Sicilia, and I. López. 2022. "The Customer Journey: A Proposal of Indicators to Evaluate Integration and Customer Orientation." *Journal of Marketing Communications* 28(5): 528–559.

Pease, G., B. Beresford, and L. Walker, 2014. *Developing Human Capital: Using Analytics to Plan and Optimize Your Learning and Development Investments.* Hoboken, NJ: Wiley.

Phelps, E.A. 2006. "Emotion and Cognition: Insights From Studies of the Human Amygdala." *Annual Review of Psychology* 57:27–53.

Phillips, P.P., and J.J. Phillips. 2023. "Essential Analytics for the Future of Learning." ROI Institute. roiinstitute.net/essential-analytics-for-the-future-of-learning.

Potter, M. C., B. Wyble, C. E. Hagmann, and E. S. McCourt. 2014. "Detecting Meaning in RSVP at 13 MS Per Picture." *Attention, Perception, and Psychophysics* 76(2): 270–279.

Raita, E., and A. Oulasvirta. 2011. "Too Good to Be Bad: Favorable Product Expectations Boost Subjective Usability Ratings." *Interacting With Computers* 23(4), 363–371.

Reamy, T. 2002. "Imparting Knowledge Through Storytelling: Part 1 and 2." *KM World* 11(6).

Rennell, T. 2021. "What Is Data Versus a Metric Versus a KPI Versus a Report?" Adverity, February 11. adverity.com/blog/data-vs-metric-vs-kpi-vs-report.

Rockley, A., and C. Cooper. 2012. *Managing Enterprise Content: A Unified Content Strategy*, 2nd ed. Indianapolis, IN: New Riders.

Rockley, A., C. Cooper, and S. Abel. 2015. *Intelligent Content: A Primer*. Denver: XML Press.

Scharf, R.E. 2017. "Pictures Tell Their Own Story." *Hämostaseologie* 37:181–183.

Semrush. 2023. *State of Content Marketing in 2023*. semrush.com/goodcontent/state-of-content-marketing/report.

Smith, T., and T. Williams. 2022. *Brand Fusion*. Boston: De Gruyter.

Soper, D.S. 2014. "User Interface Design and The Halo Effect: Some Preliminary Evidence." *Proceedings of the 20th Americas Conference on Information Systems, Savannah, Georgia, August 2014*. danielsoper.com/research/papers/soper-2014_amcis-user_interface_design_and_the_halo_effect.pdf.

Stanovich, K.E., and R.F. West. 2000. "Individual Differences in Reasoning: Implications for the Rationality Debate?" *Behavioral and Brain Sciences* 23(5): 645–665.

Stipeche, C. 2023. "How Customer Journey-Mapping Guides Brand Growth." MarketingProfs. marketingprofs.com/articles/2023/48867/how-customer-journey-mapping-guides-brand-growth.

Sweller, J. 1994. "Cognitive Load Theory, Learning Difficulty, and Instructional Design." *Learning and Instruction* 4(4): 295–312.

Tam, K.Y., and S.Y. Ho. 2006. "Understanding the Impact of Web Personalization on User Information Processing and Decision Outcomes." *MIS Quarterly* 30(4): 865–890.

Toonen, E. 2024. "How to Use the Readability Analysis in Yoast SEO." Yoast, January 3. yoast.com/yoast-seo-readability-analysis.

Tuch, A.N., E. Presslaber, M. Stoecklin, K. Opwis, and J. Bargas-Avila. 2012. "The Role of Visual Complexity and Prototypicality Regarding First Impression of Websites: Working Towards Understanding Aesthetic

Judgments." *International Journal of Human-Computer Studies* 70(11): 794–811.

Tyng, C., H. Amin, L. Izhar, and et al. 2019. "Exploring EEG Effective Connectivity Network in Estimating Influence of Color on Emotion and Memory." *Frontiers in Neuroinformatics* 13. doi.org/10.3389/fninf.2019.00066.

Um, E., J.L. Plass, E.O. Hayward, and B.D. Homer. 2012. "Emotional Design in Multimedia Learning: Effects of Shape and Color on Affect and Learning." *Learning and Instruction* 22(5): 323–332.

Ungerleider, L.G., and M. Mishkin. 1982. "Two Cortical Visual Systems." In *Analysis of Visual Behavior*, edited by D.J. Ingle, M.A. Goodale, and R.J.W. Mansfield. Cambridge, MA: MIT Press.

Van Vulpen, E. n.d. "Employee Lifetime Value: All You Should Know." Academy to Innovate HR. aihr.com/blog/employee-lifetime-value-eltv.

Vora, A. 2023. "15 Call-To-Action Statistics You Need to Know About to Increase Your Conversion Rate." HubSpot, July 14. blog.hubspot.com/marketing/personalized-calls-to-action-convert-better-data.

Walkington, C., and M.L. Bernacki. 2018. "Personalization of Instruction: Design Dimensions and Implications for Cognition." *Journal of Experimental Education* 86(1): 50–68.

Walkington, C., and M.L. Bernacki. 2020. "Appraising Research on Personalized Learning: Definitions. Theoretical Alignment, Advancements, and Future Directions." *Journal of Research on Technology in Education* 52(3): 235–252.

Ware, C. 2010. *Visual Thinking for Design*. San Francisco: Morgan Kaufmann.

What'stheBigData, 2024. "Internet Traffic From Mobile Devices Stats." whatsthebigdata.com/mobile-internet-traffic.

Zak, P. 2014. "Why Your Brain Loves Good Storytelling." *Harvard Business Review*, October 28. hbr.org/2014/10/why-your-brain-loves-good-storytelling.

Ziewiecki, S., and L. Ross. 2021. "Like, Comment, Share: Choosing the Right Influencers and Platforms for Influencer Marketing Campaigns." in *SAGE Business Cases*. Thousand Oaks, CA: SAGE. sk.sagepub.com/cases/like-comment-share-choosing-influencers-platforms-marketing-campaigns.

Zwaan, R.A. 2016. "Situation Models, Mental Simulations, and Abstract Concepts in Discourse Comprehension." *Psychonomic Bulletin and Review* 23(4): 1028–1034.

Index

In this index, *f* denotes figure and *t* denotes table.

5 Moments of Need, 90

A
Abel, S., 97
A/B testing, 146, 162, 225–227, 238
adaptive campaigns, 222–223
adoption strategies, 115–120
Agius, A., 64
AI functionality
    content quality and, 123
    data collection and analysis, 40, 48, 52, 85, 262
    learner persona creation, 59
    marketing campaigns, 229–230
ambassadors, 118–119
asset levels, learning personas and, 56–57
Atomic Habits (Clear), 239
audience, target, 28, 107–108, 193–194
    See also learner personas; segmentation
automation activities, 235–238

B
Beresford, B., 259–260
BI (Power Business Intelligence Dashboard), 257–258
billboards, 155–156
Brain Rules (Medina), 14
brand consistency, 157, 179, 185, 188
Breeze, J., 171
Brinker, S., 234
Brown, T., 27
buzzwords. *See* jargon and buzzwords

C
calendars, editorial, 109
calls to action (CTAs), 140–141, 143–147, 151–152, 220, 238
cause-related campaigns, 205
channels. *See* controlled versus noncontrolled channels; touchpoints, interactions, and channels

Clear, J., 239
CLTV (customer lifetime value), 251–253
cognitive biases, 9
cognitive load, 129, 135, 160–163
collaboration, 101, 123, 205
    See also crowdsourcing content; stakeholder alignment
communication strategies, 38–39, 115–116
    See also email marketing campaigns
consistency, 71–74, 179
    See also brand consistency; content strategy
content, content types, and content channels, 97, 98, 108, 113–114
content atomization. *See* repurposing content
content audits, 103, 104–107
content makeover activity, 184
content strategy, 96, 98–126, 135–136
contrast, 10, 166–167
controlled versus noncontrolled channels, 71–73
Cooper, C., 97
cost per acquisition or cost per action (CPA), 250–251
CRM. *See* customer relationship management (CRM) system
crowdsourcing content, 103, 112–113
CTAs. *See* calls to action (CTAs)

customer journeys, 63, 64, 65–68, 70, 75, 76–80, 189–190
customer lifetime value (CLTV), 251–253
customer relationship management (CRM) system, 69, 250–251

D

Damasio, A., 15
data, 101–102, 242, 243, 246, 256–258
    See also employee data; learner engagement data
data analysis, 48–52, 261–265
    See also feedback; metrics
data collection, 40, 258, 261, 262
    See also interviews; progressive profiling
data-driven decisions, 74–75
    See also feedback
data protection and privacy, 233, 258
data visualization activity, 267
deliberative thinking, 6–9, 21
deliverables, 194–195
design thinking, 27, 55–56
Diety, D., 33

E

editorial calendars, 109
elaborative encoding, 135
ELTV. *See* employee lifetime value (ELTV)

email marketing campaigns, 198–200, 212, 216–227, 230–234
email subject line activity, 237
emotions
    in learning design, 9, 13, 15, 21–22
    resonance and, 136–138
    sentimental analysis and, 255
    visuals and, 156, 176, 177
employee data, 36, 38, 47–48
employee lifetime value (ELTV), 251–252, 253
engagement, 254
    See also learner engagement; social media engagement and sentiment analysis

F

the face, impact of, 170–172
    See also human-centered images
feedback, 74–75, 85–86, 88, 225
    See also data analysis; data-driven decisions; metrics
file naming conventions, 124
5 Moments of Need, 90
Flesch, R., 130
Flesch-Kincaid readability scores, 129–130, 132
flexibility, 70, 180
Floor, N., 90
focus groups, 36–37, 39–41
Franklin, B., 98

funnel approach. *See* marketing funnel

G

Gero, J., 7
Getto, G., 97
goal completion rate (GCR), 253–254
Google Analytics, 121, 253, 264

H

headlines, 141–143, 150
high versus low performers, 36
how-might-we questions, 56, 82
How-Now-Wow Matrix, 84–85, 89
human-centered images, 176–177
human-centered learning, 30–31, 70–71
    See also learner personas

I

ID (instructional design), 18–21
ideation, 83
impact, of the face, 170–172
impact, visuals and maximizing, 174–180
impact measurement, 197, 240–245, 258–266
    See also metrics
influencer and social media campaigns, 202–204
instructional design (ID), 18–21

interactions. *See* touchpoints, interactions, and channels
interviews, 35, 36–37, 39–46
intuitive thinking, 6–15, 18–19, 20, 21–22

J
jargon and buzzwords, 133, 135
Jordan, L., 164
journeys. *See* customer journeys; learner journeys

K
Kahneman, D., 2, 5, 6, 7, 8
Kandinsky, W., 176
Kannengiesser, U., 7
Kelvin, Lord, 243
key performance indicators (KPIs), 242–243

L
landing pages, 228
leading and lagging indicators, 248–250
learner engagement
    content strategy and, 101–102, 135–136
    CTA and, 143–146*t*, 220
    omnichannel strategies and, 72
    tools for, 12, 16–17, 154
    See also customer journeys; learner journeys; visuals

learner engagement data, 52, 120–121, 241, 247, 251–256
    See also data collection; metrics
learner journeys, 65–67, 69–90, 92–94, 100, 186–187, 191–192
learner outcomes, 197
    See also impact measurement; metrics
learner personas, 28, 29–60, 100, 101
learning campaigns, 186–187, 191–197, 205–207, 208
learning design methods, 8–18
lecture-style presentations, 6, 9, 11, 13
low versus high performers, 36
LX Canvas, 90

M
mandatory training, 106–107
    See also onboarding activities
marketing approach to training, 1–2, 5, 9, 11, 13, 14–16
marketing campaigns, 185–190, 197–206
    See also email marketing campaigns
marketing funnel, 91–92, 99
marketing technology (martech), 209–230
    See also email marketing campaigns
Mayer, R., 162, 173

measurement. *See* data analysis; data collection; impact measurement; metrics
Measurement Map, 259–260
Medina, J., 14
memorableness, 12–13
　See also retention improvement strategies
metrics, 224–227, 242, 243, 247–258
Morin, C., 9
Mosher, B., 90
multimedia learning principles, 162–163

N

net promoter score (NPS), 255–256
Nica, I., 229
noncontrolled versus controlled channels, 71–73

O

observation checklists, 37–38
observations, 35, 37–38, 47
off-the-shelf content, 109
omnichannel strategies, 67, 72
　See also controlled versus noncontrolled channels
onboarding activities, 24–25, 61, 94, 126, 237
onboarding automation, 214
opt-in choices, 258
Orwell, G., 131

outcomes, 197
　See also impact measurement

P

The Persuasion Code (Morin & Renvoise), 9
Poor Richard's Almanack (Franklin), 98–99
positioning, 35
Power Business Intelligence (BI) Dashboard, 257–258
prioritization tools, 84–85
problem statements, 81–82, 87
progressive profiling, 245
prototypes and testing, 196–197

R

readability tools, 129–130, 132, 134
registration pages, 145
relevance, 70–71
Renvoise, P., 9
repurposing content, 103, 110
retention improvement strategies, 10, 34–35, 138, 139, 158–159, 165, 176
　See also cognitive load
Rockley, A., 97
rollout strategies, 115–120
Rule of Thirds, 172–174, 182

S

sales enablement platforms, 228
scheduled campaigns, 220, 221f

Schmitt, B., 200
segmentation, 28–29, 34–35
sensory engagement, 157
sentiment analysis, 255
SEV (student engagement value), 252
simplicity, 131–133, 135, 157, 178
social media and influencer campaigns, 202–204
social media engagement and sentiment analysis, 255
spreadsheets, 37, 40, 48, 105, 106t, 107
stakeholder alignment
   content delivery and, 98
   impact measurement strategies and, 259
   learner journeys and, 79, 80, 81, 82, 84, 93
   learner personas and, 32–34, 35–36, 38, 39, 54
stereotypes, 52–53
   See also cognitive biases
student engagement value (SEV), 252
style guides, 179
SURE principles, 129–139, 140f
surveys, 36, 37, 47

T
Tableau, 265
targeting, 35
Techniques of Visual Persuasion (Jordan), 164

testing. *See* A/B testing; prototypes and testing
texts, 198
Thinking, Fast and Slow (Kahneman), 2
touchpoints, interactions, and channels, 66–69, 74, 81, 83–84, 86f
   See also controlled versus noncontrolled channels
Tufte, E., 181

U
user-generated content. *See* crowdsourcing content

V
visual hierarchy, 159, 166, 168, 183
visuals, 158–181
voice, active versus passive, 132–133

W
webinar platforms, 228
webinar registration pages, 145
whitespaces, 71
writing content design tips, 129–147, 149–152

Z
Zapier, 211–212

About the Authors

Bianca Baumann is a seasoned L&D strategist with more than 15 years of experience. She is passionate about consulting on effective new solutions to serve learners' needs. She's developed processes, methodologies, and frameworks to help organizations meet their growth targets with the help of innovative L&D approaches. Bianca has helped dozens of organizations with their workforce transformations, as well as onboarding and reskilling programs. She has also spearheaded multiple projects in the marketing, automotive, financial, and events industries, creating award-winning programs along the way. Bianca speaks at international conferences and is a facilitator at the Ontario Institute for Studies in Education.

With more than two decades of experience as a learning consultant, **Mike Taylor** has been a driving force behind transformative instructional design and organizational performance. Known for his captivating speaking style and influential newsletter, Mike is dedicated to making learning more engaging, accessible, and effective. As a faculty member in Franklin University's Graduate Instructional Design and Performance Technology program, he bridges the gap between academic theory and real-world practice, equipping future learning professionals with the skills to excel in today's dynamic landscape. Mike's innovative approach and infectious passion are redefining the way we think about learning.

About ATD

atd The Association for Talent Development (ATD) is the world's largest association dedicated to those who develop talent in organizations. Serving a global community of members, customers, and international business partners in more than 100 countries, ATD champions the importance of learning and training by setting standards for the talent development profession.

Our customers and members work in public and private organizations in every industry sector. Since ATD was founded in 1943, the talent development field has expanded significantly to meet the needs of global businesses and emerging industries. Through the Talent Development Capability Model, education courses, certifications and credentials, memberships, industry-leading events, research, and publications, we help talent development professionals build their personal, professional, and organizational capabilities to meet new business demands with maximum impact and effectiveness.

One of the cornerstones of ATD's intellectual foundation, ATD Press offers insightful and practical information on talent development, training, and professional growth. ATD Press publications are written by industry thought leaders and offer anyone who works with adult learners the best practices, academic theory, and guidance necessary to move the profession forward.

We invite you to join our community. Learn more at **TD.org**.